Online Learning and Teaching in Higher Education

Online Learning and Teaching in Higher Education

Shirley Bach, Philip Haynes
and Jennifer Lewis Smith

 Open University Press

Open University Press
McGraw-Hill Education
McGraw-Hill House
Shoppenhangers Road
Maidenhead
Berkshire
England
SL6 2QL

email: enquiries@openup.co.uk
World Wide Web: www.openup.co.uk

and Two Penn Plaza, New York, NY 10121–2289, USA

First published 2007

A catalogue record of this book is available from the British Library

ISBN-10: 0 335 21829 6 (pb) 0 335 21830 X (hb)
ISBN-13: 978 0 335 21829 5 (pb) 978 0 335 21830 1 (hb)

Library of Congress Cataloging-in-Publication Data
CIP data applied for

Typeset by YHT, London
Printed in Poland EU by Ozgraf S.A. www.polskabook.pl

The *McGraw-Hill* Companies

Contents

Foreword   vi
Acknowledgements   viii

Introduction   1

1 Drivers to Online Learning   5
2 Where to Begin with Online Learning   32
3 Appraising the Quality   62
4 The Design of Online Learning Environments   92
5 Transforming Learning Methods through Online Teaching   124
6 Applying Online Learning to Teaching Practice in Higher
   Education   148
7 Conclusion   181

Glossary   191
Bibliography   193
Index   203

Foreword

By David Watson

This is a work of considerable imaginative and synthetic power. Shirley Bach, Philip Haynes and Jennifer Lewis Smith have pulled off the trick of both explaining the point where the university world has arrived in response to the challenges posed by an online environment and charting a nuanced but potentially highly productive future pathway.

The imagination lies in their understanding that Information and Communication Technology (ICT) is no longer a subject in its own right; something, as it were 'over there' for students and staff to deal with as a bounded or sealed proposition. Instead, as they say, it is deeply 'entangled' in the contemporary academic world in very nearly all of its activities. The synthesis comes from their subtle appreciation of the dynamics of continuity and change in the learning enterprise. The 'bonding of information with technology' will require not only a wide appreciation of how subjects, disciplines and professional areas themselves use ICT, but also a harnessing of the traditional values of respectful discourse and personal reflection in the higher education process.

As a consequence they have written an accessible, highly informed account of what living with online learning in higher education could and should be about. Like the best guides to an uncertain future, they steer us between the alternative poles of what Hannah Arendt called 'desperate hope and desperate fear'. Online learning and teaching is not a panacea, nor does it represent a fundamental attack on traditional values and ways of working. Instead, the careful analysis in the book offers a substantial middle ground of constructive possibilities.

Along the way they offer some hard truths for their most important readers. Teachers will (generally) have to adapt more than their students to the ways of working with what Jason Frand calls 'the information age mindset'. Managers will have to acknowledge that innovation is often expensive and rarely risk-free. Policy-makers and funders will need to appreciate the dangers of simplistic assumptions about global markets and local skills gaps. For those with a concern about the value of universities and colleges in the modern world, there is confirmation here that such institutions are now deeply implicated in the ways in which knowledge is created, tested and applied.

Whichever category you fall into, and many will be represented in more than one, I encourage you to read on.

Professor Sir David Watson is Professor of Higher Education Management at the Institute of Education, University of London.

Acknowledgements

Many people have inspired, encouraged and assisted us in our quest to develop online learning. In particular we would like to thank: Sue Bernhauser, Les Ellam, Mark Erickson, Peter Frost, Tony Gove, David Harley, Jane Knight, Stuart Laing, Tessa Parkes, Stan Stanier, David Taylor, Marian Trew, Marco Troiani, David Watson and Michael Whiting.

Introduction

In writing this book the primary concern of the authors is how technology can be applied to learning, rather than the use of the technology itself. The focus we have chosen is to examine the role online learning has in higher education rather than e-learning. E-learning is deemed to include any technology that can assist learning; therefore it must include radio, television, digital projectors, computers, and so on. Online learning is more concerned with the medium of communication that technology creates, rather than the technological products themselves, for example the networking of computer-based communication. Nevertheless there is some overlap between the concept of e-learning and online learning, and this is where the authors believe this book can assist academics in evaluating, for their own teaching and learning purposes, the role technology can play in planning and delivering courses and programmes relevant to their distinctive subject areas.

There are many books about e-learning and online learning, so why did the authors decide to write another one? What makes this book different is its synthesis of online leaning and an attempt to locate online learning alongside the wider evolution of higher education policy and practice. It is our view that online learning cannot be seen in isolation from these wider important transitions. This book seeks to locate online learning and its arrival in the wider context of what is happening in higher education and practice. It deals with the entanglement of online learning and technological change with other major social changes and already-existing important developments in learning theory.

The book provides an assessment of where online leaning has got to, given that it is now over a decade old. It evaluates the vision and 'hype' of the early days of online learning and the predictions that it would close university buildings and campuses and convert much learning to distance-based approaches. Clearly this has not happened on a grand scale, although there have been some significant additions and improvements to distance learning in certain niche markets. *One key aim of this book is to attempt a timely and realistic evaluation of online learning, to reassess its overall impact and direction in higher education.* By 'realistic evaluation' (Pawson and Tilley 1997) we mean a critical and wide-ranging assessment of the educational impact of online leaning in higher education, without confining the evaluation method to an instrumental and reductionist paradigm where there is a limited and narrow measurement that is based on prior assumptions (Taylor 2005).

A further aim of this book is to move beyond a description of what is happening in practice and to integrate learning theory and practice. In this sense *our aim is to consolidate the approaches to learning and teaching in higher education of recent decades and to review their current and likely impact on the use of online learning in higher education.* We are aware of a growing body of international empirical literature on the use of online learning and have tried to draw on this wherever possible, again, with the aim of creating a synthesis of where it is leading us. *A further related aim is to consider the impact of learning theory – and philosophies about how adults learn in experiential ways – on the successful adoption of online learning.*

There are some case examples in the book and these are presented as illustrative examples of how online learning is changing policy and practice in higher education. This book is not meant to be solely a hands-on manual of examples of 'how to do it' (readers will be aware that there are many such books already on the market and one of the problems with these is that technologies change, so the books can become out of date). Where reference is made to case studies and practice examples of what has happened, these are used to help reflect on what works in practice and what has been more difficult to establish as part of the routine of modern higher education teaching. *The aim here is to take a reality check on what is being taken up and used in practice, and how ideas of 'good practice' are evolving.*

Technologies improve rapidly and will continue to do so. Practice takes more time to become established. Initial ideas often are experimented with and then refined. This seems to be why this is such a key point in time to reflect on the first decade of online learning, as it is important to make an assessment of what practice has survived from the proliferation of innovation that started in the early 1990s. Nevertheless, technological change will continue to be one driver of learning practice, even though its impact in the short term can be overstated. *For this reason a further aim of the book is to assess the role of online technologies in the development of learning philosophies and the likely impact of further innovation,* such as the arrival and popularity of wireless communications.

The three authors of this book have been involved from the earliest days of the implementation of online information into higher education. They have seen the arrival and impact of email in universities, and then text-based browsing, swiftly followed by the first windows and image-based browsers. In the mid-1990s the authors were centrally involved in one university's response to trying to experiment and implement a pragmatic approach to online learning. We have seen the use of online learning move from the domain of a few early experimenters with novel approaches, to the much wider adoption by the majority of academic staff, this being assisted by the purchase of major technological online resources. These activities rapidly led us to become involved in a national and international network of people involved in the same challenges and dilemmas. In addition, as our careers progressed in the professional and managerial areas of higher education, we also began to experience the organizational dilemmas of institutional policy and resourcing, as universities sought to encourage and support the best examples of online learning practice while avoiding costly mistakes. Therefore the book attempts to provide both professional insights on learning and teaching, and managerial insights that embed these reflections in the realities of resource constraints and competitive pressures.

What follows is an overview of the narrative of the book and its progress through the key aspects of this important evaluation.

The first chapter examines the drivers for online learning and evaluates in a holistic way the global pressures for change in modern higher education. It is argued that technology is not a single driver for change, but that technological change needs to be understood alongside other key social and economic changes. In part, technology is assisting the evolution of higher education, as it seeks to respond to large-scale growth and global competitive pressures. Technology is not just a driver for change, but also makes bold claims to be part of the solution to providing a quality educational experience in a mass higher education world.

Chapter 2 examines how institutions and academic teachers approach the issue of beginning with online learning. It examines what environment, resources, skills and learning styles are associated with the development of an online learning approach. The chapter argues that online learning has brought a convergence of ideas from distance learning and face-to-face learning, with the result that teachers are increasingly encouraged to be 'facilitators' and managers of an educational process rather than expert producers of knowledge and content. This also creates pressures on both teachers and students to develop new skills for the new environment. The chapter explores the issue that there is also a need to reflect carefully on how adults learn best and how to approach this in the online environment.

This evolving of teaching practice that online resources encourage can lead to fragmentation and creativity, given the abundance of online materials and information. This has created a significant challenge for institutions as they seek to ensure the quality and coherence of such a change. In one sense there is a 'moral panic', as institutions struggle to control and regulate online teaching and examinations, and deal with difficult issues such as increased plagiarism. Chapter 3 takes an overview of these institutional and quality issues, and concludes that while institutions need to be keenly aware of the issues and how to manage new risks, in fact the managerial issues are really a transformation of previous regulatory concerns that have existed in higher education for many years, but that the new version of these manifestations demand some careful thinking and new resources. The challenge here is as much about the extra quantity of demand in higher education and how to provide good supply-side standards, as it is about specific online changes in learning and teaching practice.

Chapter 4 reflects on what has been learnt about the human, physical and virtual design of online environments and how they best create a useful online learning community. This is developed from existing literature about the detail of building and maintaining online environments and the need to see these as collective human experiences rather than as simplistic repositories of content.

In Chapter 5 the focus is on how the traditions of teaching and assessment in higher education are evolving, given the arrival of online resources. The analysis here looks at examples of experiential and constructivist learning, in addition to considering how traditional approaches like lecturing are being changed by ICT. The constructivist approaches had already been well argued for prior to the online revolution, and an assessment is made of the ability of online resources and processes to contribute to these modern ideals. It is argued that the online environment is also making a significant impact on the traditional monologue of the lecture.

Chapter 6 examines the development of learning in an online case example. It provides a holistic panorama of the development of an online course and the ways in which students and academics respond. The aim here is to capture some of the important detail suggested by the more holistic themes of the book, to illustrate that an important longer-term process and educational change is at work, rather than a simple standardized process.

The book concludes that on balance there is much that is positive about the online learning option and that it can assist with a continuity of new and innovative learning developments in the formidable knowledge management processes of mass higher education. But the challenges and changes are demanding and unpredictable, making the management and resourcing of higher education as difficult as it has ever been.

1

Drivers to Online Learning

Introduction

This chapter examines the growing evidence of the impact of the Internet and World Wide Web on social systems and, in particular, the education system. Some of the impact on the latter is shown to be different to that first expected. Nevertheless, it is argued that the arrival of online learning is part of the modern transformation of higher education. It is not the only transforming factor and must be carefully considered alongside other important aspects of change, such as globalization and the rapid growth of higher education in many countries. Some suggestions are made about the likely evolution that these combined changes will cause in the future and the likely issues for those working in higher education.

Economic, political and social change

Figure 1.1 shows that the World Wide Web is a growing international phenomenon with a particularly strong presence in North America, Western Europe and East Asia. The web is having a transforming effect on the developed world of Europe, Asia and North America, where it impacts on both business and social life. It is also becoming an important influence in less prosperous countries, where it is playing an important part in economic and social development. The Miniwatts Marketing Group argues that from 2000 to 2005 the number of people using the Internet across the world increased by 183 per cent (www.internetworldstats.com).

Transforming change is often described as having a wave-like effect (Urry 2003). Intense periods of change are followed by short periods of consolidations that are then followed by more intense change. The transforming impact of the Internet will increase further in the next decade. The first wave of Internet activity in the mid-1990s started to change the nature of business advertising and transactions. Political events and the experience

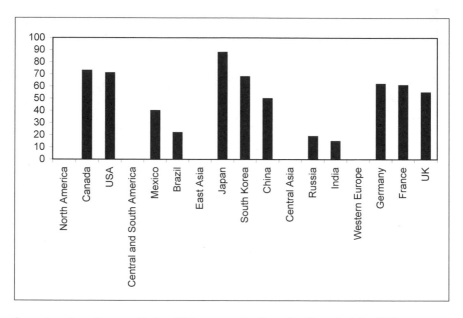

Source: based on data provided at Clickz.com and collected by Ipsos Insight, 2006

Figure 1.1   Global Internet usage, 2005 (percentage of people who had used the Internet in the past 30 days)

of education (as we argue in this book) were also significantly affected. Email and mobile phones become a mass form of communication in the developed world, experienced by the majority of people. Huge sums of money were invested in speculation about how technological developments would drive economic change and a new world marketplace. Then the Internet 'dot.com' bubble burst and technology stocks took a major tumble.

The second wave of Internet activity, in the first decade of the new millennium, followed the shaking out of the overindulgence of new investment in the 1990s. The impact of technology on business had been over-hyped, but fast progress was still being made with the underlying technology available. Broadband has delivered faster online access, and multimedia is available through video streaming. Mobile phones have started to deliver digital images and movies and access to online services. Personal computers (PCs) have increasingly connected to wireless networks. The impact is not just on the marketplace, but also on the rest of society. With this increasing availability of visual images, commentators have started to show more interest in the impact of the World Wide Web on political and social events, alongside their concern about world markets.

Future change will see the Internet and its associated technology become more dominant as the norm for these mass technologies becomes wireless and portability. Mobile phones and PCs are starting to converge to exploit this potential. The amount of business done on the Internet will increase. The proportion of communications using the new technology rather than face-to-face meetings, postage and traditional wired phone lines will further increase. The Internet is very much here to stay.

The rapid rise in Internet access has had a major impact on business. In the late 1990s the number of businesses with Internet access and web sites increased exponentially. In the UK, this resulted in 61 per cent using a web site for advertising and marketing purposes by the beginning of the new millennium (Williams 2001). Many also created an Internet sales facility where customers could purchase on the Internet. Established businesses, such as the UK supermarket chain Tesco, are noting a rising percentage of their sales as being to Internet customers. Williams concluded that in the UK over 12 per cent of sales and purchases were carried out online, resulting in takings of £118.5 billion. While the end of the first wave of activity in the Internet revolution saw many Internet companies trading solely on the web go out of business, those that survived are major global players with innovative ideas and sales: examples are Amazon, eBay and Google. The market value of the information search engine web site, Google, became big news in 2004 when it entered the stock market with a market capitalization of about $28 billion (significantly more than Amazon.com value at that time of $16 billion) and instantly making it one of the most powerful international companies. The second wave of Internet activity is also characterized by the success of long-established brand names who have adapted well to the Internet environment (Henley Centre 2001). For example, traditional institutions such as the clearing banks have adjusted to the new technologies, resulting in 24 per cent of the UK population using bank web sites (MORI 2002). Traditional brand names that have not adjusted to rising Internet sales have suffered. Finch (2006) reported that HMV lost out to Internet competitors during Christmas 2005, resulting in falling profits and the resignation of the chief executive.

The availability of immediate information online simultaneously to millions of people is changing the nature of politics. It is much harder for governments to limit people's perceptions of the world. Information banned by one government is often leaked onto a web site in another country. The availability of the Internet has changed war reporting and terrorist behaviour. Information spreads more rapidly and it is easier for the public to check multiple accounts of events, see events unfold and view the way in which they are portrayed by different nation states, newspapers and other media outlets around the world. With the recent war in Iraq and resulting occupation by Western armies, manipulation of the media has taken a new and sinister form. There has been the direct front-line reporting from journalists with coalition forces and the digital video recordings of the beheading of captives by terrorist groups, this shown later on web sites. Ideological competition to gain favour with an audience becomes a central activity as lots more information is available. The political management of information and propaganda becomes more difficult.

Governments are looking to use information technology (IT) and the web to make public services more accessible and efficient. The UK has an e-government programme, promoting the delivery of good quality information to the public and the provision of services such as the payment of tax, and eventually the purchase of driving licences and passports, online. The Inland Revenue offers an online software product that allows self-employed people to input their own finances and have their tax calculated automatically for them, before they decide to formally submit a tax return. In September 2004 the UK general government information gateway, www.direct.gov.uk, received 586,046 unique user accesses, up from 44,065 in February 2002. During 2005, the UK government reported that its direct gateway had received over two million visits in a single month.

In an information-rich world, the ability to access information becomes an important source of social capital. Social capital is defined as the networks and social relationships that give individuals access to human and social resources. Sociologists are troubled about the plight of those who do not have such access. There is a global concern about the increased polarization of 'information rich' and 'information poor'. To be information poor will lead to becoming increasingly marginalized, socially excluded and disenfranchised. Medical services report some users who attend consultations armed with printouts from web sites and demanding that public funds are used to deliver them the latest clinical technology and drugs which they have discovered online. The information poor cannot make demands, despite their needs. There is a danger that those who have the information with which to ask searching questions get the best service. The web is becoming an increasingly important media for the accumulation of information and knowledge, and this provides social capital to those who are able to use such a network. Online networks cannot fully replace human interaction and relationships, but they are an important supplement that can aid social cohesion and communication.

Technological change

Segal (1995) has written of how a period of three years from 1991 to 1994 saw a number of critical technological issues resolved that changed the whole way people used computers and thought about the communication possibilities that this offered. He argues that three foundations were established: common standards of computer systems and programme languages, the availability of affordable hardware in the mass consumer market and, finally, a move towards cooperation within the industry to allow free information technology intercommunication. Therefore, at the beginning of the 1990s, personal computer usage was transformed as computers were increasingly interlinked with telephone technology and networks.

Higher education (HE) was well placed to build on this technological revolution. It had provided some of the key scientists involved in designing the communication protocols that had founded the World Wide Web. The HE sector became one of the first enthusiasts to embrace both email and text-based Hyper Text Mark-up Language (HTML) the latter as a form of online information. But the early versions were based on UNIX, and text and command lines were not easily accessible to non-science-based academics who were only just beginning to adjust to the desktop-based, user-friendly, word-processing computers. But the arrival of the image-based web browser, Mosaic, in 1993 started a dramatic increase in use of the web. Mosaic made use of the web technologies more user-friendly. The first browser worked with UNIX but it was so popular that Marc Andreesen quickly wrote a version for PC and Mac. By the end of the year the phenomenon was so successful that the world's press were taking note. What followed was central to the whole Internet revolution: competition between browsers, the anti-competition argument against Microsoft for packaging Explorer free with other software products and the growth of the multi-billion dollar search engines – organizations such as Yahoo and Google that have quickly become global institutions.

Browsers and search engines had started to deliver information in a single global network on a scale that was previously unimaginable. Educationalists soon realized that this would have implications for them. Schools and universities started to increase the hardware and software available to staff and students, and to encourage their communities to use the technology and to explore the new information highway. But events were moving so quickly that it was hard to have a plan or strategy to respond to what was happening and to the overload of available information. By 2002 the Internet had 200 million Internet provider (IP) host addresses and in excess of 800 million users. Estimates for 2006, from internetstatistics.com, claim that over 1 billion people have used the Internet. The speed of the change in the past decade overtook the input of training in many organizations, with staff having to learn 'on the job' as the technology was delivered (Haynes et al. 2004).

Change in higher education

In the same brief period of history, higher education in most developed countries was already undergoing its own revolution as demand for higher education increased and governments struggled with how to fund provision. The percentage of graduates with university degrees (or an equivalent qualification) rose in many countries, particularly in the developed world. Table 1.1 shows the results of the global expansion in higher education for five of the world's top economies and the proportion of adults with a degree nearly doubles.

Countries have used a variety of policies and funding mechanisms to cope

Table 1.1   Percentage of 25–64-year-olds with higher education qualifications

	1991	2002
UK	16	27
US	30	38
France	15	24
Germany	22	23
Japan	30*	36
Average	16.6	29.6

Notes: * 1998 figure
Source: OECD (2004: table A3.4a)

with this rapid demand, but most have tried to raise the productivity of output as a result. In other words, input costs and resources have been reduced in relation to the number of output graduates. Some countries such as the UK have raised sharply their outputs in relation to inputs, and this leads to tensions in the sector with anger expressed by staff and concerns about the quality of provision. Lecturers are faced with teaching larger groups, and universities must equip staff with the skills and technology to deliver in this new environment. One common result is to focus on providing less classroom teaching input, and to make sure what remains is of a higher quality. The aim is to promote the value-added to student self-directed learning outside the classroom. Technology can play a key part here, in terms of linking classroom activity and core reading through online information, discussion and formative testing of what has been learnt. These themes are explored in more detail later in the book.

Influence of globalization

Globalization refers to the situation where processes, cultures and products developed in one region of the world become exported to other countries to the extent that they begin to circumvent what occurs in the local place. As a result, working patterns and behaviours, the food eaten and products consumed, and the cultural patterns demonstrated become more similar. One possible outcome is the levelling out of the culture and behaviour of all people, but equally as likely is an increasing diversity of subcultures within any one nation state and tensions about agreeing what are shared and collective values.

The role of capitalism and monetary economics is seen as a dominant partner in the process of globalization. The influence of global markets is a powerful determinant of social and educational life. For years the USA has been dominant in this respect. The US economy is by far the single biggest economy in the world. So great is its dominance that one of its states, California, has the fifth biggest economy in the world (when compared with other nation states). American companies have developed what were seen as many of the first global products, for example Coca-Cola, McDonald's fast food, Ford cars, Microsoft software, Nike shoes and Disney media. The Nobel prize winning economist, Joseph Stiglitz (2002), has argued that globalization is not a simple spreading of free market ideas and open trade, but rather a process by which the world's most powerful countries help promote unjust rules and regulations that lead to an unfairness and discontent about the process.

The global images of Microsoft in the computing world illustrate how much of the globalization of Internet communication is dominated by American business and culture. These have been closely followed by the taking up of Internet brand names into larger media brand names – for example, America On Line into Time Warner. Many of these companies each have greater wealth than the world's poorest countries.

Since the start of the new millennium some commentators have looked for the increasing importance of other continents to balance the business-driven Internet networks. China and the Far East have grown exponentially. In January 2004 a journalist, Jim Wagner, reported for clickz.com that China had 79.5 million web surfers, and that it had overtaken Japan in terms of its contribution to the total world population using the World Wide Web. But America remained in first position with 165.75 million surfers. Nua.com ran a credible web-based longitudinal market survey of the Internet and web-based products. They have noted that parts of Europe have strengthened their web-based competitiveness against the USA. In April 2003 they reported that Sweden and Denmark were better positioned to use Internet-based business transactions and had overtaken the rankings of the USA and the UK. The European Commission in Brussels has been concerned in the past decade to make sure that the countries of the European Union increase their ability to use online resources to make a profitable industry from the new technologies available. The 2006 data from Miniwatts Marketing (www.internetworldstatistics.com) shows that Internet-user growth was higher in Europe from 2000 to 2005 than in North America, although the latter still had a higher total penetration into the population. The same survey shows very rapid growth in Africa, the Middle East and Latin America, but from a much lower starting point than the more prosperous continents.

Higher education has not escaped the pressures of globalization. Although some aspects of education will always remain culturally specific, such as art and language, other disciplines are by their nature international and global in their concerns. For this reason students will be attracted away from the host nation to build their network overseas, adding important educational experience, and for many there is the possibility of adding further language skills to their personal achievements. The English language has evolved as dominant in this respect because it is the primary educational and business language in the USA. It is the most used second language in the world.

Mass higher education

A definition of mass higher education is when a society moves from a position where an elite minority of its population experience higher education to one where this becomes a large minority, or close to a majority (Scott 1995). Many developed countries have moved on this trajectory in the past two decades. Some Scandinavian countries now report very high proportions of their population engaging in higher education. Arguably it has been slightly easier for these countries to arrive at this outcome in advance of the more heavily populated Western countries because the volumes are smaller, given their smaller populations, and investment in resources is less exponential. Nevertheless the ratio of gross domestic product (GDP) spent by these countries on higher education is impressive and has often been met by high taxation that is largely tolerated by the public.

The Scandinavian experience can be contrasted with the UK, where the funding of expansion has proved problematic. Major expansion first started in the late 1980s and early 1990s, at a time when the government was committed to reducing the GDP ratio of public expenditure. As a result, the ratio of funding per student collapsed and many institutions struggled to maintain quality. Industrial relations were strained and a significant debate began about how better to fund the system, independent of general taxation. One of the first casualties of the UK funding crisis was maintenance support for poorer students, and many young undergraduates began to work part time, while studying for a full-time degree (Winn and Stevenson 1997). These issues have affected other countries to varying degrees. The UK is not unique in facing a reduction of the per capita resource base. Resource constraints are even starker in the expanding sector in developing countries where new technology facilities and support can be scarce. Despite the cost of investing in technological equipment, Daniel (1996) argued that when contrasted with the other social and economic cost factors facing expanding higher education, technology offers many advantages for adding value to the mass HE sector. This is because the quality and unit cost of technology is improving at such a rapid rate.

There is some cynicism about the growth of HE into a mass society experience. Critics suggest it is of low quality, increasingly confused with training and technical skills-based education (such as further education in the UK) and will result in an increase in over and inappropriately qualified people in semi-skilled and skilled work, rather than in professional, managerial and technical employment. Despite these criticisms, there is little international evidence that the long-term outcome of higher education is negative. Instead, there is important evidence that higher education qualifications reduce the risk of unemployment and substantially raise earning potential over the student's lifetime (Eurostat 2002). There is also evidence from international organizations such as the Organisation for Economic Co-operation and Development (OECD) that nations with a strong HE sector perform better in both the manufacturing and knowledge/service sectors, thus increasing the performance of their economies.

Managerialism and a new bureaucracy in higher education

In the past two decades commentators have noticed a worldwide movement to organize the public sector around market- and business-based models of organization and management (Hughes 2005) For some this movement was seen as an opportunity to revolutionarize public services and to make them more efficient and effective (Osborne and Gaebler 1992). Market language and concepts have increasingly dominated the culture and practices of public services. Writers such as Hughes have referred to this change as the new public managerialism (NPM). In areas such as higher education it has led to devolved budgets and unit costing, in particular the attempt to get money to follow the needs of individual students and research contracts, so that local departments and research units are rewarded accordingly, in line with the immediate demands for their services. This attempt to replicate a market environment has made the higher education environment more competitive and, in some cases, this leads to closing of departments and making staff redundant if high costs cannot be justified by market criteria. There is a concern that market- and business-based criteria do not always equate with the general social, educational and public good (Clarke and Newman 1997). Markets often create short-term reactions. There might be a demand for thousands of students who want to take media studies, but in the long term the public good demands an adequate balance of science and language students. There can be a need for some subject disciplines and research questions to be promoted by a country and society over the long term, regardless of short-term market- and consumer-based desires. The general public good might be more important than what the consumer market demands.

The practice of NPM has also placed emphasis on a new bureaucracy that supports devolved budgeting, the costing of individual units of provision (to assist financial transparency) and the development of related business targets and performance monitoring. There is a desire to link government block grant funding of higher education with specific output targets, for example the percentage of students completing courses or the number of quality research publications achieved. An example of this method of government funding is the UK Research Assessment Exercise (RAE) that seeks to audit academic publications over a period of years and then allocate block grant funding for research on the basis of output performance.

The desire to link financial costs to activities has led to a move to measure the quality of such activities. An audit and inspection of higher education is implemented seeking to demonstrate the efficiency of inputs to outputs.

For example, in teaching inspections there is a desire to show that teaching and resource inputs are carefully linked with learning objectives and assessment criteria so that efficient student outputs are achieved. Many academics are cynical about these market-driven regimes (Laughton 2003), believing that they oversimplify the complex nature of higher education activity and, at worst, distort university activity towards meeting unhelpful and ineffective targets.

Some writers directly link new public management practices with the use of IT to standardize complex professional processes into bureaucratic information system processes. Critics are concerned that this is inefficient if it ignores professional expertise and judgement, and reduces the flexibility of professionals (Furedi 2002).

This new bureaucracy of markets and quality and performance assessment has become a defining feature of modern higher education and can be linked with globalization and mass higher education and the preoccupation of politicians with delivering more higher education to the global population for a reduced unit cost. Managers and politicians can see technology as a solution to these challenges without considering the complexities.

Technical challenges

The rapid technological change experienced in the past decade has come alongside already established major social and economic change. The argument we are making is that these changes need to be understood together, rather than examined in isolation. These combined transformations in society present higher education with a number of technical challenges.

The first challenge is to make available good quality information and suitable information systems in higher education. There needs to be adequate investment in IT products. Higher education cannot stand outside the information revolution provided by the Internet. In general it has not done this, indeed it has been central to the revolution, nevertheless there are formidable challenges for the higher education sector to be able to invest adequately in technology and systems so as to keep at the forefront of the revolution and its benefits.

There are two elements to this investment. First, obtaining adequate levels of expenditure, but then using them wisely. Research, in both the private and public sector, shows that it is all too easy to misjudge technological change in the short term and to waste money on the wrong IT equipment and systems (OECD 2001).

In general, universities in wealthier countries have done quite well in providing staff and students with hardware and software. Research showed that a high percentage of academic staff in the USA had access to a computer at work (Web-Based Education Commission 2000). Similarly, most academics in the UK have personal direct access to hardware and software (Haynes et al. 2004). Some of this is achieved by significant collaboration and partnership with the industry (see the section on collaboration near the end of this chapter).

Using money wisely to invest in effective technological growth is difficult. Many UK academics complain that the arrival of personal PCs at a time of great expansion in student numbers and a reduced per capita funding ratio resulted in academics doing much more of their own administration, given that the ratio of administrators to students also fell. Some academics felt that they were becoming well paid administrators who were unlikely to be effective given their frustrations at not being able to spend enough time on teaching and research and not having been trained primarily in organizational and administrative skills. Research has shown an uncoordinated approach to the development of IT skills in higher education (Tomes and Higgison 1998). The danger is that things will only improve slowly as a younger generation of IT-literate staff moves in. This does not fit well with the age profile of higher education, it being a profession where staff are recruited and peak relatively late in their adult life when compared with other professions.

Similarly giving staff and students access to online facilities such as e-books and e-journals does not necessarily result in the recipients using them effectively. Training and incentives have to be provided to assist them to see the tangible benefits. Some academics report that having to teach themselves to search for materials online is a frustrating and unrewarding process with the temptation being to revert back to one's traditional skills of making a physical search of the library and calling on paper-based interlibrary loan requests.

In some cases spending more money on online information has resulted in less money being spent on books for the library shelves. Staff and students who are not personally experiencing the benefits of online resources, for whatever reason, feel marginalized and excluded and that their traditional information sources are being eroded.

It is difficult for universities to forecast where the information changes will lead. They are both at the forefront of change and having to respond to it. Debate is intensifying about encouraging academics to submit materials to open source electronic journals and books. The UK Joint Information Systems Committee (JISC) funded a project in 2006 with the *New Journal of Physics*, the International Union of Crystallography and the *Journal of Medical Genetics* to explore with them how to promote open access models of publishing. Microsoft are working on a mobile electronic tablet product that they claim will make paper redundant in the educational environment, with all paper-based writing being digitalized and viewable through an electronic reader. Bill Gates has outlined his vision that small tablet PCs and much more sophisticated mobile phones will transform education and young people's ability to access educational content by 2015 (Gibson 2005). Several companies are working on related ideas. E Ink (www.e-ink.com/) is an innovative approach that arranges thousands of tiny black and white capsules to form what looks like a printed page. Philips are rumoured to be working on a related product that can be rolled up like paper, while Sony has demonstrated a reader device that can store a huge amount of material behind a 6-inch screen (Smith 2006). McCrum (2006), citing a leading commercial publisher, predicts a dual market for books and e-books, but one where half of all book sales will be downloads in just ten years' time. While materials will be more widely and easily available to students, the costs of organizing such a digital system are likely to be carried in other ways, via institutional payments to large multimedia and information companies, or via commercial sponsorship from the users of knowledge and research. These commercial pressures pose some risks to the public sector ethos of civic universities and the knowledge they create. One of the first further education (FE) colleges in the UK to implement online learning on a large scale has invested to encourage its staff and students to use tablet PCs (JISC 2005a).

The second challenge resulting from this change is primarily about knowledge management. Knowledge management refers to not just the setting up of an information system and the transmission of information, but how information is converted into knowledge and that knowledge used to good effect. Knowledge is more abstract in quality than information. It implies a value judgement, a tangible benefit from information or an applied use of information. It can be highly contested. This concerns questions of what knowledge is, how it is evolving and how it should evolve in future. These knowledge management questions are at the centre of most academic disciplines and have been so for many centuries. Although knowledge management is a recent development in business studies, it was arguably already central to the higher education task and always will be. The use of information systems is secondary to knowledge management, although increasingly an important aspect of the discipline. Knowledge can be defined and applied *without* the use of information technology (Haynes 2005). Universities have managed knowledge for hundreds of years without the use of computer-based information technology. The dominance of information technology in the past decade as a vehicle for knowledge management is therefore a key challenge for higher education. It needs to make sure that the focus on technology does not distract from the focus on knowledge, knowledge creation, its evolution and application. Information technology must be used to add value to this process, rather than to frustrate it or, even, prevent it. The seeking of knowledge comes first, not the desire for technology. In many situations the two issues are entangled. Brown and Duguid (2000) argue that the key role of universities in the information age is to validate knowledge. Some have predicted that the Internet and information revolutions will transform universities beyond recognition by weakening their elitist hold on the definition, ranking and provision of information (Sutherland 2005). While it may well be the case that they will have less direct control over the provision and sharing of information (the Internet has already had this effect), it does not follow that they will lose their institutional status of defining and ranking the importance of knowledge products. Knowledge management for universities certainly looks likely to become more chaotic and complex, giving the institutions some serious challenges to navigate.

The third challenge follows on from the other two. Higher education staff and students need new IT and information skills. In the UK children are leaving school with a much higher level of IT skills than five years ago. Universities are also focusing on developing these skills further and bringing any mature students up to an acceptable benchmark. This means that academics cannot afford to get left behind. Schools routinely use the web to encourage children to research topics. University students will expect to use the web in a similar way and will need assistance in finding quality sites that can enable them to digest good information and develop complex knowledge management skills. Academics should not be surprised and dismayed at students' use of the web and mobile devices, but look for ways to add value to these skills, so that information-processing skills become advanced. Universities report that popular student demand is driving much of the rapid growth of digital resources and online content.

A final element is the overall challenge of the culture of technology. Culture here refers to the values, beliefs and logics that become formulated in the public and specific social groups. Of particular relevance is the mobile phone. Mobile phone use has grown hugely in the 1990s and is a global phenomenon. It is very significant among young people who form the majority of those in formal education. It is clear that the mobile phone is not just a technological tool for mobile communication, but is also a status symbol, a fashion icon and a key part of many young people's way of life and identity. Mobile phones that include web browsing, email features and the potential to watch online television programmes are now routinely available. Learning technologists are keen to think of creative ways of tapping into this communication, so as to meet young people within this new medium.

Developed economies are experiencing an increase in the use of personal digital assistants (PDAs) that double up as mobile phones and can also be used for basic software access and web browsing (Cole 2005). Mobile network costs are predicted to fall in the next few years and these devices will become more popular with students. Their take-up is difficult to predict, given that networked PDAs are more complex to use and marginally more cumbersome to carry around in a pocket. They might have less youth culture appeal to young people partly because they are able to manage more complex material, rather than being a symbol of personal and private peer-based communication. Standing on a street corner talking into a PDA might not look that 'cool'! Smart phones, which are smaller than PDAs, are likely to prove more popular.

A key factor recently with the marketing of mobiles to young people has been reduction in physical size. Not surprising then that much of the research and development with these devices is now focusing on their design appeal as much as their technological functions. Another factor influencing this market is that the price of laptop computers with wireless networking has also been falling rapidly. Public spaces increasingly offer wireless networks, and they are cheap and easy to install within a private home. The availability of wireless networks is set to rise rapidly. It will be some years before all universities can invest in making wireless networks a full reality on campus, but around 2010 this is likely to become the norm for all academic communities.

There are currently efforts to tap into the mobile phone medium by sending short message service (SMS) text messages and so on to students, but the educational value for this alone seems limited. Another recent idea is to use mobile phone technology so that students can vote on formative tests during lecture presentations. Some large lecture theatres have previously been set up to allow this interaction, with small remote control devices that are given out in the session and that are not dependent on student mobile phones. These systems are marketed as classroom performance systems. Students can then be given formative test questions during a lecture presentation, or asked to vote at the end of a debate. More could be done, for example using mobile phone game technology to offer a simple learning content exercise, but this requires considerable up front resources that, traditionally, the HE sector does not have unless it can see a long-term return for large numbers of students. The move to wireless PDAs, laptops or tablets offers universities lots of potential for quickly and easily passing more dynamic learning content to students (Kukulska-Hulme et al. 2005).

There have been some interesting pioneering experiments on campuses in some parts of the world that give an indication of what is likely to happen everywhere in four to five years' time. The Further Education College of Ealing, Hammersmith and West London has attempted to target its resources to offer such a vision ahead of time (JISC 2005a). Some staff groups are provided with tablet wireless PCs. College learning is developed flexibly around a wireless, multi-site, managed learning environment (MLE). The pivotal role of purpose of such integrated IT learning systems is discussed more extensively in Chapter 2 and beyond.

Desktop technology and the wired Internet certainly made their mark on HE in the past decade. An internal survey of a UK university conducted in 2002 found that the majority of students had access to an Internet wired desktop PC at home. All students in UK universities now have access to shared computer pools if they do not have access at home. Similarly in the USA, a major study for the Web-Based Education Commission (2000) found that there was one computer for every 2.6 university students, making access to online resources relatively easy where students did not have access to their own computer. At some point soon the move to wireless will also impact on the majority. The convergence of television and computer technologies is also assisting online access in some countries. Digital television has begun to make an impact in the UK in the past few years with 56 per cent of the population reporting use of digital television in 2004 (MORI 2004). It is not clear, however, whether this is leading to an increase in Internet use that is independent of PCs and laptop computers.

Learning content and technology-based learning processes must be designed to be available to the majority of students, not to an elite and well-resourced minority. This will restrict the use of some technologies in the short term, while they become mainstream. Teachers sometimes have to be curtailed from experimentation in this respect. Universities should do more to ensure that all their students have access to new technologies as they become available and to offer assisted purchase schemes and advice about what to purchase.

Changing technologies and the increasing availability of online communication provides HE with some important opportunities for responding to the challenges of a rapidly expanding HE sector. The increase in staff to student ratios has led to changes in learning and teaching methods. The creative use of technology and good access to online information is one creative resource that can assist academics in the new difficult working environment of mass higher education. Children are growing up with a culture that associates technology with communication, content and learning. Many young people arrive at university with a high level of IT experience and skills, and are ready to adapt this to the demands of self-directed learning and higher education.

IT skills

Pettigrew and Elliott (1999: 1–2) proposed a number of principles for the teaching of IT skills to students: flexibility, regular use, attitude, adaptability and complementary materials

Flexibility is the skill of being able to adapt to different hardware and software versions as people move between institutions and employers and face upgrades in equipment. Regular use is important because skills only become used and applied with confidence if they are used regularly. Sending emails and browsing the web are skills rather like driving or operating other sophisticated machinery; regular practice increases dexterity, judgement and confidence.

People's feelings and attitudes towards technology and the pace of technological change need to be taken into account. Some people have strong emotional reactions to using information technology. They find the experience de skilling and threatening to their personal construct. Such students need a lot of reassurance and have to be helped to make an accurate assessment of what can be achieved in a given timescale and the strengths and weaknesses of using IT as a working method.

In order to be able to work in a self-directed and independent environment in the future, students need to be encouraged to experiment with different ways of doing similar tasks and to see the variety of methods that software offers. This will encourage students to be adaptable and to cope with future IT change. This involves some degree of experimentation and will enable students to get the maximum of added value from using IT products that emerge in the future.

Most students will experience a wide range of teaching methods supported by complementary materials, and this can help them to learn effectively. Methods can include books, manuals, demonstrations, face-to-face advice, on-screen help and various forms of electronic multimedia. This will allow them to find the best methods that suit their own learning needs and to evolve their learning at their own pace. This is particularly important given that students now arrive in HE with a diversity of prior experience of IT in primary and secondary education.

Student skills

In the 1990s there was a rapid transformation in the IT skills levels taught at school in most developed nations. By 2004 this meant that many more students were arriving at university with a high level of IT skills, often faster and more adaptable with technology than their older teachers. But there are dangers in making universal assumptions. There have been concerns in many countries about the ability of school teachers to prepare children with the computer skills they need. In America, the Web-Based Education Commission (2000) concluded that two-thirds of teachers were not trained to assist children with developing such skills and that children from poor neighbourhoods were most likely to be disadvantaged.

On arriving at university, mature students can find themselves deskilled and at risk of dropping out prematurely if there are no opportunities in the first year of study for updating IT skills, or even learning them for the first time. It cannot be assumed that all new undergraduates and postgraduates have the necessary IT skills in place when they arrive. Universities need to deal with this situation effectively.

Many universities undertake some kind of IT skills assessment early in the induction process. Those without the necessary skills will be offered introductory classes, perhaps leading to a basic IT qualification such as the European Computer Driving Licence (ECDL). Some of these courses are made available via distance learning or are taught online (or via CD media) using products such as Electric Paper. These media demonstrate software skills via on-screen movies and then ask students to repeat skills. Regular formative testing is included and final summative tests can also be offered when the student is ready. Although the licences for such products can be costly to universities and colleges, the ongoing costs can represent savings against employing numerous specialist IT teachers who have to demonstrate software from the front of the class. Some human support for such learning methods is always needed, especially for induction, to get students started and to pick up any motivational or specific problems that individuals encounter. This type of approach to learning and teaching IT skills has become very popular in the UK and makes the most of using technology to promote self-directed learning. To be successful and to prevent high drop-out rates it needs to be supported by some human contact and tutoring advice. Universities may enter into arrangements with partner further education colleges to provide such learning opportunities and testing. They often already have more expertise than the HE sector in providing the teaching of basic skills and may have already invested in the capital equipment for IT skills learning.

Staff skills

Research into the IT skills of staff in higher education shows the importance of offering a wide range of opportunities to staff, that are both flexible and allow them to consolidate and improve their skills. Academic staff often have had to teach themselves to use computers, without any formal training. In such a situation the introduction of IT increases staff stress and is perceived as adding to their workload. Universities increasingly are introducing a variety of training strategies to help older staff learn the skills they need. A lack of staff IT skills and a lack of support for academics can be one reason why online resources and methods fail to be perceived as a useful strategy for dealing with the pressures of mass higher education. The academic community in the UK has a large proportion of its full-time staff in the age group 50–64 and the sector has had difficulties in recruiting younger people to new posts.

Students' lifestyles

In the UK student lifestyles have been changing in the past decade as a consequence of social and economic change. The number of students undertaking paid work alongside their studies has increased (Winn and Stevenson 1997). Students are more likely to remain living at home with their parents or to choose a university nearer their home town (Humphrey and McCarthy 1997). Students are less likely to use the transition to university to cut their social and economic ties with the family, although this is still a reality for some. It is more likely that students continue in regular contact with their parents and see their studies as one component of their time, alongside economic activity. But, while student's social and material existence has suffered, because of the rapidly falling relative costs in technology and their increasing availability, large numbers of students have access to PCs in accommodation (whether in parental home or halls of residence).

The growth of part-time work among full-time students is another driver for the need to increase the quality of the time spent in class at university. Teaching contact needs to help students to focus their understanding of core concepts and then direct them towards private study activities that will promote their learning and critical independence. Students spend less time at university. Technology and online resources are needed to help increase the quality of the limited time that students do spend on studying activities.

International HE market

In the late 1990s governments and universities became increasingly concerned about the effect of globalization and the expanding Internet on higher education. It was acknowledged that if the higher education experience was less based on a physical experience situated at a campus with other students, and become based on a new form of distance learning with only limited visits to a physical site, nation states might find that the international HE market suddenly became much more competitive. With hindsight this anxiety ignored the already competitive market for distance learning and some of the cultural subtleties attached to it. Key providers of distance learning such as the UK Open University had emerged many years previously and part of their mission and success was to apply new learning technologies as they appeared. In this sense, specialized distance learning universities are ahead of the game in terms of understanding the impact of technology and the Internet on the future of learning. But in the late 1990s too many assumptions were being made that rapid changes in technology would drive rapid changes in how people learn.

What was new was a belief that distance learning was likely to become more popular than face-to-face teaching if technology made it more attractive and enabled it to replace some more dynamic aspects of traditional higher education, such as synchronous human contact and conventional library searches.

A number of writers predicted the demise of the traditional university and created a vision of a competitive international distance learning market fuelled by part-time students who spent most their time at a computer terminal surfing the web to find the best providers of content (Pearson and Winter 1999; Sutherland 2005). Learning processes were seen as important, but somehow secondary to a consumer empowered digital content marketplace.

In the USA, Palloff and Pratt (2001) documented the growth of distance learning from the late 1990s onwards. The US National Centre for Educational Statistics had recorded a doubling of enrolments in distance learning educational courses between 1995 and 1998. There was an association between this growth and the availability of more courses online (Palloff and Pratt 1999). Enrolments on such courses were also observed to be associated with students over the age of 22.

A more recent large survey of universities in the USA (Allen and Seaman

2005) found that there was significant growth in the delivery of online courses. The definition of an online course was having at least 80 per cent of the process taught online. Enrolments across America of students taking at least one online course increased from 1,602,970 in 2002 to 2,329,783 in 2004. Many universities were tending to offer courses in both a traditional face-to-face and online mode, implying a choice of delivery. The reports noted a steady growth in the percentage of academic leaders who see online education as critical to their long-term institutional strategy (rising from 49 per cent in 2003 to 56 per cent in 2005). Business studies was the discipline most likely to be studied online, as compared to psychology and the social sciences where traditional face-to-face delivery was significantly more popular.

In the UK a key statement of reflection came in the form of the Committee of Vice-Chancellors and Principals and the Higher Education Funding Council for England (CVCP and HEFCE) (2000) publication, *The Business of Borderless Education: UK Perspectives*. This found difficulty in drawing up a clear strategy for UK higher education in such an evolving and unpredictable marketplace. The report conceded that there would be an increasing consumer market influence that would exert as much, if not more, influence on the provision of higher education than national policy and levels of state funding and bureaucratic allocation of state subsidy and places. But the report was reticent about the impact of technological change on the international education market. Important distinctions were recognized between training for industry- and professional-specific training as compared to discipline- and research-based higher education. It seemed unlikely that the traditional HE market would be as exposed to sudden unpredictable marketization as much as would the training market.

Technology was more likely to have a dramatic impact in the short term on the training sector, because of its short-term delivery focus and explicit knowledge. This made it vulnerable to a rapid digitalization of content where legal and production changes could be better presented on video and CD formats rather than in 'dry' textbooks. These content-based changes were less likely to have a dramatic effect on higher education where the process of reflective learning and self-directed study were more important.

It emerged that the central issue was protecting the brand of long-established higher education institutions and products, adding value with technology to centuries of tradition and reputation. The real opportunity was seen to be in the top end of the international market in academic excellence, with increased competition for English-speaking courses for the expanding market of international students. This international student market was projected to grow from 1.75 million students in 2000 to 2.7 million in 2010. Such a market not only offers precious income against low levels of state subsidy for home students, but also rich pickings in inward investment for national governments. The majority of overseas students travel to the USA. Although the UK has traditionally done well in this market, attracting well over 100,000 students per year who often contribute fees of close to £10,000 each, other countries were noted as being increasingly competitive for the English HE market, namely, China, South Africa and Australia. The decline of the dollar against the pound and the euro has made the market more difficult for UK-based universities. One method for dealing with this is for the largest and most reputable universities in the UK to establish long-term partners and franchise operations abroad, something which is seen to hold nearly as many risks (in terms of to brand identity) as rewards. Nevertheless some UK universities, such as Nottingham, have now moved firmly in this direction. Much of the conclusion of the report leaves the reader feeling that the most important thing is for the UK HE sector to protect its reputation via regulation and branding, rather than to try and compete with the buoyant and expanding e-learning training-based businesses of the USA. In the USA a concern is expressed by traditional universities that have not been built on a distance learning tradition, that the pressures of marketization and social change require them to cut costs while improving quality and accessibility (Rhodes 2001).

Universities that specialize in distance learning, such as the UK Open University (OU), are increasingly exposed to international competition and this is in part driven by the rapid advances in global technologies and web communications. In its favour, the OU is an established world leader and is a well-placed social institution working alongside similar bodies such as British Broadcasting Corporation (BBC). It has been, and will continue to be, a major catalyst for learning technological change in other UK universities, both in cooperative projects and through competition with other providers. In this sense, technology can strengthen the collaboration between traditional and distance learning institutions, if they respect each other's niche markets.

While distance learning and international students (who are willing and able to choose between countries for their subject discipline) have created a segment of higher education that is international and fiercely competitive, the market in traditional home-country higher education is more stable, certainly in the short term. It continues to be protected to some extent within national borders by state regulation, funding and an element of cultural differences.

But within national borders, the market for traditional learning is also becoming more competitive in most countries. The internal UK market is set to become more competitive with increased, but 'capped', fees being charged from 2006 onwards and universities competing to offer variable bursaries and incentives. Ironically, then the most competitive factors will be 'internal' to the UK market and here learning technology will play a key part in adding value to the conventional higher education experience and raising the profile of individual institutions against the provision of others.

The UK New Labour government of 1997 and 2002 took a less hesitant approach to the challenges of online learning to the UK HE sector when compared with the reflections of the CVCPs. It launched bold initiatives in both the national and international marketplace. None of these initiatives is noted for its success; indeed, much of the outcome is disappointing. The government sought to launch a number of special initiatives, at first outside the traditional UK institutions, while hoping that these new initiatives would build good cooperation and partnerships with the already well-established university providers. These new approaches predominantly focused on professional training and the business e-learning agenda. The first projects were the University for Industry and the NHS University. Although not specifically set up as online universities, their mission was always to have a strong online element.

In addition the e-University was set up as a £62 million, three-year, pioneering approach to international distance-based online learning. The e-University worldwide was established as a private company financed by the HEFCE. The aim was for the project to eventually break even from monies recouped in fees and charges to students recruited with partner universities. The project was to establish distance learning degrees in partnership with the UK's elite institutions, to firmly put such institutions at the forefront of the global e-learning marketplace.

In 2004 the e-University closed having been unable to demonstrate any likelihood of recovering its expensive high-tech costs. Much of this money was spent on a platform it developed in collaboration with Sun Microsystems who also contributed funding. More significantly the recruitment of students onto its e-learning courses never reached planned targets, despite the fact that courses were offered with prestigious institutions such as Cambridge University. On 2 August 2004 the *Guardian* reported that partner universities were likely to lose monies totalling over £2 million according to the financial services group responsible for the winding up of the e-University company.

The account of the UK e-University is a sobering tale of what can go wrong in the heady world of rapidly evolving new technology and ideas of online learning. Technology itself can look impressive, but to what extent can it really aid mass higher education and learning? When questioned in the House of Commons about the failure of the project the Higher Education Minister Kim Howells commented that not enough had been spent on marketing or content. But a different analysis might be offered. Little thought was given to the process of learning and related cultural aspects. Indeed, according to the marketing experts at Heist (www.heist.co.uk) the biggest single reason why overseas students come to the UK is the added value of studying in the English language and a closely associated factor is the physical experience of living in an English-speaking country. International distance learning courses do not offer the chance to maximize one's experience of living in the host country. At best, one will only visit the host country for occasional summer schools.

Failures of such bold visions are not exclusive to the UK. The online university for Europe also failed to establish itself, despite grants of over £2 million from the European Social Fund (Baty 2003). In America, online universities have had more success where they have been clearly linked with a segmented distant learning market that is strong in its vocational and professional focus, often delivering to a dispersed geographical community. The best-known example is the private University of Phoenix (www.uopx online.com/) that has a strong professional and business ethos. Established in 1976, Phoenix is a distance university that offers many distance-based courses via the Internet. Consortium and collaborative approaches can also work in the right context. For example, Open Learning Australia (www.o-pen.edu.au). The geographical features of Australia mean that online and distance learning will be particularly attractive to isolated communities.

In the international context, the role of online learning then becomes about adding value to the experience of international students living in a new country: allowing them to remain in regular contact with their home, allowing them good access back to their university when they travel home for vacations, promoting better learning and teaching access to written English content and translation of the written word alongside the spoken word.

One cannot down play the importance of the web and the Internet in advertising higher education, both in the internal national and continental markets and in the wider international markets already discussed. These media are increasingly the first point of reference for young and old alike who seek information about complicated educational products. Again the key is in using the web to enhance the impact of traditional methods such as open days and glossy leaflets.

Reviews into the future of higher education

The Web-Based Education Commission in the US concluded a major review of the impact of online learning on education in 2000. It noted the key strategic importance of information technology and online learning as a major method for learning that offered important transferable skills for the knowledge economy. The commission encouraged investment in technology to assist growth of online learning and expressed concern about poorer institutions and communities being left behind if they were not given sufficient resources and incentives. Computer training for educators was seen as a core issue.

Because of the rapid growth of higher education in the 1990s and the resulting resource difficulties experienced by institutions and their students, the UK government set up the National Committee of Inquiry into Higher Education under the chair of Sir Ron Dearing. This resulted in a very substantial report that demonstrated a core interest in the role of information technology in higher education. It recommended that increased use of IT could reduce relative costs and increase the flexibility of teaching and its ability to respond to diverse learning needs.

Throughout our report we identify scope for the innovative use of new Communications and Information Technologies (C&IT) to improve the quality and flexibility of higher education and its management. We believe these give scope for a reduction in costs. In the short term, implementation requires investment in terms of time, thought and resources, and we make recommendations about how this might be achieved.

(Dearing 1997: para. 65, summary report)

The report recommended that all students and staff should have access to laptop computers by 2006, a recommendation that looks unlikely to be achieved in most UK universities. The Dearing report was arguably the most important government review of higher education in the UK post-1945. It has led to a major change in the financing of tertiary education and looks likely to consolidate and institutionalize the expansion of the sector. It was totally committed to the central role that technology will play in the higher education environment of the twenty-first century.

The earlier review into postgraduate education in the UK by Lord Harris (1996) highlighted the geographical dilemma and paradox with the provision of higher education in an Internet age. It concluded that the future of highly specialist and professionally based postgraduate education was not to make it all distance based, but to keep some sense of geographical identity.

Nevertheless, existing statistics mask the fact that, increasingly, PG learning may be validated or provided by an HEI, but the student may actually be based outside the institution, such as in the workplace or at home studying, for example, through distance learning. While information technology (IT) and other new media are also increasingly important in the delivery of PG education, in a context where lifelong learning is becoming increasingly prevalent, many people at work will continue to need access to some forms of PG education near their homes or places of employment. The increasing provision particularly on a part-time basis by HEIs in dispersed locations spread across all regions is most important to the successful spread of lifelong learning.

(Harris 1996: para 3.21)

Allen and Seaman (2005) conclude that postgraduate education is the level of education that has seen the biggest area of growth in online provision in the USA in recent years.

The tension between both distance learning, multi-site learning and keeping some geographical links with a university campus is arguable now central to the mission of mass higher education. While the international student market is set to expand, this expansion is relatively small when compared with the national distribution of home students within any single country. There will continue to be a signficant national proportion of wealthier and most able students who travel long distances away from home to study at elite institutions in their own country. However, the biggest single impact on higher education will be a local and regional market where students can continue to live at home with their parents or return easily to parental homes at weekends for support. Indeed, this is likely to be the biggest segment of the expanding higher education market in many countries. These students will need access to technology-based content and learning processes to ensure the quality of their experience and to maxmize the efficiency of the time they spend developing knowledge. The Internet can add value to local and regional communication (Brown 2000). It is a paradox that we now look to technology not only to provide quality learning at a distance, but also to provide enhanced value for locally and regionally based students.

Collaboration – shared experimentation and risk management

One way in which higher education can maximize its use of technology in the face of limited public funding and high social and economic expectations about what can be achieved, is to encourage cooperation on a large scale to achieve economies of scale and the shared risk of technological failure. This can reduce duplication and wasted competition. Cooperation can be between public institutions and may also involve private bodies. Cooperation and risk sharing can also be important within large institutions, for example between different university departments.

In the USA, Internet2 is a consortium encouraging over 180 universities and 90 companies to cooperate and share the advantages of technology. It works closely with another partnership project called Next Generation Internet (NGI) This has allowed a more rapid dispersal of advanced technologies such as broadband, so that the educational and civic communities benefit alongside big business.

In the UK the Joint Information Systems Council was established in April 1993 to achieve economies of scale with information networks and services. This included development of the Joint Academic Network (JANET). This means that the JISC is funded directly by the Higher Education Funding Councils to provide a sophisticated IT communications network, both in the UK and with universities abroad. The specification of this network has had to improve rapidly in the past decade as the volume of traffic on the network has grown. For example from 1993 to 1995 the volume grew from under 50 gigabytes per day to over 350. In the same period its budget only grew from £29.9 million to 32.4 million (JISC 1996). More recently, the JISC has been at the centre of developments and debates in e-publishing by making a small number of scientific journals available freely on the Internet to UK academics. Prior to this the JISC has often negotiated to make electronic access easier for universities, again aiming to reduce costs and achieve economies of scale in negotiations with publishers, where possible.

The use of electronic journals in digital formats (such as Adobe pdf) has grown in the last decade. Electronic access often allows students of universities that subscribe to a publication to have access at home, and it encourages academics to obtain access via their desktop computer without having to make a physical visit to the library. These kinds of resources can be used to promote self-directed learning and to reduce a student's dependence on visits to a campus. Behind these developments is the debate about open-access publishing, where the academic community can take effective control of publication resources, either by paying the publisher for a completely open licence, or by covering all the costs of publication within the academic community. Many academics have been keen to progress such forms of open-access publishing via the web. One reason is that academics rarely get paid for contributing to journals, whether it is in the form of submitting articles, contributing to peer review or assisting the publisher with editorial decisions. More significantly, academics would welcome a world where good quality academic material was easily and widely available. There has always been a danger with expensive paper-based academic journals that their high selling price guarantees the publisher a profit when circulation is likely to be low, but has the opposite effect on increasing readership and wide dissemination of academic ideas. Open access offers the scope for using the technology of the web to widen access and knowledge dissemination. The problem with academic journals where the production is managed almost exclusive by the academic community and cutting out conventional publishers is that academics find it hard to commit the considerable time needed to digital production and often do not have well-developed skills for this. A danger is that presentational quality might suffer, even if the standard of the content is high. Similarly, the reputation of journals takes decades to establish, and new electronic journals find it difficult to compete for attention immediately they are launched. If commercial reasons for open access emerge, such as backing by leading scientific companies to get research into the public domain, then change may happen more quickly (Wray 2005).

International cooperation

The Bologna agreement between European Union (EU) countries is typical of the increase in international cooperation between universities that is likely to increase and drive change in the next two decades. An agreement in 1990 by the European Ministers of Education commits member countries to a comparable framework of undergraduate and postgraduate degrees with increased opportunities for courses to be shared between institutions and across Europe. Standardization in quality has already been partly achieved through the European Credit Transfer System (ECTS).

The increased use of information technology in higher education across Europe will help facilitate this interaction. Academics can now communicate and work together on innovative teaching and research projects more than ever before. Virtual communication such as email and online discussion makes this easier. Regular continental travel is less necessary. Continental cooperation is set to increase in future years as technology such as email, video conferencing, online discussion links, and so on make this easier. More EU students are likely to travel to another European country for a proportion of their studies. Technology will increase the ease of this movement and make it more straightforward for students to live in another country and culture. Universities that cooperate in European or international movement will find important benefits in raising their international profile and brand image, probably bringing them more opportunities to increase and diversify their revenue sources.

Conclusions

This chapter has illustrated the complex web of factors that make technology and online learning increasingly important to the future of higher education (Figure 1.2). It is argued in this book that it is not possible to resist technological change, but that the important task is to maximize the opportunities it brings to increase the quality of learning and the student experience. How to make best use of technology is not straightforward and requires careful consideration by each university and its various departments. 'A technology strategy is now a key component of the business strategy that can give competitive advantage to a university. A good strategy

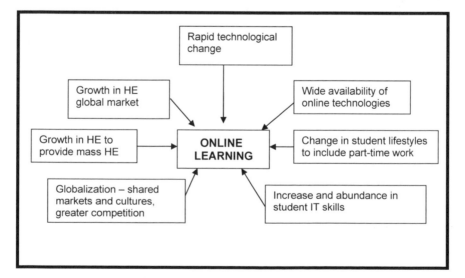

Figure 1.2   Drivers to online learning

must blend appropriateness and commitment, so its development requires debate, time and leadership' (Daniel 1996: 162). Formulating an appropriate strategy in a complex civic institution such as a university is far from straightforward, given the multitude of stakeholders and influences (Watson 2000).

What is clear is that online learning is not solely about distance learning. Its impact goes much wider. Academic practice increasingly focuses on blended learning (also known as hybrid learning or augmented learning). This integrates online learning with classroom- and face-to-face-based activities. University education has always required a maximum of self-directed learning, and online resources and processes can assist with helping a student to make progress on this difficulty journey. This path of independent lifelong learning is now followed by the majority of the population in many developed countries. But mass higher education does not remove new entrants to HE from their regional and local communities. It is one of the great paradoxes of the Internet and online communication that local and global are still closely interlinked. People are just as likely to send an email to someone in the same corridor or street, as they are to send one halfway around the world. Technology is not just about opportunities to learn at a distance, but also opportunities to learn in a new way not available to previous generations.

Mass higher education has resulted in a drive to prevent input costs rising, while increasing the efficiency of inputs to outputs. This is normally achieved by reducing the time spent in the classroom and by reducing small-group and individual tutorial teaching. Alongside this policy and management activity to increase outputs, academic professionals have sought to increase the effectiveness of outputs to outcomes, thereby maximizing the real long-term benefits of the teaching delivered and learning achieved. This often means changing the structure of degree courses so that knowledge and education gained has a high long-term social and economic value. Transferable skills are at a premium. In short, this is increasing the effectiveness of learning and teaching activities. Technology has much to offer this challenging environment. It is not the sole solution. The real solution lies in how academic teachers and their institutions engage with technology to use it creatively to raise the effectiveness of learning.

While technological change and the online environment is one of the drivers of change in higher education, it is also one of the responses to other changes. It offers new opportunities for adapting learning and teaching to the mass higher education environment. It offers opportunities to improve the quality of the learner's experience.

2

Where to Begin with Online Learning

Introduction

This chapter explores the way in which the Internet has become a learning and teaching resource and how information and communication technology (ICT) is now used in higher education as a mainstream method of learning communication. The aim is to examine practical questions such as the use of technology and the changing role of the tutor and teacher. The chapter then progresses how the online medium impacts learning behaviour and styles. These are the issues that academics must begin to face as they consider implementing online learning.

New opportunities

The development of the Internet began as a communication network between computer facilities and departments. Access to this communication was only open to those who were comfortable with computer programming command line language. But soon access to the Internet became user-friendly with the development of text-based hyper-linking on the World Wide Web that enabled one document to contain pointers to many others. Web browsers such as Netscape Navigator and Microsoft Explorer were born and these have subsequently been developed to display high-quality images, animations, video and audio media. Today the Internet is a form of mass communication that includes wireless and mobile phone contact. This has created an opportunity for the delivery of multimedia anywhere in the world. In addition, this networking of devices allows easy personal interaction across the globe. Universities and colleges across the world have seized this opportunity to widen access to higher education content and learning processes (George 1999), as new opportunities are presented for lively and interactive approaches to self-directed learning

(Hilton 2006). The Internet has altered how people access information and also how much information is available to individuals. Local, wide area and wireless networks now promote the Internet as a learning resource with software tools that enable sophisticated communication (Bernard et al. 2000). Online learning, then, not only produces new and dynamic approaches to the presentation of content, but also offers exciting new ways for students to interact and share learning.

Bernard et al. (2000) evaluated the effect of the availability of multimedia impacting on educational communities, learning materials and institutional practices. They define the changing characteristics of the learner population, with no single homogenous age or social class predominating. The network of new learners includes distance students who are not willing to carry on passively receiving information with minimal interaction and feedback. They also articulate the changing nature of the workplace that has created an increasing need for a knowledgable workforce which can work across continents and regularly update its skills through part-time study. The postmodern evolution of a service-driven society has made knowledge and its complexities a powerful product. Bernard et al. state that there is a need to examine how learning in such contexts occurs and how instruction can best be facilitated. The latest web 2.0 technologies (Alexander 2006) and e-learning 2.0 approaches (Downes 2005) claim to promote *informal* knowledge sharing and interaction that will further revolutionize learning and offer many more opportunities for self-managed learning that is not necessarily teacher directed.

In the USA and the UK major reports have promoted the use of information technology as a learning tool (Dearing 1997; Web-Based Education Commission 2000). The promotion of ICT created a variation in response from staff and higher education establishments. Some felt threatened, some were anxious and others did not have the time to address the issue, but many have taken on the issue whole-heartedly. This diversity of response was highlighted in a major review of online learning in American universities (Allen and Seaman 2005).

New structures

At the one end of the spectrum, universities such as Phoenix (www. phoenix.edu) in the USA specialize in delivering whole courses online and have become 'virtual' universities. Phoenix is a private institution that primarily offers online distance learning to a commercial market that seeks professional, managerial and business education and training. At the other end of the spectrum, many universities still deliver their educational experiences through geographically located face-to-face encounters between academic staff and students. These traditional institutions increasingly see technology and the Internet as helping them to adjust to a more interactive and dynamic method of learning. The mixed use of face-to-face learning with online learning is frequently referred to as 'blended learning' (sometimes also referred to as 'hybrid learning'). This approach is proving very popular and now affects almost all higher educational institutions. Under the umbrella of blended learning there will be considerable diversity in the mix of traditional face-to-face methods and online methods that are used. We discuss this mix further throughout the book. In essence what is happening is that elements of the new online approach to distance learning are being used in part to augment face-to-face learning. This offers new opportunities to encourage self-directed learning.

Modes and levels of online learning

Similarly, online learning can be located into the categories web supplemented, web dependent or fully online, depending on how much online content and learning process is used in any one module. Therefore a flexible approach to learning is interpreted to meet the needs of the institution, faculty, school or individual and online learning should be applied with sensitivity to a particular educational and student context (for a more detailed explanation see Chapter 4).

Table 2.1 illustrates the wide range of online learning, moving from the simple distribution of content to fully functioning online courses with integrated activities and online communication. This illustrates the potential application of online learning to a wide range of educational situations and why it cannot be criticized as merely content driven and leading always to surface learning. Online learning has the potential to be used in many different ways, and can also support deeper levels of learning (for definitions of surface and deep learning see page 52).

Table 2.1   Simple to complex use of virtual learning environments

SIMPLE	A quick and easy way to use the web to distribute course materials and carry out course administration.
	A gateway to additional online materials.
	A means of communication between students, tutors and outside contributors.
	A 'shell' for computer-based learning resources.
	Provision of examination practice and administration of summative examinations.
	Provision of additional support and practice for campus-based students.
	A platform for collaborative student projects.
COMPLEX	Delivery of complete online courses with fully integrated activities, e.g. distance learning courses.

Source: adapted from O'Leary (2002: 2)

Online learning environments

Since 2000, many universities have tried to implemented a virtual learning environment (VLE) or managed learning environment (MLE) that will provide a unified technology platform from which to embed ICT in learning and teaching. These resources are usually available to all courses, modules, staff and students in the institution, and raise expectations that academic staff will provide some level of online resources to their students. These types of standardized technological approaches therefore aim to deliver online learning, albeit in some basic form, to the majority. They consist of a robust hardware servers and web-based database software. The VLE is an integrated package of software tools and features which aim to facilitate a complete learning experience (O'Leary 2002). The VLE often forms part of a larger MLE. The difference between the two is that the MLE interacts with a range of information systems, for example student records, credit accumulation management, information services (such as an online library), finance, and so on. In most cases the purchase and delivery of a standardized online learning environment provides a more even distribution of resources and opportunities to all staff in an institution or network of organizations. Table 2.1 summarizes the phases of development. Online learning can be delivered without commercial VLE/MLE software, but large educational institutions that can afford it increasingly look to purchase and maintain such a system. The alternative is for web-based materials to be developed within the institution by its own staff. Prior to the arrival of commercial VLEs, 'home grown' online learning often required skills in the use of hypertext mark-up language or HTML editing, using software packages (such as Dreamweaver) in order to create vibrant attractive web pages. But busy academics were often reluctant to learn the complexities of these editing skills in addition to the other demands of their job.

In online learning, the VLE is used to present course materials. It provides a means of communication between tutors and their students, and between student peers. It provides an opportunity for self-assessment, monitoring of progress, submission and return of assignments. Online learning course materials are easy to create on commercial VLEs, as they can remove the need to have prior knowledge of HTML web programming and make the use of web pages as easy as possible by using simple text and image editors and basic web buttons and submission forms. The more ICT-capable academic may complain that such packages reduce the level of creativity available to the user, but the important trade-off is that the majority of staff can easily use an online web-based system.

The arrival of online learning platforms created and packaged by leading software manufactures has made the use of VLEs much more of a possibility for all academics. Examples of such packages are Blackboard and WebCT. In addition to the commercial products there are some self-funded developments and open source applications. While there are some differences between the main commercial online learning platforms, they tend to have common features, which are explored below.

Before moving on it is important to mention the definition of learning management systems (LMSs) that have some overlap and similarity with VLEs. A number of universities have been cooperating on an international project to develop an LMS that is suited to creating and managing learning activities in an academic environment. Traditionally, LMSs have been used for managing complex organizational training. The key difference between an LMS and VLE is that the LMS provides more detailed, creative and interactive control for the participants in how the visual presentation of content and learning experience takes shape. As they tend to handle relatively more complex interactions in a seamless way than VLEs, LMSs are more expensive. At the time of writing LMSs have not become mainstream resources in universities, although they have been used by a number of commercial organizations for managing training programmes. In the future they may influence the evolution of VLEs. Finally, a slightly different resource is the Learning Activity Management System (LAMS) developed by an international not-for-profit (open source) partnership (www.lamsinter national.com/) and this offers the academic environment a specialist resource for building online learning activities.

Individualized student and staff entry portal

A personal home page is displayed after logging on that gives a welcome to the user and lists online courses or modules upon which the student is enrolled (or which the tutor will be teaching). The user will only see courses and modules listed which are relevant to their studies or teaching. Some systems allow students to alter the presentation of their home page and what information is summarized there. Tutors get an additional button on their home page that takes them to a control area where they can set up the learning content for their students and manage and monitor their progress.

Message board

Once the student clicks into a specific course or module, the entry point or opening screen can be set by the tutor. It is helpful if this opening screen is the message board (sometimes described as *news* or *announcements*) as it ensures that any messages are visible to the student straight away when logging on. It may be used by the tutor to point out the posting of new information, and links are available to direct the students towards these or to give out other announcements. In our own institutions, student pigeonholes and pin-up notice boards are disappearing from corridors as more information is given out through these virtual notice boards.

Area for posting course information, for example timetables and course handbooks

This is sometimes referred to as the 'online filing cabinet'. It is used to house course documentation, regulations, and so on. It is a useful repository of information and is generally considered to be much more environmentally friendly than printing out course handbooks and photocopying them. If course handbooks are to be used online it is a good idea to break down the information into smaller chunks and to post these on the VLE as single short units of text, rather than one long course document. Examples are assessment schedule, module outline, course specific regulations, links to the university's General Examination and Assessment Regulations. This saves the student having to trawl through a long document to find the piece of information required at any given time. Many staff simply attach course documents as word-processing documents, but it is important that students can open attachments with relevant software on their own computers. Many higher education institutions prefer staff to convert files into the standard portable document format (pdf), so that they can guarantee all students will be able to access attachment files with freely available pdf readers (for example, Adobe Acrobat Reader: www.adobe.com). Portable document format converters for download can be found by searching on the Internet, but it is best to check if your institution is recommending you use a particular version (for the importance of student use of pdf, see Chapter 4).

Area for lodging course materials, for example learning resources

This is where information for online learning or to support face-to-face learning can be stored, and is the best place to store presentations, lecture notes, digitalized reading material and multimedia files. Students can access this information easily and print off what they wish or otherwise save and store the information electronically. Again this is a greener option than printing out handouts for students. The information is readily accessible, but some tutors will be concerned that this causes the cost of printing to be transferred from the university to the student and may wish to continue to produce some materials as hard paper copies. Sometimes hyperlinks are posted to identify learning resources elsewhere that cannot, for copyright or similar reasons, be posted directly. Where multimedia content is used, for example digital video or audio 'podcast' material, it is important to make sure that students have access to multimedia software (such as Windows Media Player, Real Audio Player or Quicktime) that will play the resource. Students who do this in a university open-access computer room will need reminding to keep a set of Walkman headphones with them.

Academics will want to organize and use these materials to develop *learning activities* or *learning units* that are bite-sized online study packs which enable students to engage with content through related activities. These are best designed using a range of text sizes and colours that are easy for the students to see and engage with. Thought must be given to linearity and ordering of the content. Virtual learning environments allow different materials to be released at different predetermined times, so that students do not get too confused or perplexed by seeing lots of materials at the beginning of their module. Learning units will often be directly linked to discussion boards (forums) or similar interactive elements that promote student interaction.

Group discussion boards and forums

This area can be used to encourage interactive debate and student-to-student reflection, and to foster the negotiation of meanings. This will be supported by academic staff. In our own institutions these facilities have been used in a range of ways: as a platform to run weekly seminars that reflect on given reading, as online action learning sets to reflect on contemporary issues, or to share the findings of problem-based learning groups who must use a range of resources to consider how best to deal with a given problem (there is further discussion of these methods in Chapter 5). Discussion boards can also be used simply as an informal means of keeping in touch with fellow students. Initially a discussion forum is set up by the tutor and then students are directed towards it. Links to the discussion can be placed in other content areas. Discussion threads are then created and students are notified when a new posting has been made so that they can read it and comment as necessary. Discussions can be synchronous (all students and the tutor online at the same time) or asynchronous (students and tutors contribute to the discussion when it is convenient to them over a longer period of time, for example a week). Asynchronous has been the dominant mode of online learning so far, but synchronous is improving. Systems are adding audio and video communication. These additions are likely to make synchronous contact more attractive. Synchronous discussion can usually be managed in a 'chat box' window (where all contributions are seen immediately they are submitted), rather than in a thread area where contributions are organized hierarchically under each thread.

One key aspect to be aware of is that online discussions take a little longer to start than classroom discussions and need much more direction from the tutor at the beginning. However, once they gain confidence, students proceed apace. The tutor needs to be very active in the discussion, contributing and facilitating the development of meaning for the students.

Our own evaluation has identified that these online discussions favour the shy or reticent student who may be reluctant to make a verbal contribution in class. Motivation for participation in online discussion has also been a topic of concern. In our own work we have found that students are strongly motivated by assessment, so asking students to write a short piece of reflection on what they have contributed and gained from online discussions as part of the assessment helped ensure that students do take part.

Opportunities for automated formative and summative assessment

This is a facility which enables tutors to devise online quizzes and tests. Although from a teacher's perspective it is often thought that tests such as this only promote surface learning, they can be useful to reassure students and tutors that learning is taking place when used in a formative manner. Quizzes and tests can be set up relatively easily. They can be multiple choice or other formats. The number of attempts a student may make and the way in which answers and feedback is given can be managed by the tutor. Feedback is immediate and does not need to be marked by the tutor. This is a very valuable means of monitoring progress in order to give individual student guidance. Types of questions need to be carefully chosen in order to meet student learning outcomes.

Links to other web sites

This type of area is useful for directing students to other online resources and could include links to other learning and teaching web sites such as those offered by large publishing companies to support textbooks or e-books. In order to encourage students to use the wide and varied resources of the Internet, it is often helpful to include some very general background information about a web site and its content. Students then widen their searching to find more specific information for themselves, having had a basic knowledge framework that prepares them to understand the more complex information found elsewhere. Links to content might be used in a similar way to which a student initially uses a general textbook and then makes selective decisions about more detailed reading.

Wikis and blogs

Wikis are open-access databases that allow users to participate by adding and editing each other's material. Some VLEs refer to these areas as teams. Wikis typically have an easy-to-use set of text-editing rules that do not require any knowledge of HTML code. They also allow easy editing of links to other wiki contributions. An example in education would be an open glossary where students can contribute to definitions of key terms and concepts on their course. The word 'wiki' comes from Hawaii and apparently means 'quick'. Academics and teachers have played a key part in establishing the world-famous www.wikipedia.com. This is an open-access encyclopedia where readers and users can contribute to the definition of words and concepts.

Blogs are online personal diaries. They are only interactive when users choose to share them with others, so that others can contribute with responses and questions to the author's thoughts and ideas. Many universities now offer this online service to their students, and if necessary can allow blogs to be developed in the context of a specific course or module, so that focused reflection becomes part of the learning experience.

Group communication tools

The software can be arranged so that a cohort of students can be managed in different ways for communication purposes. For example, groups can be set up so that a tutor can send one email to all of his or her personal tutees, to a seminar group or to an individual student. This is a very useful tool which saves a great deal of time. Discussion boards, wikis and blogs can also be set up within small group sub areas of a course or module.

Tracking and managing learning

The course or module area on the VLE can also be set up so that student activity can be tracked. Statistics can be produced to monitor student online attendance, registration, contributions to discussions and conferences, and assessment of performance in online quizzes and tests. This information can be useful in evidencing student performance and in personal or academic tutoring as formative feedback to the tutor. It is also possible to set up online student evaluation forms that provide an automatic compilation of results.

Further considerations about designing online learning experiences follow in Chapters 4, 5 and 6.

The evolution of online learning

In the 1990s, some universities allowed their academic staff to take the initiative in developing the integration of ICT into programmes of education. There was a common belief that a bottom–up approach was more likely to be supported by staff than a perceived enforced top–down method of introduction. Development funding directed at a few pinoneering academics established many first projects. The enthusiasts moved the boundaries forward. However, within such universities, members of staff working individually or in small teams could find themselves working in isolation using a diverse range of hardware and software applications to deliver learning experiences to students. At first these isolated communities of practice were reluctant to pool any resources or share a great deal of information or experience. This led to many wheels being reinvented, and some areas of development having huge resources (possibly inappropriately) and others trying to develop projects on a shoestring budget. By the late 1990s students arriving in higher education, all with good ICT skills, were increasingly placing demands on their universities for online-based resources and content. As a result, universities have made online learning resources mainstream and sought to establish resources that are offered to all staff and students (see Table 2.2).

Table 2.2 Phases in the development of online learning

Phase	Aspects
Pioneer phase	A few academics invest hugely in experimenting with online learning, but the majority are sceptical.
Communities of practice phase	Pioneers begin to cluster and mutually support each other; best practice is identified and grows.
Standardization phase	University managers recognize the best practice and seek to implement it with all academic staff.

There is an assumption that this integration of technology structures with learning activities is both what students require and what the academic institutions will support. Will the academic staff have the skills (technological and androgogical) to make use of this brave new world of ICT? What will any students who choose to take advantage of this mode of delivery feel about their experiences? The process needs to be evaluated from a range of perspectives in order to ascertain what is working and why, and what is not working. We need to build on strengths and improve any areas of weakness. We will now begin to explore some of these important questions.

Orientation to online learning

Online learning is not appropriate for all students, tutors and subject material. In practical terms some hands-on type of skills still need to be learned in traditional classrooms or laboratories on some occasions (Kearsley 2002). Simulation may reduce the need for real-world practice, but it cannot completely replace it.

Students and teaching staff who are not comfortable in the use of ICT are unlikely to become exponents of online learning without first being able to see considerable benefits and before investing time and risking their esteem by embarking on an online adventure! Some students will have to be persuaded of the benefits, as is the case with any type of learning activity. Table 2.3 summarizes the barriers to good online learning that are discussed in this section.

Table 2.3   Barriers to online learning – dealing with some of the assumptions

Diagnosis	Prognosis
No previous computer skills:	Skills are increasingly taught at school.
Anxious and cynical about the usefulness of computers:	Difficult to maintain such a view given the proliferation of ICT and the wide acknowledgement that they have some benefits.
Forced choice – use of computer-based learning seen as the only (poor) method for taking a learning process:	Raises student anxiety, lowers motivation and is likely to reduce chances of experiencing good learning.
No easy availability of computer:	Rapidly changing situation, with universities experiencing a proliferation of devices.
Academic staff	
Need for multitasking when there is insufficient time available:	Academics overwhelmed with the pace of change and so need positive support and training from the academic community.
Need background ICT skills:	Training needed that is relevant.
ICT cannot replace other personal interactive and augmentative skills:	Academics engaging in online learning need to feel enthused about its possibilities for creating interactivity.
Managers	
Online learning can efficiently replace some classroom and small-group activity:	Replacement is not easily achieved because the opportunities of online learning are complementary and play to different student strengths.
There is less pressure on scarce physical resources, and journeys and travel to the university can be reduced:	But student will need training and induction into how to get the most and best out of online learning, and some will need access to ICT resources.
The university can easily widen its catchments to out-of-region and international students by using a virtual environment:	Some students want to travel long distances to study in a new physical environment, so they can experience new cultures and make new friends. Online learning is misunderstood if it is seen primarily as a distance mission.

In order to participate effectively in online learning students need to possess some qualities of self-discipline and initiative. They need to be able to develop a study schedule and stick to it. Not all students have these attributes well developed when they arrive at university and may, if given the choice, prefer traditional face-to-face teaching (Kearsley 2002). In the face-to-face environment there can be behaviour associated with earlier school experiences, where regular attendance is reinforced alongside group experiences and participation. However, it could be argued that traditional learning and teaching is also increasingly placing the responsibility more firmly with the student in the spirit of developing autonomous learners who are able to move forward and practice self-directed lifelong learning. Allen and Seaman (2005) found that a majority of academics sampled in the USA thought that students needed more discipline to succeed in an online course when compared with a traditional teaching course. This can be a problem if a student who is undertaking online learning is only doing so because it is the only means of accessing a particular module of study and they have no choice in the matter. An evaluation of students' performance and learning experience by the authors has led us to believe that these students seldom do well. They feel at a disadvantage and have very low expectations of what can be achieved through ICT.

Students need access to a computer with an Internet connection. There can be problems if students are sharing a computer at home as there may be insufficient time to access participation in learning activities such as online discussion groups. Part-time students who may wish to use a computer at work to engage in online learning activities may find that there is no protected time at work and demands begin to conflict. Homes which only have one phone line and use a dial-up connection often experience conflict among household members when the phone line is tied up for long periods of time. Broadband is becoming more competitively priced and is often offered now in a package with cheaper telephone calls and cable television channels. Universities provide increasing numbers of open access computer pools where students can use a shared computer. Larger numbers of students are buying their own computers and laptops. Universities need creative policies to encourage students to purchase computers and to use appropriate software. It is surprising that the sector has not done more to work with companies to negotiate good deals and interest-free loans, although there are some examples of this. There are limitations if students are encouraged to buy cheap reconditioned machines that will not be able to work at speed or in wireless settings.

Universities are starting to provide wireless networks, within university buildings and across campuses, that are accessible to students with their own laptops and similar devices The advent of G3, WiFi and WiMax networks means that the Internet can also be accessed in airports and on trains, and therefore will be useful for students who are commuting or on the move. In time, access can only become easier. In future, universities may need to give clear recommendations about the kind of mobile phones or similar devices that students should purchase, so that these can be used collectively as technological tools for learning (Leon 2004). This may include negotiating attractive deals with commercial suppliers on students' behalf.

Computer literacy is a key skill required for online learning. Students and staff all need a basic understanding of word-processing and at least email, file attachments, pdf files and web browsing before embarking on study. Knowledge of how the Internet works is also important. Students usually need a specific orientation programme for their online learning in addition to any general induction they may have received. There are likely to be difficulties if students do not know how to apply and adapt their skills to an online learning environment. A number of universities and companies have online questionnaires that give a basic assessment of a person's computer skills. At the time of writing Miami university (www.miami.muohio.edu/ – search 'computer skills') had a public example. A further simple example can be seen at the Community College of Rhode Island (www.ccri.edu/ distance/computerskills.shtml). Many universities now have personal study skills modules at the start of longer courses, to ensure that students do have the right prerequisites before they commence substantial periods of study. These early experiences need to support and develop the ICT skills necessary for online learning. Oblinger and Hawkins (2006) caution against making assumptions that new, young students have all the technological skills they need and suggest that academics and universities regularly re-evaluate what is required because of the fast-changing nature of digital resources and information provision.

Online academic tutors also need a good degree of computer literacy as they often have to spend time trouble shooting student or system problems. They need to have the flexibility to spend time online in order to facilitate learning effectively and have a sound understanding of computer tools and delivery systems. Information and communication skills can be developed through staff training and development (Haynes et al. 2004) and there is sometimes a second line of support for online tutors, such as a learning technologist or technician. It should, however, be acknowledged that many excellent classroom teachers would not automatically make good online learning facilitators. The tutor needs to enjoy technology to be an enthu-siastic online tutor and a transition to the new medium will not work if they are in a high state of anxiety about using it. Institutions need to provide staff development support and training.

University managers have sometimes stated the following views about online learning that they perceive as obvious advantages over traditional face-to-face delivery:

- No classrooms or other onsite facilities are needed.
- Students do not need to travel to the university and no parking is needed.
- It is possible to reach student markets anywhere in the country or the world.

- An infinite number of students can be serviced at no significant extra cost.

However, our experience of the reality is somewhat different. Online learning offers different and complementary learning and teaching strategies that can only be realized by prior investment rather than rapid changes of direction that are poorly resourced.

Good progress across an institution therefore depends on the following:

- An Internet platform for delivery needs to be available (the most effective MLEs or VLEs are usually bought in from outside the university and reputable systems are costly).
- The purchased MLE or VLE is likely to need its own designated staff to support it and ongoing investment and technical servicing.
- Some face-to-face delivery may still be deemed necessary (for example, for induction or blended learning).
- It will be possible to enroll students nationally and internationally but the online modules or courses offered need to be suitable to meet student's cultural needs. Some national and international online learning markets are very much niche markets, rather than generic ones, and these markets have to be understood carefully.
- Issues of language and learning culture may be problematic with an international audience and therefore require extra resources.
- Clear marketing and promotion of what is happening and what is being offered is required, so that new students know what to expect and enrol on suitable courses.

It cannot be assumed that online learning is likely to be a more effective mass learning method than sitting in a large-group lecture that breaks for small-group exercises. It is not easy to work effectively with infinite numbers of students en masse in any environment. Large numbers of students also need to be broken down into smaller groups for online work (this is similar to what needs to happen in large-group teaching). Working on smaller group sizes increases the potential for interaction between group members and facilitates easier management of class activity and learning. The tutor needs good organization and management skills in order to deal with initial technological difficulties that students experience and to coordinate the learning process at the same time as managing the usual demands of being a tutor. There is no reason to assume that online learning is a 'magic solution' for solving the challenge of teaching large groups, but it does offer useful new resources and new creative opportunities.

It would be easy for a misinformed manager or academic to think that once an online learning environment is set up, it can be left to run itself and will therefore be less resource intensive. Our experience is that online learning needs to be facilitated skilfully by experienced tutors, with material being frequently updated, and this takes considerable time. It does not run itself and the management of an online learning process is as resourceful and skilled as managing a face-to-face learning exercise. Allen and Seaman's (2005) large survey of online learning in the USA found that 72 per cent of academics were neutral about whether online courses saved faculty time and effort, with only 23 per cent believing time savings were guaranteed. Feedback from students who are experiencing online learning needs to be taken into account when making these changes in order to limit student attrition. Students who are struggling to learn online need to receive regular encouraging emails and feedback, and need to be encouraged to give each other such feedback. Later in this book we argue on several occasions that personal encouragement and feedback for students is vital for successful online learning, particularly in the early stages of a course.

Preparing students

What do we expect from our online students? Hrachovec (2000) states that attaining computer literacy is an important educational goal. He defines the main features of this as the ability to:

- Interact with an operating system;
- Use word-processing software and accounting software;
- Search the Internet.

We anticipate that students will form tutorial relationships with tutors and each other through email, web-mediated file exchange and asynchronous computer conferencing. This is quite different to both the traditional model of distance learning and face-to-face learning. Tuition is conducted in personal interactions through the written word. Students and tutors do not necessarily meet. They may not be in the same institutions or even in the same continent or time zone (Blake 2000).

In our experience students need extra induction into online learning. Induction needs to be at two levels

1   *First level of induction.* This is for those who do not have much experience of using IT and who may not have studied for some time. These students need a short programme of study skills relevant to the online environment that enables them to begin to manage their own learning, and an induction to ICT skills so that they can meet the prerequisites for the programme, that is, to word-process a document, send an email with an attachment and log on to the web. Younger students who have come through the education system recently are more likely to have these skills and may not need this level of induction; however, it is our experience that mature students often need something of a confidence boost in this area. This level of preparation needs to be focused on the student's individual needs. Some universities encourage students to bring their skills up to a given benchmark IT qualification level early in

their time at university (for example, the European Computer Driving Licence).

2   *Second level of induction.* This comes at the beginning of the module or course which is to be delivered online. This needs to introduce the cohort of students into the modus operandi of the VLE and the way in which the different facets of the VLE will be used to support learning in the module or programme they are about to tackle. Essentially this type of induction enables students to feel confident about finding their way around specific online resources. It needs to include familiarizing students with more advanced online search techniques (see Box 2.1) and the use of pdf text files. It needs to equip students to use online video and audio if this is a requirement for learning.

Despite the challenges we have discussed, online learning has been developing steadily over the past 20 years and, despite initial resistance, online learning has gained respectability and is becoming commonplace. It is seen as being more flexible, more convenient and, in some circumstances, cost-effective. Our experience is that to compare online learning with face-to-face learning is not always appropriate. It is not better, but different. It comes with a key benefit for those who choose to use it: added technology and Internet communication skills.

Learning styles and online learning

All students learn in different ways and each individual has his or her own preferred learning styles (Kolb 2000). Students are different in the way they prefer to learn, however, Kolb's research argued that it is possible to group students into 'types'. Familiarity with personal learning style can assist learners to understand the way in which they learn and it will certainly enable the tutor to design effective learning experiences if they are aware of the range and variety of learning styles to be accommodated. Online learning may involve teachers in encouraging students to modify their preferred learning style and to develop new styles and approaches, and this will make them more adaptable in their learning in the future (Zywno and Stewart 2005).

Laurillard (1987) described how students use a range of concepts in learning according to the context in which they are operating. This would indicate that students are not either one kind of learner or another but that they vary their approach to learning according to the situation in which they find themselves. If students have the ability to call on different learning styles and can learn to adjust, then they can use differing strategies in different situations.

Students need to be helped to have insight into their own learning styles and to find ways of becoming more adaptable (Howarth 2004). These are important transferable skills for the working environment. One study

---

Box 2.1 Online information search techniques

Students need to understand the different types of online search services and how to get the best from them.

Search engines

Generic examples:

> www.google.com or www.google.co.uk
> www.yahoo.com or uk.yahoo.com/

Advanced areas of search engines

Like http://scholar.google.com/

Using the search engine **advanced search** *service*

Make students aware of **advanced search** links at these web sites.

- Learn how to search for **exact phrases**.
- Mixtures of given words: **at least one** given word; or **without** a given word.

Indexing and abstracting services

More specialist academic services that will give access to quality material.

Boolean search terms that will work with most services, and are useful to some extent with web search engines:

- Use of **AND** to link two or more key words – so the search is more focused. *For example, computers AND teaching.*
- Use of **OR** to widen the search. *For example, computers OR teaching.*
- Use of **NOT** to narrow the search. *For example, computers NOT teaching.*

Many services have *search tabs* that allow author names to be mixed with combinations of key words, title words, words in journal titles, and so on.

(Drennan et al. 2005) found that students with autonomous and innovative learning styles were more likely to express satisfaction with flexible online learning opportunities. In this 'before and after' research study of several hundred students, positive perceptions of technology were also a contributory factor to an expression of satisfaction. This suggests that online learning fits well with developing learner autonomy and innovation, but it may present formidable challenges to learners who are not confident with technology and who are used to passive teacher-led learning. Some learners will need considerable support in order to acquire the benefits that online learning offers and to make the necessary adjustments.

Making sure that resources are matched with learning styles can maximize the learning experience for students. One of the most well-known instruments for assessing learning styles is Honey and Mumford's (1992) learning styles questionnaire. Leopold-Lusmann (2000) explored learning styles theory related to VLEs and concluded that a large proportion of educationalists are aware of learning styles and the value of applying the theory to the design of learning materials. He believes that pressure of work, high student numbers and lack of learner needs analysis often means that tutors do not use their knowledge and skills to assist learners. This occurs in face-to-face learning as well as online learning. Leopold-Lusmann (2000: 8) maintains that: 'The application of learning styles theory to online learning is highly relevant as the teacher cannot directly observe how students utilise the teaching strategies provided.'

Online learning may have a strong congruence with autonomous and active learning (Thiele 2003), but teachers will have to work at making it a successful interface for all students (Dixon et al. 2005; Pena-Shaff et al. 2005).

Andragogy

Andragogy was a term introduced by Knowles (1980). He believed that adults learn differently than children. Pedagogy is a term often used to describe techniques of learning and teaching. However, the word 'pedagogy' is linked to the Greek word for child. Knowles defined the term 'andragogy' to give a name to this learning process related to adults. Knowles noted that one of the features of adult learners is that adults tend to be motivated to learn what they need to know, when they need to learn it. This must affect the way in which learning experiences and curricula for adults are designed.

The advent of the potential to deliver online learning experiences has begun to change the view that open and distance learning are the primary role of certain specialist institutions (Beaty et al. 2002). This has led to many higher education institutions looking to deliver learning experiences via ICT and online technologies, and to offer some elements of self-directed distance and online learning alongside a resident university experience. It is clear that the provision of technology alone is not enough. Tutors need to be able to translate their tuition skills to the ICT medium. Questions immediately arise as to whether tutors actually understand what they really do in face-to-face encounters with students. If they do not understand the androgogical issues here, they are going to have great difficulty in effectively using ICT to support learning and teaching and also in designing online learning experiences. 'The way we use technology to support and/or provide learning environments reflects the educational assumptions and philosophy underlying design and has implications for the quality of the student learning experience' (Beaty et al. 2002: 2).

Beaty et al. propose that the significant capabilities of online learning are the ability to support collaborative interaction and dialogue and to support information-rich resources. They place heavy emphasis on the community of scholars involved in online learning, rather than an ICT network acting as a repository of knowledge, like an online filing cabinet. The relationship here between tutor and student is based on collaboration and co-construction of knowledge. These authors feel that tutors will need to adjust to a change in role and engage in critical and reflexive evaluation of their own practice. They hold (and our experience confirms) that this needs to be supported through professional development time for tutors. They call for a policy for online learning based on educational values and research. There is a danger that online learning and e-learning is used to present sophisticated content without much thought about the learning process of how that content is used and understood by students. Many commercial companies have moved into the e-learning content market in recent years, but universities need to keep the process of learning at the centre of their reflections on how this new content is actually used.

Learning philosophies and new technologies

Educational philosophers raise concerns about ICT. Lyotard (1984) feared that any form of knowledge which cannot be digitized will be abandoned. In 1984 this would have been a realistic fear, but as technology advances it becomes difficult to imagine what information could not be digitized. The world's biggest information companies have recently talked about an alliance to digitize all known written documents (Sutherland 2005). But the process of using information to create knowledge still remains at the heart of the creative human endeavours of higher education institutions. This creative process cannot be automated by technology. Tacit knowledge is resistant to easy quantification and expression in any teaching medium. It is a reality that at the present time surgeons can practise complex techniques in simulated and real procedures using guidance and mentorship simultaneously from skilled practitioners in another continent on the other side of the world (Blake and Standish 2000). In this type of online learning, shared human experience of knowledge is more important than the presentation of passive information content. Online learning is not about an instrumental approach to learning, but should be about a creative evolution of knowledge through interaction. It should enhance good learning philosophies.

Lyotard (1984) expressed concerns for the effects of new technologies and the ways in which they would change the status of knowledge. Among these were concerns that the availability of knowledge as an international commodity would become the basis for national and commercial advantage within the workforce. This leads to knowledge being exteriorized in relation to the knower. The status of the teacher and the learner is transformed into a commodity relationship of supplier and user.

Writers such as Lyotard are worried that in the new knowledge economy and global society (as discussed in Chapter 1) we will see the commodification of knowledge and that this will undermine traditional university values and supersede learning with a market-based value system. Only knowledge that is valued by the market will be valued by higher education.

While the growth of higher education has been linked to the integration of theory and practice in this way, with an increasing focus on vocational degrees and professional technical competence, this does not necessarily mean that higher education becomes only a market commodity. The debate about the vocational practice of learning and its relationship with traditional higher education pre-dates the debate about the usefulness of online learning. In this sense, anxieties about the marketization of knowledge and the impact of technology are not new.

The implications of Lyotard's concerns are discussed by Lankshear et al. (2000) The state's role in promoting and providing learning could change, given the possible future relationship between the state and information-rich multinational companies. There are concerns about the fragmentation of learning and teaching. 'The relationship between what students learn and the ways in which they learn it versus what people actually do and how they do it in a world increasingly mediated by ICTs has become increasingly tenuous' (Lankshear et al. 2000: 43). This suggests that there are problems with the ICT-based automation of learning and that ICT-based mediation can be 'disconnected' from the learning process.

It is certainly important to understand how knowledge relates to working practices. Lankshear et al. (2000) speak of a performative epistemology where knowing leads to making, doing and acting. Thus there is a relationship between knowing and mastery of technique. Ulmer (1985) defined a process of:

- Bricolage – the assemblage of elements into a specialist curriculum.
- Collage – the practice of transferring materials from one element to another (so thinking through how it will work in an online medium).
- Montage – the practice of disseminating borrowings into a new setting (placing learning materials and learning processes into the online environment).

In this book we argue that there is no deterministic reason why online learning should undermine active, interactive and creative learning philosophies. It does not have to be exclusively linked with narrow market definitions of knowledge- and skills-based competencies. Indeed, we present an argument that online learning can, in certain conditions, improve the complete range of learning opportunities available and promote assertive, critical and creative approaches to the generation of knowledge.

Deep and surface learning

In 1976 researchers in Gothenburg, Sweden, developed a new approach to educational research that they based on phenomenography. This qualitative approach aimed to explore the process of learning as experienced by the learner rather than from concepts imposed by the researcher (Marton and Saljo 1997). Using this approach, educationalists were able to explore the *outcome* of learning as well as the *approach* to learning taken by the individual learner. As a result of this Marton and Saljo developed the concept of deep and surface-level processing. Surface-level processing would be characterized by the learner undertaking superficial activities such as memorizing facts, while deep-level processing would be characterized by a concern to understand the material being studied (Biggs 1999). In other words, deep learning would construct and internalize a deeper personal meaning.

It is our experience that the promotion of deep learning is highly appropriate as it increases the student's ability to transfer learning for use in varying situations. Students will always need to memorize some facts, and surface-level strategies will be used for this. Using the Internet for learning and teaching has led to concern among some theorists who believe that although the Internet has provided a huge resource for instantly available information, it does not foster understanding and the deeper levels of learning.

Our experience is that much depends on the design of the online module or programme. There is no reason why online learning should not be used to promote deep learning (Rosie 2000). A thorough understanding of the potential of the VLE coupled with skill in adapting the required outcome of learning with the elements of the VLE can promote deep learning. For example:

- Surface learning – online quizzes may provide a useful formative assessment to give students an idea of how their knowledge of facts is progressing in a given area.
- Deep learning – online action learning sets can be used to support a work-based learning initiative using skilfully facilitated asynchronous discussion, or blogs and wikis can present learners' reflections on the materials they are considering.

Lifelong learning

Lifelong learning is the idea that learning should occur in numerous places in society and throughout the life course. It should include formal and informal learning and different learning methods. It is a holistic approach that is often used by governments to describe the need to learn new skills throughout working life.

New technologies, notably ICT, have made a huge impact on employment in the past 20 years, leading to great rate of change in many spheres of modern life. Employment patterns and the working environment have been transformed. The new 'learning society' needs to be made up of individuals who are flexible and can cope with change in order to enhance participatory citizenship. The limitations of traditional education need to be addressed. Forms of education and training need to be able to cope with diverse learning needs. This involves a wide range of stakeholders: pre-school-leaving education, further education, higher education, adult education and continuing professional development, employing organizations and the government (Edwards et al. 1998). The concept of lifelong learning has become linked to the rapidly changing environment of the modern global economy and the idea that people need to be flexible and able to change jobs by learning the skills required to create new economic conditions.

There is considerable controversy over the relative importance of participation, equity, social integration and economic success in the design of policies and programmes of learning. There is a concern among academics that the demand for a 'learning society' is a market response to economic issues rather than a social imperative, and that catering for the learning needs of society is too important to be left to market forces. It is feared that it will lead to a further fragmentation of society. Social divisions have been found to affect participation in learning. Tett et al. (1998) state that it is mainly people under the age of 35, from skilled or professional backgrounds, who have a positive educational experience and therefore are motivated to continue with their learning. In many countries there is a concern about widening access to higher education to the poorest and most disadvantaged groups. In the UK this has inspired the 'Widening Participation' policy of the New Labour government.

It is felt that older age groups, ethnic minorities, the long-term unemployed and semi and unskilled occupations will become excluded from educational opportunities. Tett believes that an important role will be played in supporting and lobbying for these groups by learning networks, community groups, voluntary organizations, social movements and youth organizations. The influence of family and peer support to individuals embarking on new or further learning is seen to be crucial. If online and e-learning are to facilitate an open and holistic approach to lifelong learning, then governments and education policy-makers must ensure that technology is widely available to the most disadvantaged of the world's population, otherwise a 'digital divide' (Castells 1996) will develop that will prevent a vision of lifelong learning from being fully realized.

Both on a national and global scale, a number of projects are under way to deliver communications technologies to the world's poorest people. An example is the work of Computer Aid International (see www.computer-aid.org/). Educationalists need to show a strong commitment to these projects so that online learning does not become the domain of the wealthy. It seems likely that lifelong learning can be aided by the use of online learning as long as society deals with the social division of digital resources.

Attitudes towards change

The relationship between academics and the landscape of HE has been described as dynamic and highly complex but far from being tightly coupled. An important role has been identified for the agency in the reception, interpretation and implementation of new policies, but academics themselves make their own responses to changing environments. Academics can be seen as similar to the 'street-level bureaucrats' in Lipsky's (1980) seminal study of public service professionals. They make their own policy on the ground, to a large extent, through the way in which they interpret the inconsistencies of government demands alongside the realities and ideals of their professional practice. Reactions to change are diverse and difficult to predict as a variety of reactions are often provoked; for example:

- negativity
- resistance
- burying one's head in the sand (waiting for a change for the better)
- enthusiastic adoption of change
- strategic undermining and reworking of change.

Technological change can lead to de-professionalization and a loss of the bonds of collegiality among the academic community (Becher and Trowler 2001). De-professionalization takes the form of new techno-professionals who take the domain of online activity away from generic academics, or increased part-time and temporary staff who are used by the new management regimes as a method of dealing with the diminishing unit of resource discussed in Chapter 1. These strategies can undermine the ability of the academic teacher to evolve and cope with the new world of mass higher education. A recent study in America suggests that key academic staff are still very much involved in the evolution of online learning, despite the increase of casual part-time staff in some areas (Allen and Seaman 2005).

Over the past century academics have been coping with a steadily changing environment. Research universities were confronted by emergent community colleges and polytechnics which delivered their own degree programmes and often evolved into new universities. Full-time teaching became augmented, and sometimes replaced, by part-time teaching. At the same time there has been a perceived shift away from research as being central to academic life, to a point where teaching assumes the key aspect of the role and research activity is in danger of becoming the specialist domain of some but not all. Many academics are fighting hard to retain the link between teaching, scholarship and research,

These changes have led to a perception among some academics that they are becoming de-skilled and that the conceptualization of knowledge has become separated from the execution of lessons. At the same time there have been changes that have created increasing bureaucratization and managerialism, with centralized control of the curriculum, extensive audit and control of work alongside league tables and performance statistics. Government regulation and inspection has become more intrusive and bureaucratic in many countries.

Within universities there has been an increase in the range and type of academic disciplines. This is evidenced in the growth of the number of departments, types of courses, numbers of journals and articles published along with a multiplication of recognized research topics and clusters (Becher and Trowler 2001). Inter disciplinary studies have become more important, but at a time when academics take additional career risks if they stray outside the boundaries of their traditional disciplines and professional roles.

Within disciplines different processes are at work. These have been defined as subject parturition, where new areas of subjects bud and then break off to become specialisms in their own right, and subject dispersion, where subjects expand to cover more ground. Through the 1990s more subjects became affiliated to universities, notably in the health professions, and are increasing in status and acceptability as a result of this. The range of what is suitable to be studied within a university is widening; new types of departments and degree courses are developing along with new modes of delivery.

Academics are under pressure to change and learn new skills, including the ability to utilize ICT, but this is in the context of transforming change in the higher education sector and the difficulties in identifying what changes should be welcomed and what should be resisted. Many academics feel under siege and not sure if they can cope with the pace of change. Although new disciplines, new practices and new technologies can be inspiring and challenging, it is easy to understand why academics often feel at best ambivalent about them.

Hanson (2002) presents views on motivating lecturers to use online learning. In order to do this she believes we need to understand the characteristics of academics that divide themselves into two broad groups:

- Innovators – who want the latest technology, are prepared to try new ideas, are strong risk-takers and want revolutionary change.
- The majority – who want to see the educational reasons for ICT use, who need opportunities provided to explore their own teaching and who need assistance to develop the confidence to make changes.

Academic lecturers will move to the use of technology and online learning at different speeds (see Figure 2.1)

Hanson provides examples that have been used to give support and professional development opportunities to the majority grouping. This has included a range of methods including a designated person to support each

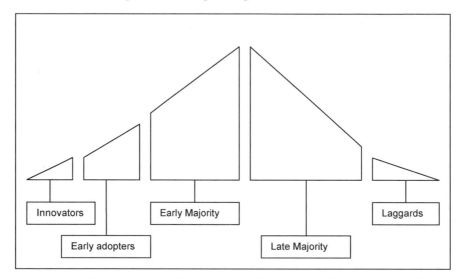

Figure 2.1   Technology adoption life cycle

faculty or school. Academics certainly will need the support of institutional
strategies that offer encouragement and support if they are embrace new
online learning methods.

A question then arises about what should be the focus of professional
development. Is it the ICT skills or the androgogical research base? Tensions have arisen in academic institutions between academic and technical
appointments and the distribution of supporting resources. The Faculty of
Education lecturers in Australia complained about the lack of androgogical
principles of educational designers who placed a focus on information
transmission rather than a constructivist learning approach. Some staff
development units for academic staff have been disbanded because they
had lost a service orientation and seemed remote from the everyday practices of front-line teaching staff. Another difficulty has been that the staff
development units providing support for online learning did not always link
well to other units providing general staff development for lecturers.

Academic teachers will need a range of opportunities that enable them to
experiment with online learning in parts of their practice that seem relevant and where online learning is able to adapt to existing pressures, processes and resources. Both technological issues and issues of learning
philosophy will have to be satisfactorily addressed and, over time, each
academic will need opportunities to assimilate the foundations of online
learning into their everyday practice.

Technology which is available or desirable

Technology and information is growing at an exponential rate. Moore's Law (see www.intel.com) is widely cited and states that the computing power of the microchip will double every 18 months. This generalization has held true for the past 40 years. As more transistors are packed into tighter spaces, microchip technology was thought to be reaching its natural limits and would have ceased to expand at this rate in around 2017. Technology is moving ahead and it appears now that a new system of layering transistors on microchips may mean that Moore's Law will soon be superseded.

Added to this rapid expansion of technology, Metcalfe's Law states that the value of a network increases as more people use it. In 2000 there were thought to be over 200 million users of the Internet with over 800 million web pages accessible to the public and many millions more protected behind the firewalls of institutions. If anyone with the skills can place information on the web, without the verifying and validating influences of peer review or traditional publishing, what credibility can the information hold? 'The exegetical reader sees bounty in the multiple sites on a given topic while the dogmatic reader sees chaos and the inability to judge good from bad' (Bruce 2000: 114).

Bruce raises other issues concerning the credibility of information on the web, notably, the speed of changes to web sites, the sheer quantity of information, commercialism, the distributed authority of web authorship and the nature of hypertext itself. He also points out that every web page draws in part from its inter textual relations with other web pages; therefore it is difficult to determine where meaning resides. Meaning is also constrained by the search engines that navigate hypertext and the relationship between search engines, and commercial or governmental interests further complicate this. These points, while challenging the credibility of knowledge on the Internet, do not diminish its importance as a resource. However, they do serve to emphasize the need for questioning, analysis and critical evaluation by its users, and the need for a facilitating guide or tutor to assist in the development of these skills. Students need assistance from academic staff so they know how to rate the quality of online sources. Examples of online resources that inform students how to make these decisions can be seen at the UK-based Virtual Training Suite (www.vts.rdn.ac.uk/). Technology and information will continue to expand at a rapid rate, and universities and academics need skills and strategies to cope with this revolution.

The role of the tutor

In this post-information revolution world, the role of the tutor in helping students to have the confidence to rate and categorize this information will be central.

A learning activity should involve both autonomy and guidance (McKie 2000). Students will still need tutors. Csikszentmihalyi and Robinson (1990) introduce the concept of 'flow theory' where an individual is so engaged within an activity that they lose the conditioning experience of linear time. This has relevance to modes of learning from the Internet. McKie (2000: 133) stresses that: 'Navigation can be a more or less individual affair, more or less goal directed with varying levels of support'.

Testone (1999) compared experiences of participating in two online courses and describes her first course instructor as having low visibility and being unresponsive, with students not receiving replies to questions for over a month. The instruction and assignments given were not conducive to online learning and student interaction. In her second course, a more positive experience for her, Testone describes the tutor as being online often, posing questions which encouraged reflection and encouraging student interaction generally. Creativity is required here in order to present learning materials in a different way and to create assignments that encourage students to work cooperatively (Cowan 1998). Testone identifies the tutor's responsibility as being to maintain the quality and to provide optimal learning environments for the students.

Testone's experience leads her to believe that instructors need to be prepared to spend more time facilitating online learning than they would a similar class in a traditional classroom setting. It would indeed be quicker to 'tell the students what they need to know' in a formal classroom lecture setting. Such a minimalist approach if applied to the online setting becomes about putting lecture notes on the web. Effective online learning needs to be collaborative and interactive (Palloff and Pratt 1999; Bernard et al. 2000). Therefore more experiential methods need to be employed and adapted for the new medium of delivery. As with face-to-face methods that seek to encourage students to take more responsibility for their learning, online learning that is good at promoting interactive learning often needs more time invested at the beginning of the course of study.

This can be quite challenging for those from a background of traditional distance learning, who are used to focusing in their educational careers on the manufacture of high-quality content and less time is spent on the tutoring process. In the new content-rich world, teaching will become more about guiding students in their navigation of content and helping them to reflect and interact with the materials they have found.

Evaluation of learning and teaching experiences

When starting the practice of using online learning it is important to build in a system of monitoring and evaluation. This is particularly the case for a new and innovative approach. Parlett and Hamilton (1972) made a distinction between the 'instructional system', that is, the course documentation which sets out how an educational programme should run, and the 'learning milieu', which is a social-psychological and material environment in which the students and teachers work together. Parlett and Dearden maintain that the innovatory programme cannot be separated, for the purposes of evaluation, from the learning milieu of which it is a part. They also hold that connecting changes in the learning milieu with intellectual experiences of students is one of the chief concerns for illuminative evaluation. They hold that: 'the concept of the learning milieu is necessary for analysing the interdependence of learning and teaching and for relating the organisation and practices of instruction with the immediate and long-term responses of the students' (Parlett and Dearden 1977: 16).

The tasks of the researcher in this model are to:

- Unravel the complex scene encountered
- Isolate its key features
- Delineate cycles of cause and effect
- Comprehend relationships between beliefs and practices
- Comprehend relationships between organizational patterns and the response of individuals.

(Parlett and Dearden 1979: 10)

Three stages are defined in the process of the model's application:

1 Observation;
2 Further inquiry;
3 Explanation.

Data may be collected from a range of sources, including observation, interviews, questionnaires and tests or documentary and background sources.

For its time, this approach to evaluation as a research paradigm was itself innovative. In the new millennium we can see that this is now an accepted practice and that interpretive traditions of research have become much more firmly established methodologies. This is relevant for the exploration of phenomena across a range of disciplines rather than, as in the 1960s and 1970s, when these traditions of research were more commonly used in disciplines such as anthropology.

Cann (1999), in an empirical study, reiterates the difficulty of evaluating single aspects of learning experiences. He states that online learning materials have been evaluated less than other forms. He believes this is due to the fact that online materials can be highly diverse in terms of format, educational content and end-users. For this reason it is difficult to generalize across institutions, as each online experience is designed to meet the needs of a unique set of circumstances. He points out that, although appropriate evaluation informs the future development of learning materials and the final stage of the authoring process, accurate evaluation is laborious and time-consuming, as so much is authoring, and should be costed into any new project development. Cann identifies difficulties in carrying out empirical studies of online learning experiences. He does concede that engagement and interactivity appear to be the major factors which distinguish high-quality online learning materials.

Testone (1999) used an autobiography of her own two online learning experiences as a student as a relevant form of evaluation. It is interesting that she points out difficulties from the beginning with one course where it was advertised as distance learning. Online learning is subtly different and students need to have the skills of autonomous learners who are highly motivated and can manage their own learning online.

Palloff and Pratt (1999) state that evaluation should begin in the planning stage and conclude with a follow-up study to confirm a programme's effectiveness. Several authors, notably Palloff and Pratt (1999) and White and Weight (2000) recommend a system of evaluation which demonstrates the following features:

1   Questions throughout the programme on:
   • How students experience the course;
   • The mode of instruction;
   • The online environment.

2   Online technology:
   • How well the technology worked;
   • If any technical support required was received;
   • Suggestions for further courses or modules.

3   Feedback from tutors:
   • Experience of teaching in the medium;
   • What is needed to improve this.

All this presumes that tutors and students are reflective in nature. Our own experience leads us to question if all tutors are reflective and what conscious understanding they have of the androgogical techniques they employ on a day-to-day basis in their interactions with students. Professional evaluation through reflecting on one's own practice is a key component of starting in a new area of teaching practice such as online learning. It is no good just collecting basic quantitative data from students. A plurality of methods is needed.

Conclusion

Our experience has taught us that it is difficult to make a direct comparison between online learning and face-to-face learning with a tutor. In many cases online learning is better than no access at all to learning. Online learning can overcome travel and time constraints. It can reduce visits to a higher education institution, while not necessarily replacing such visits completely. It is certainly a more enriching experience than traditional distance learning. Academics think of study as a private activity but tend to presume that, for teaching to be effective, it needs to be face to face. Online learning offers a potential for a new study environment where it is relatively easy to make contact with other learners during a private study process and at one's own convenience. 'Like cohabiting species, face to face work and online tuition complement each other in complex ways. We have not yet begun to explore their ecology' (Blake 2000: 215).

It seems that online learning is more likely to be effective with tutors and students who have significant prior experience of face-to-face work and understand student interaction. This involves the coordination and management of a system of learning that is complex and multifaceted (see Figure 2.2).

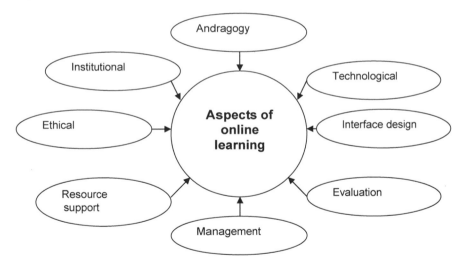

Source: adapted from Khan (2000)

Figure 2.2 Aspects of online learning

3
Appraising the Quality

Introduction

One of the many challenges in higher education today is not only increased access to information through the Internet and new communication technologies, but the ability to keep pace with developments in knowledge, scientific discoveries and emerging technologies. Trying to meaningfully assimilate the quantity and quality of this information and make judgements on its credibility and value is a dominant issue in higher education. This explosion of, and access to, information creates anxiety and yet is also a powerful driver to seek reassurance that the educational environments in which students will learn are sound and supportive. One means of achieving a greater sense of security is to consider the quality monitoring and enhancement of the new approaches to teaching that are required to manage this breadth and depth of information. In one sense, this involves the evaluation of learning; its processes and outcomes. In another, it is concerned with the standards that provide a guide to sound pedagogic practice and benchmarks for future practice. In this chapter we consider changes to the quality management process in mass higher education and their relevance to the expanding use of online learning.

Quality as a theme in Higher Education

The theme of quality in UK higher education entered a new phase in 1997 with the birth of the government agency, the Quality Assurance Agency (QAA), for higher education. This body was established by central government to inspect and assure standards in the sector. It uses a system of peer review, but has been criticized for its bureaucratic culture and institutionalized view of education (Hodson and Thomas 2003). It has been unclear that the professionals working in the sector are fully committed to such a regime (Laughton 2003). The arrival of a new agency to manage quality in higher education in the UK was driven by concerns about the speed of growth of higher education and a concern that standards would deteriorate as a result.

The national system is based on occasional planned visits to institutions to examine the provision for a particular discipline. Documentary audits are produced around a self-assessment exercise where a department reveals its own strengths and weaknesses and proposes how it will deal with the latter. The visiting peers then probe to see if the self-diagnosis and prognosis are fair and accurate. Critics complain that the system creates large amounts of paperwork and documentation and amounts to over-regulation, given the system of external examination and internal student evaluation that already exists in UK universities. In response to these criticisms, the QAA adjusted its inspection regime in 2002 and moved to a 'softer touch' process, with less regular visits to those institutions that had already demonstrated quality provision.

The activity of the QAA in the UK and similar quality management activities in other countries in the later 1990s needs to be seen alongside the transformational themes affecting global higher education discussed in Chapter 1. In particular the 'moral panic' about quality has been driven by increasing movement of students across global markets, the increased proportion of populations studying in the sector (which we argued in Chapter 1 cannot usually be matched by a proportionate growth in units of resource) and the move towards new methods of teaching and learning, including online learning, as methods to cope with this transformational change.

One reason why there is so much interest in using online learning technologies is that they are regarded as a cost-effective way of expanding higher education. Some believe they are the only realistic way to respond to the increasing numbers of students in higher education institutions (HEIs) and widening participation initiatives. An ardent champion of online learning was the UK Dearing report (1997) which modelled comparisons of staff time for different alternative teaching methods. For example in one module (unit) of a course traditional teaching contact time in lectures and seminars was 30 hours. If student numbers double, it could be argued that this teaching time needs to increase to 60 staff hours, if the institution is offering similar lectures and seminar sizes to the additional students. However, by using strategies such as larger lectures and large-group teaching, and removing small-group seminars to replace them with distance or online learning, teaching staff contact hours might actually be reduced. In order to provide accessible education and sustain quality experiences in this equation the challenge is to meet these demands, with mixed modes of learning and teaching, using combinations of face-to-face and learning technologies. The impact on universities thus far to meet this challenge is to transform the way knowledge is packaged, delivered, accessed, acquired and, ultimately, measured. The challenge then becomes how to reduce quantity of staff teaching contact while increasing the *quality* of learning.

Not everyone is convinced that the shift to new modes of teaching and learning driven by learning technologies will meet the demands of the twenty-first century and the new generation of students. Resistance to online teaching has been recorded and attributed to psychological variables such as lack of confidence, feelings of loss and a lack of awareness and training in the new approaches (Panitz and Panitz 1998). There is a concern that many younger students now entering higher education are not skilled and motivated to use self-directed approaches, even though they have good ICT skills. Others fear for the demise of the universities as they know them. This leads to a state of anticipated loss among academic staff who are apprehensive about losing their status and power, and remain cynical about the real benefits for students. Noble (1999) took a strongly opposed and controversial view that universities are becoming commercialized and teaching is becoming a commodity, undermining the academics' control, knowledge, skill and livelihood. In spite of both substantive concerns about the pervasive role of learning technologies in academic life, most institutions have incorporated some, if not many, aspects of these technologies. Online learning as a method of delivery for higher education and training has, on the whole, gained many supporters, and the reasons for this are evaluated in this book.

Yet, the medium of online learning has introduced a new instructional paradigm in universities and offers possibilities for academics to develop learning that is more flexible. To benefit from these possibilities the academic becomes entangled in a network where information and IT, web design, educational design, teaching delivery, learning support and assessment are all interwoven. Traditionalists and others perceive this as the fragmentation of instructional paradigms. There are some who argue that online learning can cause a reduction in quality as students use the Internet to find the easiest option and do not search in depth and to make informed choices (Fuchs and Woessmann 2004). To choose a course of study that meets their personal learning needs students, of whom many are increasingly part time, independent and adult learners, may face a bewildering range of options. These range from choosing between different learning methods, different levels of online learning involvement, to selecting from thousands of options in the online learning market in order to study in their own time, or with the option to study from a distance.

In summary, in online learning education there is a variety of electronic technologies that claim to deliver learning. But, according to Roffe (2002: 41) when appraising its quality:

the 'e' term has less to do with electronics and much more to do with other, equally valid, 'e's. These are the

- Engagement of the learner;
- Enhancement of the learning;
- Experience of exploration;
- Ease of use;
- Empowerment of the learner to control the learning schedule; and
- Execution of the learning programme.

This chapter examines the impact of online learning on institutional and regulatory frameworks, and evaluates the known and likely impact on the quality of higher education experienced. Before beginning, is it useful to reflect on some of the quality appraisal synthesis frameworks that are used in modern higher education?

Guidance on assuring the quality and standards of higher education programmes of study by means of distance education programmes is provided by the QAA (1999) under the direction of the Higher Education Funding Council (HEFC). These general areas are structured under six headings:

- System design;
- Programme design, approval and review;
- The management of programme delivery;
- Student development and support;
- Student communication and representation;
- Student assessment.

Avedis Donabedian first used such an overview to quality in the public health and heath-care organization sectors in 1980. The systematized model of structure, process and outcome that was developed (Donabedian 2003) has been used extensively in other fields to clarify thinking on quality appraisal. It has relevance to any large organization where quality, value efficiency and effectiveness require analysis and strategic planning. The principles underpinning the model are

1 Efficacy;
2 Effectiveness;
3 Efficiency;
4 Optimality;
5 Acceptability;
6 Legitimacy;
7 Equity.

This second synthesis offers an overview of the values that should underpin any managerial analysis. Donabedian's model provides a framework for analysis in this chapter which begins by exploring definitions of quality. We also explore issues such as teaching, assessment, attendance and plagiarism.

Quality assurance

There are several definitions of quality and these can be summarized as total quality, public or user satisfaction, performance based, or minimum standards. Total quality is built on the idea that the commitment to the delivery of a quality product and service should be at the centre of an organizational culture and everything should follow from this (Morgan and Murgatroyd 1994). The reports of the service user (in education's case, the student) are seen as paramount and much effort is taken in collecting these, understanding them and responding to them. Managers try to institute a culture in the organization that is based on a value that all gains, such as promotion and pay rewards and so on, only come from a better understanding of the customer or service user. All other management approaches and regimes, such as strategic management, performance management and so on, are supposed to be driven by this core idea. Such approaches are difficult to implement in many public services where the 'public good' (the well-being of all) is as important, or partly as important, as the individual experience. For example, in education the standard of education required in society and by employers has to be weighed against the interests and aptitudes of an individual 'customer'.

Public satisfaction or user satisfaction is a limited subcategory of Total Quality Management. It is much more focused and seeks to measure satisfaction with a specific aspect of provision. For example, do students feel satisfied that a learning technology has helped them learn? Public satisfaction alone can be too simplistic for understanding complex public sector outputs such as education. For example, students might like a particular series of lectures that prepares them well for examination and assessment, but this may not necessarily give them adequate professional practice for development of the employment skills they need on graduation. In other words, external stakeholders may be under-represented by focusing too much on specific user criteria.

Performance-based approaches to quality are designed to focus on whether a particular target or performance indicator is achieved. An example in higher education is a target to increase the number of students enrolling in higher education from poor family backgrounds, or a target to reduce those who withdraw from courses. Targets do not in themselves ensure depth of quality for the individual and there are real concerns that they distort policy and management practice, leading to too much focus on certain activities. An example is that to increase the ratio of computers available to students is no guarantee that their learning will improve as many other steps must be taken to ensure that the technology is used appropriately.

Quality based on minimum standards has some benefits. It makes clear definitions of acceptable practice and what all individuals should expect from university provision. Examples are minimum contact hours with academic staff that students can expect, response times for requests for tutorial support, and the minimum content that must be included in the curriculum for a specific discipline. Minimum standards can inform benchmarks, although these are more positive in that they seek to replicate best practice and give professionals reasonable attainable goals and templates to use for practice, rather than being based on a minimal level of provision. Minimum standards are sometimes refined with reference to complaints data, in other words, seeing where educational systems are failing and then trying to set standards that prevent such failure.

Most modern universities take a holistic approach to quality that has aspects of Total Quality Management practice within it. Rather than focusing exclusively on the narratives of the students and their account of education and learning, the systems seek to balance a range of inputs: external peer review, internal peer review, dialogue with professional organizations that experience the outcomes of student graduation, reflection on a range of performance statistical targets and, of course, lots of feedback and input from current students. The holistic approach is pursued as the optimum approach in the following discussion in this chapter.

Appraising quality in innovative teaching methods is not new. Prior to the explosion of Internet communications and IT, institutions offering both distance and face-to-face teaching were expected to develop quality assurance methods to demonstrate that their open and distance courses were of equal quality to these offered in the traditional classroom environment. To provide reassurance and evidence that the necessary quality assurance methods are in place, institutions have tended to focus on output measures which are able to demonstrate the value to the student participation in the learning process. International distance universities, such as the Open University in the UK (OU), Indira Gandhi National Open University in India (IGNOU) and the Open University of Hong Kong (OUHK), are quality-systems driven organizations in the same way as are traditional historical universities (Hope 2001). They work in the context of the global higher education external market system and must demonstrate credible quality in order to survive and prosper in the marketplace. The issue of scrutinizing and peer-reviewing the design and validation of courses are applied in the same way in distance universities as they are in traditional universities. There will be some exceptions, for example the so called e-universities or corporate universities that promote workplace skills and industry-related qualifications. Training and vocational online learning may not necessarily be constrained by these kinds of quality procedures, but many student customers will be able to discern the difference. There are some risks to potential customers in a growing market place, but in the main, these have been overdramatized. For many years unscrupulous companies have existed who will send a dubious university certificate for a nominal fee, but such market distortions existed long before the arrival of online learning.

It is a myth to think that online learning educational processes mysteriously escape the scrutiny process in higher education. In many cases it is likely that they will be subject to greater scrutiny because they are new and different, and academic staff seeking to navigate such approaches through university committees will need to have robust and informed arguments about the learning benefits that new technologies and methods can bring as well as being prepared to address the issues of the potential for plagiarism and the sensitive issues surrounding intellectual property rights and copyrights.

However, these quality indicators are not only required for the home markets. In order to flourish against global competition, institutions need to establish the quality of their online learning in a competitive global education market. It is important for institutions and for agencies involved in the accreditation of courses to seek to develop what John Randall (Chief Executive of the QAA), describes as a 'global currency for higher education qualifications'. The driving quality assurance method that resulted was an evaluation of learning outcomes with reference to agreed minimum standards and benchmarks within the academic community. These created clearly defined exit levels (Randall 2001). The role of learning outcomes as a means of standardizing the quality of education is emphasized in the proposals of the European Bologna Process. These proposals accentuate the need for harmonization of higher education curriculum through their use across the European Union. This is most recently referred to in the Berlin communiqué 2003 and is the focus of discussions around Europe (Adams 2004; Moon 2004). As a result of this important policy, the role of learning outcomes is discussed later in this chapter.

The emergence of online learning provision as a new learning method in universities means that, in the UK, QAA guidelines for conventional open and distance education need to be interpreted in the context of the new learning environment. Blended learning – that is, the use of online learning alongside traditional face-to-face paradigms – forces some convergence of the quality assurance agenda for open and distant learning.

In the first instance, the Internet environment requires measures to support the provision of information for students that is at a quality of service level above that normally delivered by a university. This entails the construction of an online library within the VLE, which can be offered to support online learning. So, in the online environment, the focus on the number and range of books in the library holding is replaced by consideration of access to online databases and digital media, including journals and books. Can students easily access online journal and book resources from their own hardware, located outside of the physical campus of the university? Similarly, there must be the application of IT to facilitate the interaction of students with information resources to ensure that students focus their limited time on the appropriate inputs, processes and outcomes.

Roffe (2002: 42) has categorized these factors for an online learning programme under the same structure as the QAA guidelines on the Quality Assurance of Distance Education (see Table 3.1). The factors are presented in the same order as the QAA guidelines, together with explicit precepts for e-delivery, in Table 3.1. The key issue for Roffe is that online learning offers 'personalization' of a learning programme where the education is adjusted to fit the needs of differing individuals and allows them to set their own timetable of study. The traditional notion of the class group is less clear. The focus on understanding quality shifts towards the individual context within the overall experience, with less emphasis on the classroom 'group' experience.

The UK Joint Information Systems Committee (JISC 2005b) suggests the

Table 3.1 Roffe's precepts for an online learning quality assurance strategy

QAA guideline	Precepts for online learning quality assurance strategy
System design	Clear governance and control throughout an organization, especially where there is a disaggregated design environment.
Academic quality and standards	Attention to academic tasks to support the online learning curriculum.
Management	Appropriate choice and effective management of technology qualifications of staff.
Student development	Electronic support for pre-entry counselling, motivation and autonomous learning needs.
Student communication	Electronic participation to address student needs as well as strategies for feedback, to contribute to meetings and to disseminate information.
Student assessment	Capabilities for online learning are applied to enhance student assessment and achievement.

Source: Roffe, I. (2002) 'E-learning: engagement, enhancement and execution', *Quality Assurance in Education*, 10(1): 43, table I. Republished with permission, Emerald Group Publishing Limited

following standard for teaching and learning with online learning: 'To be effective, ICT must be places in the context of a professional approach to teaching with a holistic view of how it will fit in with the learning objectives of the topic, overall course design and the assessment and feedback procedures'. Here the role of the academics' professional responsibilities is emphasized and explicit within the triangulation of learning objectives, course design and assessment processes. Feedback has become a crucial feature of online learning, and is discussed in Chapters 4 and 6; however, here it is appropriate to mention that the success of the engagement between students and e-moderators is predicated on the interactions gained through effective feedback. The JISC also acknowledges that not only are there more diverse teaching methods in this milieu but there is a need to meet the challenges of new student demographics, among other contemporary pressures in the twenty-first century. For example, students' expectations of online learning are generally high. They believe it to be a magical alternative to classroom learning that will take less time and be more entertaining than conventional learning. Many are accustomed to using the internet for support with homework or authoring web pages, as 78 per cent of UK households with 16-year-olds having computers or laptops (DfES 2002). Consequently, their expectations of what they need to fulfil their learning choices, coupled with their judgement on the quality of feedback, the speed of delivery and flexibility demanded from contemporary expectations, will also be high. Quality issues and online learning share many similarities with issues in traditional face-to-face learning, but the experience of the individual and his or her ability to find a personal experience of quality within the technological structures is all important.

Structural issues

It is acknowledged that ICT has become an important aspect of the teaching and learning strategies of many universities. While there has not been a complete shift away from bricks and mortar – from bricks to clicks – the term 'virtual university' is now widely used and there has been heavy investment in, for example, electronic resource centres (Ryan et al. 2000). The implications are, however, that new technologies will alter higher education's core production and delivery processes. Currently, there appear to be three levels of application of learning technologies in universities: (1) as the primary teaching mechanism for one or more courses, (2) as an enhancement to traditional face-to-face courses, and (3) as a forum for discussion, information exchange with peers and experts, and a means of accessing online resources. However, the very flexibility and diversity of online learning provision raises questions about how its relative effectiveness can be gauged.

One of the first questions to ask any academic or institution is 'Why are you attempting to place these resources or activities into an online context?' If they are unable to provide an explicit answer, then it could be argued that the strategic intent or rationale for the learning process has not been defined adequately. Without a clear understanding of the purpose, the chances of success are reduced (Sims et al. 2002).

Noble (1999) suggests that online learning can be erroneously seen as an economic solution to government cuts and increases in staff to student ratios. It becomes imperative that senior academics have a clear philosophy that links online learning to new approaches for quality learning and that this is manifest in an explicit university strategy. Once the strategic intent has been defined, members of the design and development team will have a foundation on which to base the various elements of an online learning environment. Online learning could then be added to a traditional learning programme for sound pedagogical reasons, for example to increase self-directed learning that is directly related to a conventional classroom approach such as a lecturer or seminar experience. It still might be possible to reduce conventional classroom contact while maintaining the quality of educational provision.

The British Learning Association (2001) developed a checklist and a step-by-step guide to set in motion online learning in an institution. It asks questions that the average academic in the classroom who wishes to embrace the emerging technologies may not ordinarily ask as they challenge the strategic intent of the institution and pose questions about the macro management of any new development. Caught up in the enthusiasm of module or course development, the questions seem far removed from everyday teaching matters. That said, the checklist raises important considerations that could, if explored thoroughly, pre-empt any obstructions or disappointments to the planning processes. The checklist suggests that developers begin with a statement about their purpose or goal for introducing online learning. This focuses the intent and rarefies the rationale. There follow ten steps, in Box 3.1, framed as questions to guide the would-be creator of online learning. Each of the steps requires an action point and any one of the steps provides a guide for future quality appraisal.

Managing the online learning environment

Because online learning is likely to be associated with institution-wide, electronic systems it is useful to have an appreciation of this relationship and why this partnership is deemed apposite. The infrastructure for online learning is complex, but not daunting when seen as a means to an end. In any organization there needs to be a method of recording information and no less so in universities where students' academic and, increasingly relevant, financial records are managed. In the world of ICT, these elements can be united within online learning environments. Thus informatics, involving electronic access to library catalogues, remote databases and archives, can be assimilated into computer-based instruction or learning, which may or may not require telecommunications, and computer or web-based communications.

The development of VLEs has brought together these threads so that they are accessible in one place. The JISC defines a VLE as the 'online interactions of various kinds which take place between learners and tutors including online learning' (JISC 2002). Commercial products are available that provide electronic environments to unite web-based communication systems with platforms to build learning units and teaching opportunities (examples are WebCT and Blackboard – see Chapter 2). The VLE provides a controlled access to curriculum that has been mapped onto units and modules. It enables tracking of students' access to online materials, activities and achievements against the elements of learning. It becomes possible for academics to guide and monitor students' online progress and to collect anonymous evaluation feedback via electronic questionnaires and drop boxes. The technological platform becomes an important resource for managing part of the quality assurance process.

The VLE offers and creates support to online learning by including access to resources, assessments and active guidance through e-moderation activities (Salmon 2004). The resources can be self-developed, authored or purchased, and imported to be made available to students. An essential feature of the VLE is communication between the learner, academic and other learning support specialists, such as those providing technical support. This communication provides direct support and feedback to students as well as providing peer-group communications that help to build up a group identity and community of interest. Although quality must respect individual difference, quality online provision will also build a collective online experience.

Box 3.1 First steps to getting started in online learning

Step 1: Be clear about the benefits

The benefits of online learning are many and varied – what do *you* wish to gain?

- Consistent delivery of programmes? ☐
- Distributed learning across your organization? ☐
- Flexibility to update and deal with change? ☐
- Opportunities for learner involvement? ☐
- Low delivery costs for large numbers of learners. ☐
- Opportunities for monitoring and evaluation of outcomes? ☐
- Access for all that need it. ☐

Actions required

Step 2: What are you trying to achieve?

You might be motivated to embrace online learning just to show that you are up to date. However, such short-term considerations rarely lead to real benefits. What outcomes will show that you've achieved success with online learning?

- Delivery of a specific programme? ☐
- Learners reporting high satisfaction? ☐
- Proven cost-effectiveness? ☐
- More employees involved in learning? ☐
- A shift in attitudes towards learning? ☐

Actions required

Step 3: Whose support do you need?

Think of those who can influence the success or otherwise of your initiative. You will need their support – so secure it at an early stage. Which groups are important to you?

- Senior management? ☐
- Middle management? ☐
- Employees? ☐
- Your HR department? ☐
- Your IT department? ☐
- Your face-to-face trainers? ☐

Actions required

Step 4: What's your strategy?

It's easy to plough ahead on a wave of enthusiasm! You also need to plan. What are the strategic issues you need to consider at this stage?

- Have you a clear business case for introducing online learning? ☐
- Is online learning aligned to your business strategy? ☐
- Is your approach flexible enough to cope with change? ☐
- How does it relate to existing learning programmes? ☐
- How will you manage this initiative? ☐

Actions required

Step 5: What type of delivery solution is right for you?

There are many issues to address and you will need to examine your rationale for each.

- Generic materials or bespoke? ☐
- Bought in or developed in-house? ☐
- What mix or blend of delivery will learners prefer? ☐
- Do you have the skills available for this? ☐
- Who will create the content? ☐
- Who will 'take on' instructional design? ☐
- Which external providers might you approach? ☐

Actions required

Step 6: What about your organization as a place to learn?

Some organizations have a history of positive employee development. To others this will be a major change. How will your organization match up?

- Is there a learning culture in your organization? ☐
- Are line managers likely to encourage take up of online learning? ☐
- Are there dedicated Learning Centres for all to access? ☐
- Are times set aside for employees to learn? ☐

- Will managers act as role models?   ☐
- Are there reward systems that support employee-led learning? ☐
- Have new flexible ways of learning been tried in the past?   ☐

Actions required

Step 7: How might others view an online learning initiative?

There are other stakeholders whose support you have already identified as a key to success. What are their perceptions?

- How does HR view an online learning initiative?   ☐
- How are new ways of learning viewed by:
  - managers?   ☐
  - employees?   ☐
- Do managers see an urgent need for new learning
  opportunities?   ☐
- Will your trainers be supportive or anxious   ☐
- Are they willing to innovate and experiment?   ☐

Actions required

Step 8: What about the ICT issues?

Online learning will require you to address a range of technical issues. Getting these right will either inhibit or enhance your chances of success with your online learning initiative.

- Do all employees have access to a PC?   ☐
- Is training required to make online learning work for them? ☐
- Is your IT Manager aware of the issues?   ☐
- Is your network suitable in terms of bandwidth?   ☐
- What IT standards are you working to?   ☐
- Will online learning require new investment in the network? ☐

Actions required

Step 9: What about adding the human touch?

Learning through a PC can be hugely enjoyable for many – for others it doesn't match so well with their style. Adding the human touch can bring an added dimension and interaction to the online experience and benefits for all.

- Are existing tutors suitable for an online support role? ☐
- How might trainers themselves be trained for online learning? ☐
- Can learners be organized into groups to collaborate on learning? ☐
- Will face-to-face workshops integrate with online learning? ☐
- Can online tutor support be provided for each learner? ☐
- Can supported off-line assignments form part of the approach? ☐
- What new relationships between learners, materials and learner support can be developed? ☐

Actions required

Step 10: Now you know what you want – start!

- Specify your programme ☐
- Be clear about your strategy ☐
- Keep others on your side ☐
- Manage the development phase ☐
- Involve learners in the pilot ☐
- Evaluate the results ☐
- Publicize success. ☐

Actions required

Source: The British Learning Association (2001) Ten steps to getting started in e-learning, www.british-learning.com. Reprinted with the permission of the British Learning Association

Managed learning environments (MLEs), however, are integrated electronic systems that unite together the technological infrastructure for organizational systems underpinning educational processes and learning environments. The JISC (2002) defines these as 'the whole range of information systems and processes (including VLE if the institution has one) that contribute directly or indirectly to learning and the management of that learning'. These are large organizational and institutional electronic systems that integrate the learning platforms with records of students' activities and academic progress. The advantages to having an integrated administrative system are manifest in the efficiency with which data can be accessed and reproduced on issues related to student tracking, for example, in modular educational frameworks. There are ongoing issues that such systems are only as efficient as the humans who input data, the provision of staff training, the willingness of staff to utilize the technologies and the potential twin fallibilities of power supply and system maintenance. On balance, the overall efficiencies achieved with integrated ICT systems are considered valuable.

Contemporary students may expect a one-stop shop to deal with their queries and support, and it is unlikely that the MLE will contain all the answers they require. Different parts of the organization will have different levels of access to information and it is here that students may become frustrated, confused or even feel alienated. This raises issues both for the students seeking support and the institution giving it. It is difficult for an institution to simplify this situation as no individual will have expert knowledge of the entire range of student queries from fee payment facilities to degree regulations, location of tutorials and possibly (even hopefully) the answer to an assignment!

Therefore, designing infrastructure with signposts to different types of information is needed at the portals to the institution. There is a tendency to veer towards giving out large chunks of information which may be unnecessary, and tracking announcements when they are posted for 'hits' can indicate the relative importance of these announcements. Otherwise, gaining feedback from students about the accessibility of information through electronic feedback questionnaires or focus groups are valuable methods for fine-tuning systems.

Student charters are another method that attempts to lay down guidelines for what the student can and cannot expect from the institution. Charters have been criticized for being window dressing and only serving public relations functions. Students can unfairly blame themselves for problems arising from their lack of understanding or knowledge of how the institution operates. This can be avoided by a well-written charter that makes the expected standards clearer and explicit, particularly for student support from the online learning environment. A charter can outline standards for response times, for example, to overcome the frustration engendered by lack of immediate responses that the modern wired world has the potential to offer. This is an example of quality management by minimum standards.

A real challenge for universities is the administrative issues that are related to an MLE. This is in addition to the academic issues in VLEs, where all the learning systems need to link up. In the MLE, the administrative functions of academic registry, credit accumulation and transfer, assessment results, library systems, and so on also need to offer the student a quality and reliable experience (see Figure 3.1).

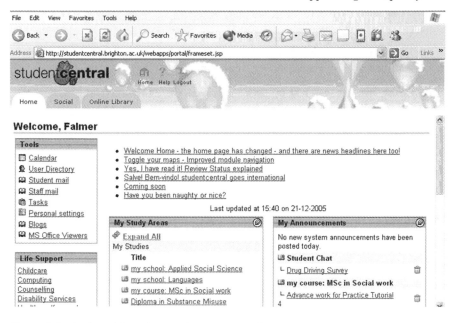

Figure 3.1 A virtual learning environment student gateway

Processes: roles and responsibilities

As already suggested in this chapter, the 'personalization' of online learning, to prevent it from becoming a depersonalized and distant experience, is all-important to the quality agenda. Adopting new approaches to teaching that fundamentally alter teaching and learning transactions can affect individuals' ideals, as well institutional philosophies towards learning. As mentioned before in this book, online learning has become a protagonist for change in higher education. It has created a paradigm shift from the 'sage on the stage' to the 'guide on the side' where students need to acquire strategies to manage the information explosion through, for example, resourced-based learning, rather than structured delivery of content. The consequences of this shift are multifaceted. It is assumed that the impact on the role of the academic is significant as it will change with the assimilation of the new teaching technologies. This is in line with the corresponding demands that education enables students to learn how to learn as well as to learn.

The expanded choices and capabilities of online learning provide an opportunity to shift towards an inquiry-based approach, favouring learner control and responsibility. Yet, the core principles and responsibilities of a traditional educational transaction remain translatable to an online learning context. Principles such as clear expectations, critical discourse and diagnosis of misconceptions are common to both online learning and face-to-face environments. With online learning there is a now a new goal, which is to construct educational environments that incorporate the development of critical thinking and self-directed online learning abilities. The result is the formation of knowledge structures, not necessarily curriculum derived, but emerging from course designs that are nonetheless coherent arrangements accommodating developmental learning and not exclusively specific topics.

Teaching presence

In addition to these changes are the effects on the roles and responsibilities of teaching, which are complex in any context. There are many facets to being an academic with different roles, from being an education designer and subject expert to that of a social facilitator. Applying these roles to the online learning arena does require an adjustment of how the subsequent responsibilities are fulfilled. Garrison and Anderson (2003: 65) describe this as the 'teaching presence', which is more than assigning control to the learner and is charged with 'shaping the right transactional balance to manage and monitor the achievement of worthwhile learning outcomes'.

Gilly Salmon (2004) has proposed a new descriptor for these roles and has identified them as 'e-moderators'. This is a term used to describe persons who preside over online conferencing or meetings. The difference between this role and that associated with the commonly understood role of moderator is the wider range of expertise that is required. Salmon (2004: 4) claims that 'the essential role of the e-moderator is promoting human interaction and communication through the modelling, conveying and building of knowledge and skills'. The role of the human factor is retained as it is acknowledged as a major influence on the success of online learning. It is also one of the main criticisms of online learning by those uncertain of the effectiveness of teaching without the personal qualities and interactions found in traditional teaching methods. The roles that are emerging for academics in online learning were discussed in Chapter 2. Here the issue is the adaptation of the traditional teaching role into one that maintains the facets mentioned above, in addition to the new roles required, to maintain student satisfaction and quality-learning experiences. It is yet another challenge for online learning but can be tackled with guidance from engaging with quality appraisal models that facilitate online learning and its underpinning methodologies. This illustrates that the quality of the relationship between academic and student is just as important to online learning as it is to face-to-face learning.

Attendance and assessing participation

Many conventional universities have in recent years developed attendance regulations to ensure that students take an active and responsible part in shared learning activities that are seen to be part of the value added of the higher education experience. Some academics will argue that this is misguided given the traditional idea of 'reading' for a degree, and that self-study is the prerogative of higher study, but many will accept attendance regulations as a necessary standard to ensure personal and collective responsibility and maximum benefit for all in an era of mass higher education. There is no reason why attendance regulations cannot be applied to online activity. Indeed, online activity can be easier to 'police', given that many MLEs have student register and log in records built in as standard.

In addition, creative teaching and learning strategies, outlined in Chapters 5 and 6, such as discussion activities and personal learning plans, can gauge participation and whether individual learning intentions have been met (Maier and Warren 2000: 109).

Issues around outputs and outcomes

Outputs are the first results of a performance process. In management practice, they are usually quantitative and easy to define in numerical terms. An example would be the percentage of students who pass an examination. But, arguably, outcomes are much more important in education than outputs. Outcomes are more long-term, qualitative form of results that are quite abstract in definition. They are difficult to measure conclusively and sometimes only occur long after the associated activity. A typical learning outcome might be expressed as a student's ability to make complex and autonomous professional assessments.

Continuing with the theme of Donabedian's (2003) structure, process and output model for quality management, we explore in this section the outputs of education and how these can be monitored. One means is to apply standards to the expected outcomes of the learning process. Adam (2004) maintains that learning outcomes are the essential building blocks of education. While reflecting on the European harmonization of higher education learning, he observes (2004: 3) that learning outcomes have applications at three distinct levels:

- The local level of the individual higher education institution (for course units/modules, programmes of study and qualifications);
- The national level (for qualifications frameworks and quality assurance regimes);
- Internationally (for wider recognition and transparency purposes).

The alternative approach uses an input-driven systems model where the curriculum is designed around content, main theories, events and processes, and where relationships are made between content and learning strategies. This approach depends upon the length of the programme, numbers of hours taught, the material to be covered, number of staff and level of resources available to support the delivery of the programme. It has many supporters, particularly where resources are a driving concern, but questions the real applicability to cover all the facets of learning and is very far from the constructivist approach, which believes in building knowledge structures from learning resources rather than providing knowledge to be learned.

> Constructivism emphasises the construction of knowledge while objectivism concerns mainly with the object knowing. It is the funda-mental difference about knowledge and learning that departs the two in terms of both philosophy and implications for the design of instruction.
>
> (Tam 2000: 51)

The likely difference between traditional, content-driven and sequentially structured design and constructivism is that in a constructivist design the content cannot be pre-specified. Constructivist designers prefer learning environments in which knowledge, skills, and complexity exist side by side. Objects and events are deemed to have no conclusive meaning; therefore the design task is to provide a rich context within which meaning is dis-covered by the learner while working with others. Designers develop learning activities in which the context of the subject plays a major part, and the learning outcomes evolve as learning progresses (Tam 2000). Thus, in complete contrast to traditional designs, real constructivists do not adopt learning or performance objectives. Instead, they look for learning tasks that relate to the subject area and let specific objectives emerge from the process of learning by the student. The objectives are therefore entirely student directed and relate to how the student constructs meaning and understanding about the subject in relation to the real world. The goal is not to teach a particular version of a subject, but to teach someone how to think like a person who understands the subject. In reality, most modern higher education management processes strongly favour the definition of learning outcomes before learning begins. This helps to structure a learn-ing process that is in an online learning environment.

Learning outcomes have implications for all stages of the learning and teaching process, if quality is to be assured. They are usually considered a crucial part of the development of twenty-first century approaches to higher education. This will mean a reconsideration of fundamental questions on the design and function of the assessment process. Specific assessment criteria are increasingly developed that help the learning outcomes to be expressed and identified. The focus is even more accented when these are applied in the online learning environment, and are discussed more fully in Chapters 4 and 5.

In an international and European context, learning outcomes have been variously defined as:

A statement of what a learner is expected to know, understand and/or be able to demonstrate at the end of a period of learning.[1]

Learning outcomes [are] statements of what a learner is expected to know, understand and/or be able to demonstrate after a completion of a process of learning.[2]

Statements of what a learner can be expected to know, understand and/or do as a result of a learning experience.[3]

Student learning outcomes are properly defined in terms of knowledge, skills, and abilities that a student has attained at the end (or as a result) of his or her engagement in a particular set of higher education experiences.[4]

Learning outcomes are statements that specify what a learner will know or be able to do as a result of a learning activity. Outcomes are usually expressed as knowledge, skills, or attitudes.[5]

Learning outcomes [are] specific measurable achievements.[6]

A learning outcome is a statement of what competences a student is expected to possess as a result of the learning process.[7]

Learning outcome statements are content standards for the provincial education system. Learning outcomes are statements of what students are expected to know and to do at an indicated grade, they comprise the prescribed curriculum.[8]

These definitions are based on a summary produced for the Scottish Executive at www.scotland.gov,uk/library5/lifelong/tehea–01.asp

The diversity of defining terms for learning outcomes raises doubt about achieving any consistency in measuring quality in any systematic way across programmes and institutions. In opposition, a pure constructivist approach would not require learning outcomes and would thus avoid this problem. Randall (2001), however, has proposed the following generic performance indicators, starting with the clear statement of learning outcomes:

- Learning outcomes have been set at the appropriate level and clearly communicated to students.
- Content and design of the curriculum and the teaching methodologies employed are effective in enabling the student to achieve the outcomes in terms of both the acquisition of knowledge and the development of related practical skills and abilities.
- Assessment is appropriately designed and rigorously administered to measure the achievement of the outcomes.

Box 3.2 Guidelines for quality programmes and courses

Acquired content skills and knowledge should be:

- Relevant;
- Transferable;
- Specific for the purpose (e.g. work or higher learning);
- Blend traditional education and applied technology skills.

Necessary learning skills are acquired for:

- Course/programme completion and success;
- Quality assurance;
- Lifelong learning;
- Self-directed learning management.

Completion takes the form of credit or credentials that are:

- Recognized by professional accreditation bodies and employers;
- Recognized by other educational institutions;
- Of the same value whether acquired through on-site or distance learning;
- Transferable within programmes and institutions, locally, nationally and internationally.

Return on investment of the learner's time, finances and energy meets expectations for:

- Accessibility as needed and when needed;
- Objective benefits and utility;
- Effectiveness: subjective achievement of personal goals;
- Efficiency: best use of resources;
- Customer satisfaction with all course/programme elements.

Source: adapted from www.futured.com/pdf/distance.pdf (Barker 2002)

Hope (2001) describes a Canadian approach, developed specifically for online learning. Barker (2002) has devised guidelines for e learning in Canada (Box 3.2).

In addition, Hope (2001: 130) summarizes her writing on quality issues with an essential overview checklist, which starts with learning objectives high on the agenda rather than learning outcomes:

- Clearly defined and achievable learning objectives;
- Relevant, scholarly and up-to-date curriculum content;
- Well-designed teaching and learning materials;
- Well-supported total learning package;
- Appropriate use of learning technologies;
- Sound technical design;

- Appropriate and necessary personnel support;
- Provision of access to additional learning resources;
- Planned resource provision;
- Outline review and evaluation cycle.

In the UK the Open and Distance Learning Quality Council (ODLQC) (www.odlqc.org.uk/index.htm) provide standards for programmes that they define as 'including any provision in which a significant element of the management of the provision is at the discretion of the learner, supported and facilitated by the provider. This ranges from traditional correspondence courses, on-line provision and interactive CD ROMs, to open learning centres and face-to-face provision where a significant element of flexibility, self-study and learning support is integral to the provision. The standards are found in Box 3.3.

The criteria all have a broad relevance to online learning if taken over a distance. There is little difference between the Canadian, QAA and ODLQC standards. The Canadian standards do reflect, intrinsically, the learner needs and requirements with regard to end results, and are laudable in this respect. All the standards could be equally applied to the quality assurance of traditional classroom-based learning. There is an ironic incongruity in that the development of online learning standards for the new learning methodologies may advance the paradigm shift towards learner-centred teaching to encompass all forms of teaching methodologies, not just those undertaken in ICT. The idea of learning outcomes is a dominant approach to quality assurance in both traditional face-to-face learning and newer forms of online learning. Outcomes and objectives are supposed to assist in focusing the assessment of learning and, so, the quality of the assessment process, as part of the output and outcome agenda, is discussed next.

Assessment and online submission

One of the myths of recent years, given the moral panic about the arrival of online learning and its affect on educational standards, has been the idea that assessment and examination are much more open to abuse online than they are in another context. We argue here that there is no real evidence of this and that a status quo, where abuses are possible in both conventional and online paradigms, is evident. The biggest myth concerns online submission. It has been implied that online submission encourages students to submit the work of others. But there is no systemic difference between online submissions and postal or similar submission of printed word-processed work in terms of their openness to fraud and abuse. Students handing in essays or sending essays by surface post have been known to pay other students to do the work for them before they attach they own name or identification number.

Many HEIs have resisted the online submission of student's work owing

Box 3.3 Standards for learning outcomes

A Each course includes a clear statement of what the learner can hope to achieve on successful completion.

B The methods, materials and support offered by the course are sufficient to achieve the intended outcomes.

Outcomes can be fully attained through open and/or distance study, augmented as and when necessary by face-to-face provision.

C Each course starts from a clearly stated level of ability and facilitates learner progress to a greater level of ability.

Courses need not assume any level of skill and understanding in a given subject at the start. Different outcomes or completion points may recognise different levels of progress.
Where possible, the course is structured to include points for partial completion.

D Statements that the level of ability inherent in the outcome can be matched to a nationally-agreed level of qualification are supported by appropriate evidence. When courses lead to degrees then those degrees are properly validated.

In particular, in the case of degrees:

a   the awarding body has Chartered or equivalent national status, regardless of the qualifications it offers, if it chooses to call itself a University;

b   those degrees are validated by the appropriate national authority;

c   those national validating mechanisms have international credibility;

d   if degree courses are offered which obtain their ultimate validation by being the degrees of another, properly accredited university, this is clear in all publicity, and the organisation offering such courses does not call itself a university unless entitled to do so under a) above.

E Where time limits for course completion are imposed by the provider, they are clearly stated, along with any possible extensions to this and related cost implications.

Where no limit is given, the provider is able to support the course for an appropriately extended period of time.

F Any assessments set by the provider during or on completion of a course are appropriate and adequate to ensure a proper assessment of the learner's ability and achievements to date, and the results communicated to learners.

Examinations should be properly marked or assessed, with procedures for ensuring security in their setting and assessment, monitoring the quality of those assessments, and providing appropriate feed back to the learner. Learners should be made aware of the procedure whereby assessments can be challenged, and whether resits are possible.

Where the outcome of an assessment is a variance with previous assessments, or with expectations on the part of the learner, reasons for that assessment are given.

Where appropriate, assessment is linked to accreditation by nationally-recognised qualification-awarding bodies. Where such links are not established, the provider does not make undue or unsubstantiated claims as to the level of skill or knowledge gained through successful completion of the course.

G Documentary confirmation of outcomes is available where appropriate to all learners on course completion.

Any certificate or diploma offered by the provider on completion of a course clearly:

1 indicates what outcome the provider is recognising (eg course completion, or assessed qualification);
2 indicates the name, nature, academic, vocational or professional recognition and other appropriate details of the awarding body.
3 does not indicate or suggest

that ODL QC endorses or validates the qualification concerned.

Any certificate of course completion provided to learners clearly states that it recognises only completion of the course, and does not imply any internally or externally validated qualification in that subject. The criteria by which 'course completion' is assessed are made known to the learner prior to enrolment.

H Where the outcome of a course is the declared competence to sit examinations offered, or be otherwise assessed, by another external organisation, the learner is informed of this, and of the respective responsibilities of provider and applicant, prior to enrolment.

Whilst the provider takes responsibility to ensure that the course fits the currently declared curriculum of the awarding body with other matters it should be made clear which are the responsibilities of the provider and which the applicant: who should ascertain, for example:

1 the on-going availability of any external qualification;
2 the nature of any prior qualifications or other entrance requirements imposed by such an external organisation;
3 the currency of any qualification offered as outcome by an external organisation

4   how, where and when any external examinations or assessments can be taken;

5   what charges, if any, will be made.

At the same time, the provider makes reasonable efforts to keep up-to-date with changes in these matters and at no time misleads applicants or learners as to the provider's knowledge of or responsibilities in such matters.

I The course and its objectives are placed in a wider educational, vocational and professional context.

In particular:

1   The relationship between the outcome of the course and any standards suggested, required or imposed by the relevant profession are made clear to the learner prior to enrolment;

2   If the outcome offers a qualification from theprovider, then the provider also takes appropriate steps to support that qualification subsequently.

3   Wherever possible, indications of opportunities for or routes towards further study are given.

Source: Copyright © ODLQC 2006

Reproduced with the permission of the Open and Distance Learning Quality Council (ODLQC), www.odlqc.org.uk/st1.htm)

to the additional burden this can impose on academic or administrative staff. The quality of the submitted work in a conventional system rests with the student. In online submission, the work is unlikely to be marked from a computer screen. If it is to be printed off in a university department there are concerns that some of the responsibility for output begins to pass to academic staff and the institution, for example, what if the work has been prepared in a programme where formatting and so on is not compatible with that available within the university.

Perhaps the biggest barrier to fraud remains the traditional unseen, sit-down examination, and it is interesting that it remained at the core of the Open University assessment regime in the UK for many years, with distant learning students travelling many miles to take their examinations. Even here, there remain some small possibilities for fraud with fake candidates appearing on behalf of others. More importantly, there are doubts about the ability of the unseen examination to assess a range of student skills in an appropriate manner.

Our argument is that while the online information environment may increase the range of opportunities for fraud in the same way as it increases the range of assessment paradigms, there is no hard evidence that it leads to an increase in fraud via online learning delivery. There, is however, reason to think that the Internet increases the total incident of fraudulent activity from students, regardless of whether they are engaged in online learning environments or conventional classroom activity. This concern is based on evidence of rising incident of plagiarism in traditional university assessment. This is based on Internet sources, but not necessarily related to online learning paradigms.

Plagiarism – authenticating students' work in the online environment

A good definition of plagiarism is that:

> Plagiarism may take the form of repeating another's [words] as your own ... or even presenting someone else's line of thinking ... as though it were your own. In short, to plagiarise is to give the impression that you have written or thought something that you have in fact borrowed from another. Although a writer may use other people's words and thoughts, they must be acknowledged as such.
>
> (Modern Languages Association 1977: 5)

One of the authors of this book, while working as a head of school in the UK higher education setting, found that during investigation of numerous suspected plagiarism cases as many as 90 per cent were concerned with allegations of copying material from web sites into students own work (rather than copying from paper sources such as books and hard copies of journals). Most of these assignments were conventional paper-based essays and dissertations, and were not related to online learning or submission. A typical offence was to cut and paste approximately 600 words (or two pages) directly from a web site into an essay of several thousand works, hoping that it would not be spotted as being written in a different style to the student's own narrative. No attempt was made to identify the source of the web site. More complex and subtle cases tended to intermix cut and pasting from web sites into the students own narrative, with some limited reference to the web site, but no proper identification of quotations from such sources. National reports in the UK press in 2006 indicated that plagiarism using Internet sources was rife at Oxford University (*Times Higher Education Supplement*, 14 March 2006). A study for the same newspaper taking a poll of 1022 undergraduates in 119 institutions found many students admitted to copying ideas without acknowledgement (37 per cent), but only 3 per cent said that they had copied word for word form a book or online source (Shepherd 2006). The media in the USA report similar problems in higher education (Argetsinger 2001)

The only good news for academic staff in his situation is that it is much easier to detect and check plagiarism when it is based on an Internet source. A typical detection practice is to place a suspected quote from a student's essay in inverted commas in either google.com, or scholar.google.com and hit the return button. If the sentence or paragraph is a direct copy there is a reasonable chance that Google will find it. More sophisticated detection methods are now being implemented, including specialist software and national partnership projects such as the UK JISC Plagiarism Advisory Service, funded by the JISC, and based in the Information Management Research Institute at Northumbria University (http://online.northumbria. ac.uk/). This technological detection system requires an electronic copy of all assessment to be submitted, in addition to any paper-based copies. The electronic copy is then compared with a very large international database of academic sources (Buczynski 2005).

These kinds of plagiarism cases appear to be on the increase (Szabo and Underwood 2004). This presents higher education academics and managers with formidable challenges. While such plagiarism is directly attributable to the arrival of the Internet society, it is not directly related to online learning paradigms and affects traditional educational delivery and assessment as much as online teaching and learning methods.

Academics need to design assessments and mixed strategies of assessments that reduce the temptation for students to use web material in this irresponsible way. From our experience there seems increased risks that students will be tempted to use material irresponsibly if academics give them limited time to do difficult creative tasks and if course learning materials lead students to a limited range of Internet-based resources rather than encouraging them to explore for themselves a full range of traditional library and Internet-based sources. The latter strategy gives students implicit permission to explore difficult subjects 'in their own way', rather than feeling that there must be a particular source that must be used, even though they do not understand it.

So called 'take away' examinations, where students have to answer short essays in a limited time period (perhaps a few days), seem to raise the pressure and temptation for students to break the referencing conventions and to risk passing off other people's work as their own (see also Chapter 5). The general setting of assessment titles and questions can also be done in such a way that it makes plagiarism less likely, if the process encourages creativity, and explicitly rewards those who use a wide range of properly referenced sources.

The manner in which assessment and examination processes are quality monitored is twofold. In the first instance internal scrutiny or moderation of examination processes and outputs should be accepted practice in all HEIs. This can be applied to online learning in the same manner. There can be digital submissions of assignments into the VLE that are receipted and acknowledged as feasible. Multiple choice or test bank forms of questioning can be dealt with in a similar manner. Scrutiny by plagiarism software is also made easy with online submission. Students can be expected to sign declarations of their own work as a testimonial; however, this declaration of faith is only as good as the intentions within which it is signed. There is a view that for each level of ingenuity that HEIs implement to guard against plagiarism, students will rise to that level with a means to subvert the method. Finding assessment methods that require students to produce work that demonstrates their own ability to understand a subject is the goal and should be the fundamental principle underlying the assessment process.

The second step is for external examiners to ensure that the process of assessment and examination is meeting the aims, objectives or learning outcomes of the module or course. All courses are required to have an external evaluation of the assessment process. In the UK universities and individual institutions are responsible with their own internal mechanisms for the standards and quality of the education they provide. As part of a national system, all institutions use external examiners to assist them in monitoring the standards of all of their degrees. These roles are guided by the standards outlined in the QAA' s code for external examining (section 4).

The external examiner system used in the UK is usefully summarized by the University of Birmingham.

The system will ensure:

- first and most important, that degrees awarded in similar subjects are comparable in standard in different universities in the United Kingdom though their content does of course vary;
- secondly, that the assessment, including examinations, and for determining the final marks of awards, are rigorous and have been fairly conducted within the University's regulations and guidance.
- thirdly, that the academic standards set are appropriate for the awards, or part thereof.

In order to achieve these purposes External Examiners need to be able:

- to participate in assessment processes for the award of degrees;
- to arbitrate or adjudicate on problem cases;
- to comment and give advice on course content, balance and structure, on degree schemes and on assessment processes.

(Source: www.ppd.bham.ac.uk)

When online learning began, lecturers and examiners were concerned that external examiners would not be involved in the assessment process in online learning, but the converse is true. It is a shared perception of many that are new to online learning that there will be a distance created between the learning materials and human interaction, which generates anxiety about the process. If it is online, it is not nearby or observable and is perceived to be 'at risk' or in a timeless, objectless universe. One of the authors has had experience of living in England, externally examining a course in Scotland and scrutinizing the assessment online of a multiple choice question examination that was set by the lecturer who was resident for part of the year in the USA. This accessibility was made possible by making available access to the VLE through a password, and the process was then freely available for scrutiny. It was possible to see at first hand what the learning materials were, to observe the structure and strategy of the assessment and to view the students' responses. Making time to demonstrate, online to external examiners, the assessments and the procedures that have been put in place to monitor assessments creates dividends for the eventual fulfilment of the external examiners' duties. It requires more detailed observation, involvement and exposure in the initial stages, but this can lead to a reduction in unfamiliarity of assessments or examinations.

Conclusion

In conclusion this chapter has shown that many of the institutional regulatory and quality management issues associated with online learning are in fact entangled with issues to do with the rapid expansion of higher education and difficulties with traditional face-to-face teaching and assessment. There is little hard evidence that online leaning dilutes the quality of higher education, or makes matters worse. Indeed, we argue later in this book that online technology actually presents opportunities to improve the experience and quality of mass higher education.

Online learning contributes to an increasing complexity of institutional processes. The rapid growth of Internet-based information and the widespread use of ICT has also made it easier for students to plagiarize, but this is an issue that effects face-to-face teaching environments and assessment as much as it is directly related to online learning.

Ensuring the quality of online teaching and learning is a difficult process, but it is no more or less difficult than finding a satisfactory methodology for ensuring the quality of any teaching provision or educational-based public service. No single method is satisfactory, and an eclectic mix of methods that look at different definitions of quality and allow a number of different stakeholders to be consulted is important. The current focus on learning outcomes should be used to encourage a quality process that looks at learning from the students' point of view. It should assist them by providing clarity of the learning task.

Notes

1   The definition used by the SEEC, the NICCAT and the NUCCAT *Credit and Qualifications – Credit Guidelines for Qualifications in England Wales and Northern Ireland*, November 2001, available at www.seec-office.org.uk/prop_guidelines.pdf
2   Final Report of the Socrates Project (Phase 1), *Tuning Educational Structures*, glossary. This is also the definition used by the European Credit Transfer System (ECTS) in the new 2004 ECTS Users' Guide.
3   Credit and Qualifications Framework for Wales, working document, June 2003, p. 8.

4 US Council for Higher Education Accreditation (CHEA).
5 American Association of Law Libraries: www.aallnet.org
6 University of Hertfordshire: www.herts.ac.uk/tli/locguide_main.html
7 Transnational European Evaluation Project (TEEP).
8 Government of British Colombia Ministry of Education.

4

The Design of Online Learning Environments

Introduction

This chapter looks at the importance of designing an online learning environment as part of the wider process of planning a teaching process. In one sense, online design follows on directly from the systematic approach to learning and teaching that should be used in traditional face-to-face learning. Online learning needs to follow many of the principals of design applied in face-to-face learning. There needs to be a synthesis and overview based on a vision of what is required, in addition to the analysis of detailed components and stages. Design is as much about considering how to achieve good learning interaction and human activity, as about the materials and content to be used.

In this chapter the design of online learning is examined first in terms of structuring and planning the human and interactive process that is needed, and then the material resources that are to be used. Design includes giving consideration of the social context of the learner and any special needs they have.

Planning a process of learning

We might summarize the stages of planning in any learning and teaching process as in Box 4.1.

Given the move towards more student-directed and constructivist approaches to learning, it becomes difficult to express the detail of a learning process as always linear, where different core skills and content are progressed each week. In the linear model, summative assessment is likely to be the end point, perhaps with some formative assessment at stages on the way. But when constructivist methods are used and more emphasis is put on students creating knowledge and learning in their own unique way,

---

Box 4.1 A typical learning and teaching process

- Decide on learning outcomes.
- Express broader learning aims that are more abstract, but are associated with learning outcomes.
- Identify core knowledge, skills and content.
- Identify available content-based learning materials that are likely to be useful to assist student learning.
- Identify an assessment strategy that will demonstrate students have acquired learning outcomes.
- Plan a learning process that will enable the learning outcomes to be acquired and demonstrated, with reference to the identified content.
- Express the learning process as specific learning activities, again with consideration to the identified learning content.

---

the learning process may become non-linear with fewer clear points or stages along the way. In this model assessment is likely to be more integrated and students will progress their individual projects and portfolios in different orders, but ultimately with similar end products. Different students may reach different key points at different times. Nevertheless there is still likely to be a clear beginning and ending in the overall process. One danger for teachers using an online environment is to underestimate the importance of a basic structure and timetable of events, even if they want to promote constructivist, student self-directed learning (Terrell 2005).

In all cases, it is a good idea for academic teachers to have a plan of how they envisage that the learning will develop, what teaching methods they will use, and by implication what kind of online learning environment they will use and at what points in the process. Many academics will prefer to break up the learning process into weekly subunits, each with their own learning aims and outcomes but more clearly related to specific learning activities. The JISC e-learning and pedagogy team (2004: 12) describe a learning activity as 'an interaction between a learner and an environment, leading to a planned outcome. It is the planned outcome which makes learning a purposeful activity.'

One writer who considered general aspects of the learning process was Moos (1974). He defined the general aspects as:

- Relationship dimensions – the nature and intensity of personal relationships within the environment;
- Personal development dimensions – the basic directions along which personal growth and self-enhancement tend to occur;
- System maintenance and system change dimensions – the extent to which the environment is orderly, clear in expectations, maintains control and is responsive to change.

These dimensions need to be represented in the online learning experience. A design which promotes ease of belonging will also be a design with ease of navigation, as even the most highly motivated students will abandon their studies after several fruitless attempts to find information or seek support. Material aspects of design are discussed in the final section of this chapter.

Designing the learning experience

It is useful to think of the learning experience as a holistic process that will normally include a number of key aspects. Juwah (2002) wrote from his experience of using online learning and ICT to support problem-based learning. He drew attention to the need to carefully design learning experiences online while ensuring that students are motivated and their needs met. He used examples of Gagné et al.'s (1992) nine events of instruction. These can be simplified as:

1   Gain attention.
2   Inform of learning objective.
3   Stimulate recall of prior learning.
4   Present stimulus material.
5   Provide learner guidance.
6   Elicit performance/provide feedback.
7   Assess performance.
8   Enhance knowledge retention and transfer.
9   Appeal to learner's interest.

This implies that the learner is an active person whose interest must be persuaded and captivated, not a passive person who is an empty vessel waiting to be filled with information. Juwah (2002) recommended that models of design should be used in conjunction with Keller and Dodge's (1982) ARCS motivational model to ensure that learning is enjoyable, meaningful and fit for purpose.

   The ARCS model ensures that students are motivated to learn. The model includes:

• Attention;
• Relevance;
• Confidence – to engage in/accomplish task and achieve intended outcome;
• Satisfaction.

This model could surely be applied to tutors developing online learning experiences as well as to the students who will learn from them. Again, not all of these aspects necessarily need to be achieved online and in many cases it is likely that a mix of face-to-face and online strategies will be used. Table 4.1 gives an example of a matrix that might help a teacher to decide

Table 4.1 Instructional events – use classroom or online delivery?

	Classroom	Online
Gain attention/ interest	Attractive module handbook, inspiring introductory talk.	Email an attractive module handbook, inspiring video clip.
Inform of learning objective	Explain objectives clearly in writing and discussion.	Use carefully timed announcement and email to make sure students see learning objectives – require response, or monitor they have been read. Allow questions – i.e. frequently asked questions (FAQs).
Stimulate recall of prior learning	Group exercise and flipchart recording, or similar.	Asynchronous discussion for limited time when students share prior learning.
Present stimulus material	Give out reading, reading list or similar. Promote related activities.	Post link to web sites, video clips, online reading, use formative test or follow up asynchronous discussion.
Provide learner guidance	Remind students in classroom where their learning should have progressed to.	Announce and circulate in an email – say what students should have achieved by key dates, provide formative self-testing.
Elicit performance/ provide feedback	Encourage self- and peer assessment.	Use formative test with automatic results or similar.
Assess performance	Submission of essay or sit exam.	Electronic submission of essay or project.
Enhance knowledge retention and transfer	Reflective exercise on how knowledge is being used or might be used in near future.	Link to web-based examples of how knowledge is being used in practice, create asynchronous opportunity to share knowledge use.
Appeal to learner's interest	Do early group work exercise to ascertain why students are studying and what their expectations are. Modify expectations if necessary.	Devise interactive questionnaire to assess learner's motivation and anxieties about doing the course. Share results anonymously.

whether to use classroom or online activities to cover a particular event and to create a good holistic learning experience.

The teacher has to combine synthesis with analysis. There needs to be a synthesis of the key aspects of the environment: context, resources available and desired outcomes. The academic needs to consider how these key aspects will interrelate. This will allow an appropriate analysis of what type of online environment to create for specific activities and events (Heathcote 2006). When trying to ensure a good overall learning experience the teacher needs to have an overview, in addition to an eye for detail.

Time management

Time management is important in all learning methods, and the online environment offers some useful structuring opportunities to assist students and academics with their management of time. Planning the timing of activities and events is at the core of any design of learning and teaching processes.

Online leaning can be a good means of keeping students on track with their learning. In face-to-face teaching, tutors have control of the timing of individual sessions, but are often frustrated by their ability to engage students in reflective and critical practice between classroom sessions. Tutors generally work to a time plan which ensures that they can achieve the learning aims and objectives of a session within the time slot available on the timetable. Academics have been challenged to look beyond the classroom and to design learning in the classroom that will promote self-study before the next teaching session.

In online learning, students do not have their facilitated learning closely time-managed by a tutor in a classroom setting. They often do not know how much emphasis to place on allocating time to different learning tasks and discussions. It is very helpful for a student not only to have navigation information within the online learning spaces prepared well ahead, but also to have some idea of how long to spend on each task. This prevents 'the task expanding to fill the time available' and helps students to spread their efforts appropriately. The technical resources in many VLEs usually allow the release of materials at set times and remind students of key dates and deadlines by announcements and emails. These are important opportunities to assist online students with their time management.

Time is an important aspect of the design of both classroom and online learning processes. The focus is different with online learning. Students may need more clear contextual guidance about how to manage their time. But there are opportunities to expand the time that students use for their self-directed study, as the boundaries of learning activities are less clearly defined, and students may have longer periods during which to reach specific learning aims and objectives that previously were met in the classroom session.

McKie emphasizes that awareness of time and spatial architecture is essential when seeking or using information on the Internet. She makes an interesting observation that deconstructing what it means for the guide, to actually be the guide, is salutary. Again this emphasizes the key role a facilitator has to play in the successful application of ICT in learning and teaching. To guide the student's experiential learning is a delicate task. As McKie (2000: 133) points out: 'The guide is a form of secondary text, one that can sometimes obscure awareness of the benefits of experiencing the terrain first hand'.

Structuring the environment and creating learning spaces

Having given some thought to the overall learning environment and type of learning process that will evolve, it is then important to begin to define the detail. When contemplating the setting up of an online course or module of study it is important to consider how to structure and segment the environment. Students arriving at a physical campus get time to find their way around before starting their studies. They identify with specialist areas such as the library, department office, lecture theatre and small-group classroom, and then begin to orientate themselves and link this with their first semester timetable of events.

Literature from architecture and surveying is being brought into play in the design of online learning environments. The design of a building leads people to behave in a certain way inside it. For example, if one enters a church, one would probably behave differently than when entering a football stadium. The first might be a place to seek peace and tranquillity, while the second would be quite the opposite when a goal is scored. Given the popularity of blended learning, university estates departments are having to give careful consideration to blending technology and online facilities into the physical environment of the campus (JISC 2006). Design therefore needs to give consideration to human and social processes in addition to presentational aspects. Examples of online places are a general chat area, an online library, a student support area an asynchronous discussion area and a place for weekly or monthly learning plans. Online places may have social meaning in the same way as real places.

Kolb (2000) emphasizes the need to create learning places online. He cites a wealth of references from architecture and planning literature and feels it is essential to create learning and dwelling spaces for 'critical inhabitation' and 'self-reflexive belonging' (Kolb 2000: 137 and 138). He reflects on Heidegger's four aspects which come together in true places or things:

- Earth – objects to interact with that have some independence and thickness of their own.

- Sky – times and changes, not always the same but varying according to its own rhythms.
- Gods – ideals and aspirations and calls to what we might become.
- Mortals – a sense that choices are meaningful in finite careers and that time makes demands and is not unlimited in amount.

A general description is proposed when a place is an extended location where a perceived (physical or virtual) expanse is linked to norms and expectations for appropriate or inappropriate actions. Virtual locations can become loci of our actions, expectations and norms. Kolb felt this must be applicable in designing learning experiences for delivery via the Internet. In order to create a sense of belonging we need a more perceptible locale, for example in the design and colour of backgrounds and graphics (Kolb 2000). Therefore graphics and logos will be helpful in reinforcing the cultural definitions of online places.

Standish (2000) supported this, describing a way in which web sites can be seen as providing a shell in which an infinite variety of material can be located. Sites are points in space but they become localities as they are given substance and links. This is what gives us reason to visit, explore, interact and revisit them to join in conversations.

Given the above comments, many university VLEs are designed with key social areas alongside course and module web sites. The social areas promote university clubs and societies and student support services. There may well be a general area for student chat and online friendship, and for posting discussions on general student issues. These kinds of materials help promote an interest and commitment to the virtual community so that academic materials are more likely to be accessed and used. Virtual learning environments need to be viewed holistically, rather than seen as separate to the general university experience. Students need to be socialized into the significance of different segmented areas and the part that these locations can play in their learning and development. It is vital to create a sense of an 'online' place.

Learning communities

Learning spaces need to be populated by learning communities. Cross (1998) maintained that we are interested in learning communities as they have the potential to create more holistic, integrated learning experiences for students. Learning community implies a bond between the people who populate a given space, and can vary from very tightly organized full-time programmes through to much looser arrangements of distance learning part-time students and those with a shared professional interest Cross defines a learning community as 'a group of people engaged in intellectual interaction for the purpose of learning' (1998: 4).

Interest in learning communities, according to Cross, can be divided into three categories: philosophical, research-based and pragmatic. Again human interaction is of great importance here and brings life to an online environment.

> A major challenge for today's online instructors involves creating a consistent level of interaction that fosters academic learning and cultivates a community atmosphere. This will require developing strategies that provide appropriate guidance and instruction for individuals and student groups.
>
> (Muirhead 2004)

In the 'virtual' online learning community the experience of personal bonds and ties takes on a new and different form (Dixon et al. 2005). Although there may be less face-to-face contact between the learners, personal interaction still takes place and becomes significant to the lives of the members. The online teacher often acts as a facilitator and ensures that student interactivity does take place. Personal feedback is a vital part of ensuring that a positive feedback loop occurs. The teacher may have to invest considerable time in the early stages of the online community to send personal feedback to encourage participation and to convince non-participants of the value of joining in. Early interactions are often social and about making introductions, rather than being purely educational, but they are necessary first steps (Salmon 2002). In time, a critical positive feedback loop will develop so the students encourage each other.

Virtual learning communities can take a number of different forms. Lewis and Allan (2005: 21) define three types: simple learning communities, managed learning communities and complex learning communities. Lewis and Allan have examined learning communities in a wide social sphere and are by no means limiting their analysis to higher education. Where there is a primary concern for the teacher to moderate and encourage interactivity (as in higher education) educationists may find they identify with many aspects of Lewis and Allen's 'managed learning community'. Here the learning community is focused and includes collaborative approaches to problem-solving.

Deciding on the use of online learning

Table 4.2 gives an example of the module process and sets out the ways in which issues could be addressed in the preparation for the use of online learning in any way – simple or complex.

Once the tutor designing the course or unit of study has decided in which direction to proceed, further in-depth consideration will need to be given to a range of factors. Much will depend on the type of online learning to be used. Although there are many means of employing online learning, from simple to complex, for the purpose of this chapter we have decided to focus on three main methods:

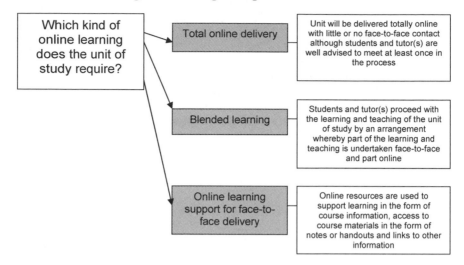

Figure 4.1   Deciding on the method of delivery

- Totally online learning.
- Blended learning.
- Online learning support for face-to-face delivery.

Delivery of a totally online learning experience

As this is the most complex mode of online learning, greater consideration will need to be given in addition to the areas highlighted in Table 4.2 in the areas of learning and teaching methods, student management, assessment, planning, development, student recruitment and student induction. This is because there is likely to be little or no face-to-face contact to support learning, and the VLE/MLE is going to be the student's only learning environment. Wherever possible it is desirable to ensure that the students and tutor have the opportunity to meet at least once during the course of their online study. In our experience this may occur during induction or in encounters on other related studies. It is a definite means of adding to the quality of future student–student and student–tutor interactions.

Learning and teaching methods will need to be especially carefully selected and applied, with excellent guidance to students on time management and clear navigation. In addition to this it will be necessary to organize the course or unit of study into sessions. If this is usually delivered in intensive mode, for example, over a week, it would probably be best, especially where the market is mainly part-time students, to consider a more extensive form of delivery so that online attendance for the unit of study is over a semester.

Another decision which will need to be made about online 'attendance' is

Table 4.2 Preparation for online learning

Stage	Reflection
Staff preparation	All tutors involved with the unit or course should undertake at least the basic level of training to use and manage the VLE/MLE and identify support mechanisms.
Validation	If this is an extant unit of study or course, ensure that it is approved for delivery using online learning in whatever form required as part, or all, of the mode of delivery. New courses or units should also be approved in this way. Often where HEIs are not very familiar with online learning and lack confidence with it, it is necessary to demonstrate an advanced stage of planning before approval is given.
Operationalization	Think through the implications of the learning outcomes and how this content could be delivered all or in part online or how online learning could be used to support face-to-face delivery.
Learning and teaching methods	Consider the learning and teaching methods which would be ideal to convey this content to students in face-to-face delivery.
Student management	Think about the ways in which you would like students to tackle the learning tasks – independently, in groups, seminars, action learning sets, problem-based learning groups, etc.
Assessment	Think about what formative and summative assessment is required.
Planning	Consider how the learning and teaching methods, student management methods and assessment match with the facilities on the VLE/MLE. How could these different areas be used creatively to create and support the learning environment and convey content material?
Development	Consider the need to develop any 'Learning Units' in HTML.
Student recruitment	How will students be recruited to this course or unit of study – will there need to be any prerequisite IT skills specified?
Student induction	What level of induction will be required by students?
Evaluation	How will the course or unit of study be evaluated? The experiences of tutors, students and any other administrative, technical or other support staff involved in delivery should be taken into consideration here.

over whether communications will be synchronous or asynchronous. For example, a *synchronous* discussion group would mean that students and tutor would all be online at the same time. An *asynchronous* discussion can be contributed to by students and tutor at any time over a prolonged period. In our experience synchronous communications are very difficult to arrange and manage. First, it is difficult to persuade a large group of busy people all to have access to a computer and the Internet at any given point in time. Secondly, when all the students and tutor are online at the same time, the communication moves very fast. Individuals can find it hard to fit a text in quickly and frustrations come to the fore. For these reasons we prefer the asynchronous method of communication.

In our universities, a module of study usually has a notional student effort attached to it of 200 hours, of which 30 hours are facilitated in the university. These 30 hours will equate to the facilitated online delivery. In our experience it has proved useful to divide these 30 hours into ten online sessions. The first of these sessions would be introductory and the last drawing the threads of the module together, while those in between would address specific issues of the module content in order to meet intended learning outcomes. Table 4.3 addresses the content of sessions.

In this scenario the role of the online tutor is to ensure all relevant material is time released and displayed appropriately, draw attention to new information being posted, set up discussion fora, explain how each forum will operate, facilitate student discussions, model the required behaviour in discussions (questioning, elaborating and so on), draw students into the discussion and deal with student questions and difficulties.

Delivery of a blended learning experience

When designing blended learning experiences it is important to consider the factors in Table 4.3. However, unlike the totally online experience, blended learning will offer opportunities for face-to-face contact between students and tutors interspersed with online learning. This gives an opportunity to iron out difficulties and clarify any unresolved issues face to face, and so is a little less stressful to the novice online tutor. The main decision that has to be made in designing the experience is how much and what to deliver face to face and how much and what to deliver online. If we consider the same unit of study as used in the example in Table 4.4, we can see how it could be adapted for a blended learning approach.

In a blended learning situation the students will be attending sessions related to several modules during any one period of time, term or semester, within the university, and engaging in online learning as a supportive activity to classroom activity which has taken place or will take place in the university in the future.

Design of blended learning experiences

In this mode of delivery it can be seen that the tutor is not entirely dependent on creating and facilitating an online learning experience for

Table 4.3 Plan for professional studies unit of study to be delivered totally online

Session content	Learning and teaching method	Online tutor and student activity
Session 1 Introduction to programme	Students introduce themselves to each other – ice breaker.	Discussion/OL conference. Sunday to Tuesday – students to put up document about themselves and reasons for being on the programme second discussion. Wednesday to Saturday setting personal aims and objectives for the unit.
	Aims and objectives + course handbook. Timetable of sessions. Focus of study.	Remind to visit course handbook and timetable on message board.
	Explanation of assessment task.	Remind to visit assessment guidance notes – set up questions and answers conference or FAQ (word document).
	Reading – core and supplementary.	Send message re reading.
Session 2 History of professional development	Presentation of history and influences on professional development.	HTML presentation created on Dream Weaver by faculty web editor posted in Course Materials.
	Questions: 1 What is driving the professional agenda? 2 How do professions develop? 3 Who are the stakeholders?	Group discussion: Sunday to Tuesday – depending on numbers – 3 × groups of 5–1 question each then share OR all working on all question OR one question each. Second discussion: Wednesday to Saturday elaborating on this.
Session 3 Historical and political context	Contextualizing nature of development of professions presentation.	Web-based written content (HTML learning unit created in Dream Weaver by faculty web editor). Narrative plus pauses, questions, reflections.

Table 4.3 continued

Session content	Learning and teaching method	Online tutor and student activity
	Selected papers for reading.	Post papers on web site in PDF format.
	Online seminar.	Discussion forum Wednesday to Saturday.
Session 4 Patterns of service delivery and effects on the professions	Group project – pressures affecting the practice of professions in organizations familiar to the students.	Discussion forum set up. Individual poster presentations (Word documents) to be posted by individual students Sunday to Tuesday. Second discussion forum to discuss effects on practice Wednesday to Saturday.
Session 5 Organizational context of professionalization (encourage students to work in pairs with someone from another profession)	Small-group work – students to link up with students from other professional groups (within the unit attendees) to analyse the pressure being placed on professional groupings.	Discussion fora – one for each group (3 groups × 5 students) Sunday to Saturday.
Session 6 Leadership within the professions	Students to provide anonymized case examples of leadership styles from practice and evaluate each other's examples.	Case examples to be posted onto course materials Sunday to Tuesday. Discussion forum Wednesday to Saturday.
Session 7 Management of challenges and changing roles in the professions	Students to identify key papers and texts to share in a 'journal club'. A journal club is a meeting where a group of people attend bringing with them a journal article which is of common interest. The individuals will have read and gained an understanding of the article prior to the session so that they can share and debate the opinions of the author in the journal club.	Online references for papers and texts to be posted Sunday to Tuesday. Forum to be set up for two groups to run as a journal club Wednesday to Saturday.

Table 4.3 continued

Session content	Learning and teaching method	Online tutor and student activity
Session 8 The impact of inter-professional education on the development of the professions	Presentations by a range of tutors sharing their experiences of facilitating inter-professional education.	Web-based written content (HTML learning unit created in Dream Weaver by faculty web editor) or enhanced PowerPoint presentations. To be posted on Sunday.
	Discussion of implications for practice.	One discussion forum Wednesday to Saturday.
Session 9 Individual professional development	Personal tutorials.	Email communication between tutor and students on one day of the week (to be arranged).
Session 10 Conclusion and preparation for summative assessment	Group work to draw unit to a close. Evaluation of learning. Evaluation of unit. Preparation for assessment.	Meet in university.

student contact. However, it must also be seen that the tutor engages in a lot of facilitation of online discussions and has the same responsibilities for ensuring information is posted on the VLE/MLE at the right place at the right time.

Delivering online student support for face-to-face learning experiences

In this mode of online learning, all learning and teaching activity is going to be delivered face to face. The VLE/MLE is going to be used to provide additional resources for learning and as a form of 'online filing cabinet' to provide information on course materials, course information and course announcements. It is clear that the role of the tutor here in online learning is to act as a coordinator, ensuring that all the information is available when it needs to be rather than being involved in facilitation of online interaction (see table 4.5).

Table 4.4 Plan for professional studies unit of study to be delivered using blended
learning

Session content	Learning and teaching method	Online tutor and student activity
Session 1 Introduction to programme	Face-to-face session.	All course documentation posted in course information area.
	Students introduce themselves to each other – ice breaker.	
	Aims and objectives + course handbook. Timetable of sessions. Focus of study.	Remind to visit course handbook and timetable on message board.
	Explanation of assessment task.	Remind to visit assessment guidance notes – set up questions and answers conference or FAQ (word document).
	Introduce reading – core and supplementary.	Send message re reading.
Session 2 History of professional development	Face-to-face lecture. Presentation of history and influences on professional development.	
	Online group discussion Questions: 1 What is driving the professional agenda? 2 How do professions develop? 3 Who are the stakeholders?	Group discussion: Sunday to Tuesday – depending on numbers – 3 × groups of 5–1 question each then share OR all working on all questions OR one question each.
Session 3 Historical and political context	Face-to-face lecture. Contextualizing nature of development of professions presentation.	
	Selected papers for reading Online seminar.	Discussion forum Wednesday to Saturday.

Table 4.4 continued

Session content	Learning and teaching method	Online tutor and student activity
Session 4 Patterns of service delivery and effects on the professions	Face-to-face experiential session in university. Group project – pressures affecting the practice of professions in organizations familiar to the students.	Discussion forum to discuss effects on practice Wednesday to Saturday.
Session 5 Organizational context of professionalization (encourage students to work in pairs with someone from another profession)	Face-to-face small-group work session in the university. Small group work – students to link up with students from other professional groups (within the unit attendees) to analyse the pressure being placed on professional groupings.	Discussion fora – one for each group (3 groups × 5 students). Sunday to Saturday to present findings.
Session 6 Leadership within the professions	Face-to-face group work in university. Students to provide anonymized case examples of leadership styles from practice evaluate each other's examples.	Discussion forum Wednesday to Saturday.
Session 7 Management of challenges and changing roles in the professions	Journal club in face-to-face session in university. Students to identify key papers and texts to share in a 'journal club'.	Discussion forum to reflect on the learning experience and its application for practice.
Session 8 The impact of inter-professional education on the development of the professions	Face-to-face presentations by a range of tutors in the university sharing their experiences of facilitating inter-professional education. Discussion of implications for practice.	One discussion forum Wednesday to Saturday.

Table 4.4 continued

Session content	Learning and teaching method	Online tutor and student activity
Session 9 Individual professional development	Face-to-face university-based personal tutorials.	Email communication between students and tutor to arrange appointments and negotiate/plan use of time during the tutorial.
Session 10 Conclusion and preparation for summative assessment	Face-to-face session in university. Group work to draw unit to a close. Evaluation of learning. Evaluation of Unit. Preparation for assessment.	Unit evaluation forms available online.

Facilitation of online learning experiences

The tutor's role in making online learning a human experience should be at the centre of any design process. They will often be responsible for initiating the early beginnings of a virtual online learning community. At its most simple this can be a time-limited asynchronous discussion.

Thorpe (2000), writing from considerable experience of facilitating online learning, indicated that interactivity in successful online learning depends on three key elements:

1   A good reason, which is obvious to the learners, as to why such inter-action is necessary to achieve the learning outcomes of their course. Linking participation to assessed outcomes is a powerful way of achieving this.
2   Support from someone who takes the responsibility for the process of interacting online – this is the academic who acts as a facilitator or moderator.
3   The willingness and resources that learners bring to it.

We have found it interesting to reflect on Thorpe's writing. These are all key factors in any experiential work, especially those part-time adult lear-ners who are also in full-time demanding employment. They are often pressed for time with competing demands of work, home and family commitments. Desirable learning outcomes are often set aside and only the essential ones, which link to assessed work are addressed. Membership of a virtual learning community and discussion group will depend on a belief that some clear educational benefit will be gained.

Table 4.5 Plan for professional studies unit of study to be delivered using online learning to support face to face learning

Session content	Learning and teaching method	Online tutor and student activity
Session 1 Introduction to programme	Students introduce themselves to each other – ice breaker.	All course documentation posted in course information area.
	Aims and objectives + course handbook.	
	Time table of sessions Focus of study.	Remind to visit course handbook and timetable on message board.
	Explanation of assessment task.	Remind to visit assessment guidance notes – set up questions and answers conference or FAQ (word document).
	Introduce reading – core and supplementary.	Send message re reading.
Session 2 History of professional development	Face-to-face lecture. Presentation of history and influences on professional development.	Announcements regarding room changes etc. Links to other web sites and documents.
	Group discussion Questions: 1 What is driving the professional agenda? 2 How do professions develop? 3 Who are the stakeholders?	
Session 3 Historical and political context	Face-to-face lecture.	Announcements regarding room changes etc.
	Contextualizing nature of development of professions presentation.	Links to other web sites and documents.
	Seminar – selected papers provided for reading.	Papers for discussion in seminar posted in advance of session.

Table 4.5 continued

Session content	Learning and teaching method	Online tutor and student activity
Session 4 Patterns of service delivery and effects on the professions	Group project – pressures affecting the practice of professions in organizations familiar to the students.	Announcements regarding room changes etc.
	Group discussion to discover effects on practice.	Links to other web sites and documents.
Session 5 Organizational context of professionalization (encourage students to work in pairs with someone from another profession)	Small-group work – students to link up with students from other professional groups (within the unit attendees) to analyse the pressure being placed on professional groupings.	Announcements regarding room changes etc. Links to other web sites and documents. Discussion forum (unfacilitated) to plan who will work with whom prior to session.
Session 6 Leadership within the professions	Students to provide anonymized case examples of leadership styles from practice evaluate each other's examples.	Announcements regarding room changes etc. Links to other web sites and documents. Case examples to be posted by students on web site after the session.
Session 7 Management of challenges and changing roles in the professions	Journal club. Students to identify key papers and texts to share in a 'journal club'.	Announcements regarding room changes etc. Links to other web sites and documents.
	Discussion to reflect on the learning experience and its application for practice.	Links to journal articles used to be posted on the web site after the session.
Session 8 The impact of inter-professional education on the development of the professions	Face-to-face presentations by a range of tutors in the university sharing their experiences of facilitating inter-professional education.	Announcements regarding room changes etc.

Table 4.5 continued

Session content	Learning and teaching method	Online tutor and student activity
	Discussion of implications for practice.	Links to other web sites and documents.
		PowerPoint presentations to be posted by the tutors after the session.
Session 9 Individual professional development	Face-to-face university-based personal tutorials.	Email communication between students and tutor to arrange appointments and negotiate/plan use of time during the tutorial.
Session 10 Conclusion and preparation for summative assessment	Face-to-face session in university. Group work to draw unit to a close. Evaluation of learning. Evaluation of unit. Preparation for assessment.	Unit evaluation forms available online.

Thorpe also gives valuable advice on using occasional face-to-face contact with tutors and other students to support online learning where relevant and practical. She gives warnings against using large blocks of text online and advocates other mixed media to support computer-based learning, for example books, course materials, audio cassettes, video cassettes and the telephone.

Salmon (2002, 2004) describes five stages of development of student activity in online working. Each stage needs to be heavily front loaded by tutor activity, with the students taking over the momentum as they gain confidence. These stages are as follows:

1 Access and motivation – technical support activity here is in setting up equipment and accessing the web. Tutor activity is to welcome and encourage students.
2 Online socialization – technical support activity here is to send and receive messages. Tutor activity is to interact, familiarize and provide bridges between cultural, social and learning environments.
3 Information exchange – technical support activity here is to search for and personalize software. Tutor activity is to facilitate tasks and support use of learning materials.

4   Knowledge construction – technical support activity here is to set up conferencing or discussion groups. Tutor activity is to facilitate this process.

5   Development – technical support task here is to provide links outside of closed conferences while the tutor is supporting and responding to student need.

(adapted from Salmon 2004: 29)

The role of the tutor in the facilitation of online learning cannot be emphasized too greatly. The tutor needs to be in and out of the module all the time that activity is occurring in the discussion, in order to carry out the roles listed above. Testone (1999) reflected on her experience of being a student in two very different online units of study. She emphasized the difference that a fully engaged online tutor made to the quality of her learning experience by facilitating and taking part in discussions, answering questions and making sure of staying at least one step ahead of the students in placing information in good time ready for use on the VLE.

Salmon examined the use of what she terms as 'e-tivities' (Salmon 2002). We have found this approach most helpful, as to give activities to be carried out online gives student a purpose for engagement with the medium. This is particularly helpful at the commencement of an online unit or course of study when students do not know each other or their tutor well.

Our experience has been that students have done well where the module has been fully facilitated by a tutor. Some shy students have said that they felt more able and less reticent to contribute to online discussions than they did in classroom situations. One colleague from another HEI has also stated that some students felt it removed a racial and cultural divide which was felt to be present in face-to-face encounters.

The time that the development and facilitation of an online unit or course of study takes is often said to be greater than that for a face-to-face learning experience. We are not sure that this is the case. Recent research in the USA showed that many academics feel neutral about this issue, and are convinced that no single method is preferable for saving time (Allen and Seaman 2005). In an online learning experience all the development has to be done in advance of the commencement of delivery. This is not usually the case with a newly validated face-to-face learning experience where sessions are often planned or updated just before delivery. There is no need for a constant tutor presence with online learning as there is in face-to-face delivery. The tutor can join in and leave the online learning experience while it is running. This dipping in and out of online facilitation can be fitted in around other learning and teaching, administrative or course management tasks.

Other writers have increasingly focused on the concept of interactivity to describe the need for quality interaction between a student and an online learning environment. Muirhead and Juwah (2004: 14–16) proposed ten different types of interactivity: object, linear, support, update, construct, reflective, simulation, hyperlinked, non-immersive contextual and the complete virtual interactive environment. Not all of these are based on human interaction.

Dealing with each of these definitions in turn:

- Object interactivity involves using a computer object like a mouse or website button to start an interactive process.
- Linear interactivity is where the student moves through a predetermined list of online content.
- Support interactivity is where a user receives a response to a request for supportive information.
- An update interactivity means that the user will receive an individually generated response to a computer-automated exercise.
- Construct interactivity aims to link theoretical ideas to real-world examples through simulated exercises.
- Reflective interactivity allows users to match their own ideas against those of others and to make their judgement about how their assessment compares.
- Simulation is similar to construct interactivity, but may provide a more normative or deterministic process through which the student must progress.
- Hyperlink interactivity allows the user to explore a range of information and knowledge.
- Non-immersive contextual interactivity is said to be a holistic online environment where users engage in work-related learning through a series of content.
- Finally, the most holistic form of online interactivity is immersive virtual interactivity. This is a complete virtual interactive environment that promotes interactions between the users and is built on numerous examples of feedback.

Online tutors have a central role in promoting interactivity and evaluating its quantity and success. It is all too easy for tutors to create a learning environment, but not to manage and encourage the creative learning process that evolves, by giving adequate support and feedback. Online tutors need to be aware that the social psychological processes that prevent people from learning, such as low self-esteem, low self-efficacy and high anxiety may take on particular forms in the online learning environment that can be associated with a lack of ICT skills and resources (see also discussion in Chapters 2 and 6). One key aspect when designing online learning and teaching is to allow sufficient time for the teacher to remain involved in providing ongoing support.

The design of the material environment

The first part of this chapter has focused quite deliberately on the human, social and interactive aspects of designing online environments, because they are the easiest to ignore. We now discuss the design of the material environment. This is primarily the use of web pages, and their associated text and images on the screen.

Online learning resources need to be as easy to use as possible. Often there are trade-offs between ease of use and technical superiority. For example, adding the availability of video will increase the attractiveness of resources for some students, but others will not be able to access the additional resource and will be frustrated as a result. It is a priority that materials are designed with the following factors in mind: ease of navigation, minimal download delay, and 24-hour reliability (Tarafdar and Zhang 2005). Mark Ward, previously BBC News Online technology correspondent, argues that the basic rules of good web site design are: 'avoid jargon, let users know where they are in the process, keep pages small to save download time and use dead space in top right for a search facility' (www.news. bbc.co.uk/ 4 November 2002).

During the past decade there has been a fierce debate in the media about what constitutes good design of online materials. International web guru, Dr Jakob Nielsen (1999) is a key exponent of simplicity, but his critics accuse him of underestimating the rapidly developing skills of Internet users, the exciting artistic design potential of new media, and the added value of online additions such as Adobe Acrobat pdf, Flash and Java. Nielson has stuck by his argument of simplicity in the face of rapidly advancing technology. His web site at www.useit.com/ lists the top ten mistakes in web design, a commentary he updates each year. His top ten mistakes of all time are paraphrased below:

1   Search engines that provide over-complex results.
2   Web links that open in Adobe Acrobat pdf files.
3   A failure to change the colour of visited links (so that the user knows what they have already visited).
4   Unreadable text that is too dense.
5   Fixing font sizes so users cannot change them.
6   Page titles that are not picked up by major search engines.
7   Including too many advertisements.
8   Ignoring commonly used web design conventions.
9   Links that automatically open in new windows.
10 Not answering users' questions.

(Nielsen 2004, www.useit.com/alertbox/ 9605.html)

In 2005 he had some new concerns; in particular about the use of Flash multimedia automated presentations and the provision of over-complicated forms for personal submission. Nielsen is defending the needs of the global majority and the vast numbers of new users who enter the online community each year. In particular he is concerned about those with relatively low-specification machines in developing countries and poorer communities, and those groups who may find it more difficult to adjust to the e-society, for example older people. His presentations and books about usability are based on numerous surveys. But his conservativism infuriates those at the pioneering forefront of the web who want to see new technologies advancing and offering sophisticated new interactive elements to the modern user who has new high-specification equipment and high expectations of what can be achieved. American web designer Joshua Davis was vehemently critical of Nielsen's approach when interviewed for the BBC *Dot Life* programme in December 2001 (www.news.bbc.co.uk). At that time he was one of a number of global web designers taking part in the 'Web Wizard: Designers Who Define the Web' exhibition at the London Design Museum.

So where do Nielsen's important and influential commentaries leave the global higher education community in terms of the use and design of online materials? On the one hand, it might be tempting to argue that the higher education community is different because it is at the high end of the user sophistication spectrum. Therefore we might conclude that more challenging and advanced online materials can be used. But this ignores the rapid growth of higher education discussed in Chapter 1 and the limitations of technology in some countries that do not have an advanced infrastructure. Overall the higher education community would be wise to be cautious and not dismissive of Nielsen's argument. There is a lot be said for his basic rules of web design, but then again rules are made to be broken. As is discussed below, it is imperative that academics take careful note of Nielson's findings on the presentation of text. But his idea of avoiding the use of Adobe Acrobat pdf files is extremely difficult in the higher education environment, given that so many academic journals and official reports are now made available in this format.

The presentation of online text

Looking at Nielson's top ten web design mistakes of all time, academics certainly need to heed his advice on the presentation of text. Neilson has found that the majority of online readers scan the web page rather than reading text in a linear fashion from beginning to end.

No single web page should have a lot of dense text on it, because the nature of the web is that links (hyperlinks) can be provided to reach a more detailed level of information behind the first page. It is therefore important to think of online learning design in terms of levels of content. If users insist on using long pages – although it is not advisable – the first part of the page should be thought of as a summary of what is coming and page 'anchor' links can be made to more detailed material provided later on the same page. Neilson calls this style of writing the 'inverted pyramid' because the conclusion, or overall summary, comes first. This style should be familiar to academics who write papers because they are trained in the art of writing a clear summary of the whole article as an abstract, and the abstract should give the reader a very clear idea of what the paper is about in only 200–300 words.

Hyperlinked words and phrases are not the only means of helping readers effectively to scan online text for key points. It is possible to draw attention to key words without them necessarily linking to more detailed text on an additional page. It is important, therefore, to consider using bold and colour variation to draw attention to key words where further links are not needed or appropriate.

The use of clear sub-headings, short paragraphs and bullet point lists is a vital part of the strategy to assist web users in effectively scanning pages. Neilson's research at www.useit.com shows that the use of sub-headings and bullet points, to reduce the density of text, is a highly successful strategy in keeping users' interested and informed about a site's content.

A key issue for the academic teacher who is designing online learning is signalling to the student when they are moving from summary virtual course information to traditional text-based materials. Neilson has raised concerns about the use of Adobe Acrobat pdf files to do this, because they perplex the user by opening new software and slowing the process down. Adobe pdf files change the visual menus for the user, with the result that users are left feeling that everything is suddenly out of their control. But pdf files are endemic in the academic community. They are the means by which traditional higher education text-based materials have entered the online environment. Therefore it is vital that students overcome the difficulties and anxieties about managing such files early on in their online experience. Online and ICT inductions must take this into account. The pdf file environment must be used to the advantage of students because it represents such a rich resource and potential gateway to high-quality material. It is important that academics communicate to students that when the online browser environment moves to an Adobe Acrobat pdf environment and the window and menus change, they are moving from an online text environment to a more traditional text-based book-type environment. It is a core and fundamental skill that modern students know how to work with Adobe pdf files.

The typical structure of a virtual learning environment

Table 4.6 summarizes the likely structure of a VLE/MLE, and summarizes material already discussed in Chapter 2. Usually teachers can control the degree of complexity of what is presented, so, for example, some basic features such as announcements will always be turned on by default, but others can be added by the teacher if required. It is clearly important to allow additional optional areas to be presented, thereby increasing the visual complexity.

Table 4.6   A typical VLE structure

VLE areas and content guide	Student activity in these learning spaces
Announcements:	• Checking for updates • Room changes • Timetable changes
Staff profiles, e.g. tutor and administrative staff contact details, work place and photographs:	• Accessing instant information about staff • Checking tutor and administrative staff roles • Clarifying who to contact about what • Checking best times to contact staff
Course information, e.g. module handbook timetable:	• Seeking and checking information for guidance and support
Course materials, e.g. glossary reading list learning units/presentations:	• Seeking and using learning and teaching materials • Carrying out learning activities and tasks
Discussion/conferences:	• Collaborative learning • Small-group work • Seminar work • Action learning sets
Quiz, e.g. self-assessment:	• Self-assessment • Formative assessment • Summative assessment • Checking that learning is progressing • Identifying strengths and needs
Links, e.g. web sites in related topic areas online books or journals:	• Widening scope of learning materials • Increasing knowledge in topic area • Gaining confidence in accessing new and wider sources of information • Using door-opening information
Communication tools, e.g. group email facilities:	• Contacting fellow students quickly and easily • Contacting identified groups swiftly, e.g. seminar group, PBL group members • Contacting tutors easily
Digital drop-box, i.e. area to post work for tutor:	• Submission of work prior to tutorials or research supervision for formative feedback

Navigation

Navigation is the means by which students move around the online learning environment. As on any other journey, students need to feel safe and secure in their movements without the risk of wandering off the planned route and becoming lost. Losing direction is very frustrating for students as they have to come right out of the programme and try to find their way back to where they need to be. This also wastes a lot of time.

Such difficulties can not only be avoided by consistency in design, as discussed above, but also by careful design which includes signposting to other coterminous activities. An example of the way navigation can be assisted follows below.

1   A student could be engaging in learning activities from the course materials area.
2   After reading a piece of text or viewing a presentation, the student should be clearly directed towards a discussion forum where they can 'meet' with other students to share thoughts and ideas.
3   The tutor needs to have set up the discussion forum well in advance of the discussion starting and to have thought through its visual working.
4   The tutor needs to have posted tasks to instigate the discussion.
5   The students can then engage in discussion facilitated by the tutor.
6   Once the discussion is over, the student can be directed back to the course information area again.
7   Activities need to have a clear timescale and date attached, so that students know when they should have completed an activity.

From McKie (2000) we have deduced that navigation should be goal directed, with support. An example of goal direction appears above but support needs to be available in many forms. For example,

- It is often better for students to use a 'bread crumb menu' situated at the top of the web page to navigate back to the sections of the web site that they need to revisit rather than using the 'back' button on the web browser.
- Links to other areas of the learning and teaching site need to be visible at all times so that the student can move freely between the areas as required
- Learning packages that have been appended to the VLE/MLE through links and links to other web sites, when clicked, should open in a new window to ease the student's navigation process.

The management of computer windows can be a key skill in helping students to manage their online learning experience better. Neilson (www. useit.com) has criticized web sites that open too many links in new windows, but in online higher education learning processes students often need to know how to work with more than one window open at a time. For example, a student may need to keep one window permanently open on their tool-bar, because this contains the core narrative of a learning exercise, while opening and closing other reference windows. This makes the online lesson more dynamic, but can result in students becoming frustrated if they do not have the core skills for managing windows. When designing an online learning exercise the teacher can sometimes help by making it clear in the instructional text when a student should open a link in a new window. Similarly some VLEs allow teachers to set a new hyperlink to open in a new window by default. There is a balance to be struck here. In our experience, students do need to know how to work with more than one window open, while engaging in online activities, but if students are expected to have many windows open simultaneously then the learning activity can become too complex and too difficult for them to manage.

There are no hard and fast rules about how the various areas of the learning environment should be used, but consistency is essential. If several tutors from an individual module are posting information inconsistently on the VLE in different areas at different times, it causes confusion for the students. There are difficult decisions for larger higher education institutions in terms of promoting consistency of design. For example should a large university try and impose rules of consistency, or should it leave this to disciplinary-based departments and schools, where staff will know what is realistic and helpful for a particular group of students. Some universities that try to enforce house styles at a high level quickly become frustrated that academics are notorious for making their own decisions. While some basic overall rules of design can be set at the centre, especially if a single commercial platform like Blackboard or WebCT is being used, more detailed criteria are best worked out by subject specialists. After all, the needs, requirements and abilities of IT degree students will be very different to general social science students.

Designing online learning activities

One approach is to simply think about replicating existing face-to-face learning activities online, as this is often seen as a safe way to begin with online learning. The material is tried and tested; previous students have used the material and evaluated it. The learning and teaching techniques will be familiar to the tutor. The only risk is in identifying how classroom-based activities can usefully be replicated online.

Table 4.7 shows how a simple classroom learning process can be replicated in an online environment. Because the activity moves from being based around face-to-face discussion, the formative assessment is more focused. This is to make sure that the students are clear as to the focus of their longer period of discussion. This also creates a learning output for their longer timescale of activity and will allow the teacher, who is at more of a distance, to assess how the group is doing.

Table 4.7   An example of replicating a classroom experience online

	Classroom	*Online*
Learning outcome	Understanding of theoretical concept.	Understanding of theoretical concept.
Activity	Reading of text followed by small-group discussion.	Reading of text followed by asynchronous discussion.
Timescale	One hour.	One week.
Formative assessment	Students define concept in their own words through discussion.	Students must post chosen quotation from reading and summarize why they think the quote helps define part of the concept.

Online activities should make the most of the variety of online content that is available to promote the added value of the medium. A number of global television and radio companies are increasingly posting useful resources on their web sites. These can often be downloaded or played by video streaming (which makes memory problems more manageable). While teachers will be worried about promoting learning activities that increase the specification of hardware, many universities in the developed world will now have open-access computer rooms where teachers can guarantee that students will have access to minimal hardware requirements to view or listen to a specific resource. In other words, if students cannot see or hear a video or audio clip at home, they can be encouraged to find time to use the college facilities to experience it.

An online learning environment needs to follow up the experience of a multimedia resource with a well-structured and clear interactive learning exercise. This does not have to be complex, and is often best kept simple, for example posting comments to an asynchronous discussion that asks to students to reflect on the content. A student group could be asked to view a number of resources between them and to post 500 word summaries of each resource. Such shared summaries should encourage the students to explore each other's primary resources. Some key sites for locating educational multimedia materials are indicated in Table 4.8.

Influence of special needs on practice and learning

Students with a disability frequently encounter problems accessing online resources. For example, those with a sensory impairment that limits their sight will need text-based buttons and links so that these can be interpreted by software that gives audible translation by reading the screen. If images are used as buttons and links by web designers, then these will need a text-

Table 4.8 Examples of multimedia content sites of interest to higher education

Web site resource	Audio	Short video
www.podcast.net/	Directory of audio files on hundred of different topics.	
nobelprize.org/		Video clips from Nobel prize-winning academics.
www.bbc.co.uk/calc/news		Short news clips, including science, health and education.
www.bbc.co.uk/radio/downloadtrial/	Numerous radio documentaries, many in mp3 format.	

based alternative. Most countries are now working actively to make sure that those with special educational needs and disabilities are not disadvantaged by the provision of online learning. A number of international standards of practice are beginning to emerge about how to make online materials accessible to those with special needs. The World Wide Web Consortium (W3C, www.w3.org) is an international industry cooperative that has been central in the argument for universal accessibility. It has a Web Accessibility Initiative (WAI, www.w3.org/WAI/) that has regularly published content accessibility guidelines. Some web-based services have been established that can make technological assessments of the usability of specific web addresses.

In many countries there are legislation and protocols that reinforce the importance of this perspective. In the USA, section 255 of the Communications Act requires providers to make services compatible with specialist resources that are used by people with disabilities (see www.fcc.gov.uk). An amendment to section 508 of the Rehabilitation Act requires government agencies to make information accessible to those with a disability, and this includes electronic information. The European Union has supported the global WAI initiative through the Euro Accessibility project (www.euroaccessibility.org). A landmark human rights case under the 1992 Disability Discrimination Act in Australia brought to court by the country's Human Rights and Equal Opportunity Commission ruled that Bruce Macguire who could not achieve access to the Olympic web site had been disadvantaged by the Organizing Committee of the Sydney Olympic Games.

In the UK, the Special Educational Needs and Disability Act 2001 required further and higher education institutions to ensure that disadvantage does not occur in any aspect of educational services. The earlier legislation, the Disability Discrimination Act 1995, is also important as it implies that public organizations are obliged to provide information in a manner that does not discriminate. For this reason the UK Disability Rights

Commission (DRC) held a formal investigation, published in 2004, into the access and inclusion of disabled people on the World Wide Web. An important aspect of their investigation was the inclusion of service users with a range of disabilities who could give a first-hand qualitative account of their experiences. The DRC (2004) noted the value of 'assistive technologies' – special products that can make sites very useful to impaired users. An example is a screen reader that converts text on the screen into audio data. The DRC commissioned the City University, London, to assess numerous web sites using technological and service-user based evaluations. The majority of web sites they visited (81 per cent) failed to delivery on the most basic of WAI criteria. Blind users were particularly disadvantaged by web sites that could not take account of their need for basic text that could be interpreted by a screen reader. It became clear that services could be improved greatly if disabled people were more directly involved in their initial design. There was a great need to make web designers more aware of the requirements of users with disabilities. This could be encouraged by a formal accreditation process or certification scheme such as a quality kitemark.

Conclusion

The design guru, Jakob Nielsen, cautions about the limitations of e-learning and online learning from a designer's point of view and makes the important point that online content is not about replacing text-based materials, such as books, with new online content. He sees the design of online learning as needing to focus on the processes – that is, where it can deliver added value to traditional learning processes.

> What is good online is a lot of experience based learning, because that's what online can give you that a book cannot give you. People could do things, try things and discover things almost by themselves, except that of course, you have carefully planned all the things for them to discover. So, whether it is simulation systems, or problem based learning, or cases where you can do calculations, it depends on the topic and what is appropriate for it. You can even get people to do live exercises, for instance, if you are teaching a social science type of a topic where you discuss current issues, you could consider making a newspaper site as material for your course. I think those are features that work well online and don't work well in a book or even in a live lecture.
>
> (Nielson 2001)

This is an important reminder that online learning is not primarily about the design of content, although the display of content is one part of the procedure.

The most important aspect of design is the creation of a holistic learning process. The design of an actual online learning environment has many similarities with the design of a classroom-based learning process. The first steps are almost identical in that they are strategic and visionary, and based around having a good overview and definition of the learning process. In particular, learning aims and outcomes need to be clearly defined and how they are to be assessed needs to be clearly thought out. Subsequently, during the process of working out the detail, decisions can be made about designing and using specific aspects of online environments. This is the part of the process that specifies the stages and units of learning over a given time frame. Many learning events can easily be adapted from the classroom to an online environment. Some aspects of learning events seem to work well on line, in particular where more time is given for reflection and the individual is encouraged to work alone as well as in a group. It is important not to underestimate the importance of giving students guidance about what is expected at different time points along the way, even where a more open and constructivist approach to learning is envisaged and desirable.

5

Transforming Learning Methods through Online Teaching

Introduction

This chapter examines how online learning is changing the traditional forms of teaching used in higher education. It is argued that, if managed correctly, online learning methods can add value to traditional face-to-face methods and provide opportunities for reducing some of the weaknesses of traditional teaching methods. Online learning is not an immediate panacea for all the difficulties of modern higher education teaching; it takes on its own forms, structures and discourse, in the same way as traditional classroom-based and face-to-face learning. What is fundamentally different is the nature of the medium and its added dimensions in time and place. The change of medium offers new opportunities to move some of the contemporary and the traditional approaches towards learning in more interesting and efficient ways. The chapter tries to evaluate the likely direction that learning and teaching will take in the future, and makes some tentative forecasts about the impact of online learning.

Lectures

The traditional lecture is where an academic presents a monologue to a large group of students. This teaching method is still very much a feature of higher education across the world, but has been questioned as a method of learning for many years. Writers such as Bligh (2002) fundamentally questioned the value of such an approach to teaching, arguing that such delivery methods are not efficient forms of learning for many students. The key criticisms are discussed, and then consideration is given to the ability of online learning to make an impact on these limitations.

> Why aren't lectures scrapped as a teaching method? If we forget the eight hundred years of university tradition that legitimizes them, and

imagine starting afresh with the problem of how best to enable a large percentage of the population to understand difficult and complex tasks, I doubt that lectures will immediately spring to mind as the obvious solution.

(Laurillard 2002: 93)

Although academic lectures last for at least an hour, the attention span of learners in such circumstances is limited to about 20 minutes. In the traditional lecture theatre there is no opportunity for engagement between lecturer and students, the physical structure almost prevents this, with the lecturer positioned alone at the front of the theatre addressing a mass of students in front. The appearance is much like a cinema or theatre, creating the impression that students will be 'entertained' and are not expected to contribute or disturb what is happening on the 'stage' at the front.

The lecture has become viewed by its critics as an elitist and paternalistic form of delivery whereby students defer in silence to the lecturer, paying too much respect to the lecturer's experience and expertise, and rarely questioning his or her judgement. It is argued that this increases the mystique of knowledge transmission rather than demystifying it, because it implies that only the academic has total understanding of knowledge and he or she alone can impart it. Given the status and power that the traditional lecture confers on the academic, it is easy to see why it has retained such prominence for so long. Many academics feel ambivalent about replacing it.

Lectures do not appear to encourage good flows of communication between lecturer and student, because the lecturer is not getting coterminous feedback about what the students understand from the presentation. Laurillard (2002) gives the example of an engineering lecture where she discovered from one student's question at the end that the person had not understood the majority of the content.

Although academics and universities have been reluctant to revolutionize the traditional lecture, much work has been done to reform it and encourage the form to evolve. If universities insist on giving lecture programmes and their students expect to receive them, what are 'good lectures' like?

Most agree that good lectures have a structure based around a few clear learning aims, a number of key points and facts, and a conclusion that revisits the aims at the end. In between, good lectures inspire students to want to look beyond the basics by raising key contemporary questions and controversies, and by suggesting reading material from which the students can become familiar with such debates. There should be a helpful reference to sources that are practical and obtainable for the student audience. A good lecture inspires students to want to research more on the topic themselves. A good lecture promotes self-directed learning of greater depth.

If lectures are to be inspiring it helps if they are delivered by inspiring academics who have a confidence and charisma about the way they deliver. But this is a lot to ask. Some academics can take time and need considerable experience to acquire such confidence and it would be unrealistic to expect anything different. Added to which, good lecturers may have sophisticated social and presentational skills that are difficult to learn quickly, although presentation skills can be taught to some extent. The pacing of delivery and material is one key aspect of presentations. A clear summary of key information is important.

Lectures and mass higher education

Given the rapid growth of higher education discussed in Chapter 1, the lecture has evolved to cope with the transformation of higher education in modern post-industrial society. Rather than being terminated it has emerged stronger and more resilient to change, often described in new language as 'large-group teaching'. Lecture halls are often booked for a two- or three-hour block, and a large group receives a number of short lectures during that time, with small-group activity distributed between the presentations. A key challenge for teachers becomes how to obtain feedback from these groups and to include it in a large session, and how to keep the whole experience dynamic and integrated (Huxham 2005). Seminal writers in learning and teaching who have tried to inspire demoralized academics with methods to cope with expanded student numbers have made practical suggestions that are linked to action research and trying to move the lecture beyond its traditional boundaries (Race 1999). They emphasize the importance of student interaction.

This encourages teachers to break up the delivery of content by means of activities. Ideally, the activities can include some kind of feedback to the lecturer, so he or she has a better sense of whether learning aims are being met. Activities might take the form of small-group discussions (or pair-based discussion), problem-based examples or, even, formative tests.

This evolving of the lecture into managed large-group teaching is one of the most important developments in the UK since the arrival of mass higher education. It has used the challenge of greater numbers as a catalyst to confront pedagogic assumptions. But there is an implicit criticism that this kind of pedagogic pragmatism lacks idealism and is based on coercing academics to accept the prevailing bureaucratic and managerialist approaches to higher education and that in reality this dilutes quality, standards and the fundamental culture of independent criticism and thinking. Such critics argue for the preservation of small-group teaching and discussion. Evolved large-group teaching is therefore in danger of promoting and providing small pieces of pre-formulated knowledge, rather than facilitating deep and independent learning. Academics are in danger of focusing on the management aspects of the classroom and educational outputs rather than the creative ability of each individual and more holistic quality learning outcomes. The communication of core chunks of information can take over from promoting confident, creative and critical reflection.

New technology and the lecture

So what impact has technological change and online learning had on this debate? A number of writers such as Laurillard (2002) note that a lecture presented with digital media, such as digital television, has the ability to be much more entertaining that the traditional lecture, added to which the student can have more control over the content. They can switch it on and off at their convenience. In addition, new technologies present the opportunity for such professional presentations to be interactive. Laurillard distinguishes between 'adaptive, communicative and productive media'. Adaptive media are media that allow the student to adjust the content delivered to some extent. For example, using digital television, or Power-Point, horizontal options are available to students, so they can choose which concepts to explore in more detail. One might add that this kind of option has always been available with reading – in terms of students' choice of reading, even if directed by the academic. The students decide in what order to read book chapters and journals, and can choose to pursue sub-topics that they are more interested in. Laurillard, with her professional history and expertise being largely developed at the UK Open University cites the value of such adaptive media in the history of the UK's leading distance learning provider. But this ignores that not all students wish, or feel confident enough, to study at a distance. Historically, distance universities such as the OU attract older, more confident and self-motivated students.

It is all too easy to replace traditional lectures with media presentations that take on similar monologue and elitist modes of communication. An example is the web site for the Bank of Sweden Noble peace prizes (http://nobelprize.org/). Here one can watch an award winner speak on a digital video clip of high quality as it is streamed to one's desk top (no need to download a large video file). In addition the viewer can see copies of the speaker's overhead summaries, even link (in some academic disciplines) to another web site with a full text of what is being said. But this does not necessarily aid understanding of the new and leading-edge concepts presented, and there is no opportunity to engage with the difficult material by asking questions. Such an online media presentation of lectures offers only minimal advantages over attending the event, the main one being that you can control the content delivery at your own pace. There are also social and psychological disadvantages with not being present – you cannot ask the person sitting next to you to help you clarify your understanding of a point, you cannot reflect with others on the content of the material in the bar afterwards, and so on. It is important not to minimize the social value of attending such educational events and these are often of a high added value.

Nevertheless, learning technology does offer more creative opportunities to present knowledge content at various levels and in different temporal zones. For example, difficult concepts can be linked to online encyclopedia or scientific dictionaries. Controversies can be linked to online journals and debates. Frequently asked questions (FAQs) can be posted. Discussion about the content can be promoted. These are all additions that can rapidly raise the learning value of content-based materials. Presentations can be linked with self-study material and interaction.

Microsoft PowerPoint has offered some improvements and benefits in the quality of lectures by providing a clear structure and increased use of visual aids. But the progress is contingent and related to other associated secondary changes, such as lecturers themselves becoming more organized with their material through use of the software.

Asynchronous lectures – experiencing it all 'after' the event

Microsoft PowerPoint and digital multimedia technology have begun to add a stronger asynchronous element to the idea of the traditional lecture. Twenty-five years ago if you missed a lecture the best way of finding anything else out about the content was to borrow another student's handwritten notes. Even a photocopied handout was relatively unusual. Today, versions of many lectures are preserved in a computer file on a university intranet. This provision is far from uniform. Not all teachers do this, but increasing numbers do. Some academics resist it, arguing that it encourages students not to attend lectures, or that it leaves them open to the theft of their original ideas. But the placing of lecture notes on computer servers around the world is an unmistakable trend in global higher education. We predict this trend will increase further. This is not to argue that it is normatively a good thing. It is no guarantee of quality learning, but it is an evolutionary trend, an aspect of the modernization and technological change in higher education that we cannot ignore. In itself, as behaviour change, it is not hugely significant. No one could really argue that the long-term availability of presentational notes via online technology has a revolutionary impact on learning. But it is an interesting behaviour change and a simple use of technology that could have long-term consequences. The important related evaluative question to ask seems to be: how can this trend, this behaviour, be developed to improve the quality of learning in higher education?

The online revolution, coupled with the modernization and increase in size of higher education, is locked in a drive to bring academic content, knowledge and concepts to a mass audience. This dictates that 'the lecture' will continue to evolve to be in part an asynchronous digital form, coterminus with its traditional synchronous version. This could have a number of outcomes. What started with lecture notes is beginning to include digital video clips and hyperlinks to related material. Lectures are being captured in a digital and online format never seen before.

Revolution – the end of lectures as we know them?

As the integration of technology improves and academics become better trained to use it, asynchronous lecture presentations might take over much more from synchronous face-to-face forms' with online video and content being suitably followed up by technologies such as asynchronous discussions (see the section on online seminars below) and with face-to-face teaching being based more on individual support in tutorials of small groups and individuals. This seems like the vision that Laurillard shares, but it is close to the form and discourse of the large distance learning universities and it rather denies the social collective experience of mass higher education that still seems to be attractive to so many young people. We think this vision is unlikely to be achieved in all modern universities. While distance learning has grown, traditional campus-based universities have grown faster.

The lecture evolves to a digital and new form

Much more likely is a coterminous evolution whereby the lecture evolves around both its synchronous and asynchronous forms. Thus the technologies used to capture the lecture (so as to offer it as an asynchronous experience in the future) are also used live – to present digital video clips and web-site searching of related literature – within the real live lecture theatre. This seems to fit the 'market model' of higher education now so common, where there is more emphasis on choice, flexibility and diversity. This is against the backdrop of students' part-time working lives and the related stress. Students will increasingly find that they can choose how they experience a lecture from one week to another. Either they take part in the lecture theatre or they receive the material later in their own time. Although at first the choice of the timing of the content may be implicit and non-permissive, suggesting to students that synchronous lecture attendance is the required norm, institutions will become less explicit about this and more accepting of student's physical absence and choice. There are likely to be some elements of chaos and fragmentation here, different courses and modules might offer varying degrees of experience and quality. Some lecturers will progress their technological skills more rapidly than others, some universities and departments will move ahead and find money for equipment more quickly than will their competitors. The move to this mode of experience will not be logically planned, it will not be equitable, but it does seem likely to happen, as a wave of gradual transforming change. The good news is that this transformation will present many opportunities to improve the quality of lectures and their integration with other aspects of learning. Activities such as seminars, reading and attendance will become more important and integrated with the content of lectures. The traditional lecture will survive, but it will be less dislocated from the holistic learning experience. Lectures will increasingly be captured with technology for a later asynchronous experience. The content of lectures will be increasingly and more easily linked to other learning experiences and exercises.

For many students, but not all, the lecture will remain important as a social educational event, as a discipline in part of the week, a catalyst to get focused input on a subject and to lever them towards the library on the way home. Yet not all students will want or require this. Some will have different learning styles and lifestyle organizations. There will be increasing numbers of students who sit in the lecture theatre less, but they will still attend other smaller face-to-face learning events and will borrow library books. They will even go on to pass essays and examinations and to graduate.

> Alternatives to the predominance of the lecture method at university such have been practised successfully for years in distance-learning universities such as Open University. These have relied on a combination of media-based learning, occasional tutorials, and individualized support from tutors via mail, telephone, and now email. For the campus-based university the balance could be similar, but with the advantage of more opportunity for contact with the tutors and with other students.
>
> (Laurillard 2002: 94)

This is not going to be an easy environment for academics to work in. The boundaries will be less clear. There will be the challenge of developing new skills, of deciding which skills and technologies to develop in one's own personal work. Institutions will struggle with finding the best support strategies to use in this uncertain world. The challenges will be formidable, but they will be interesting and dynamic. Higher education in the next 20 years is not a place for the faint hearted. New technology with multimedia will become more central to teaching methods and experiences, but institutions will struggle to find a single dominant learning and teaching paradigm that exploits new technology.

Seminars and small groups

Seminars are defined here as small-group discussions where students take a key role in presenting and discussing material. Groups are interactive and more student led than lectures. They facilitate peer-to-peer learning, in circumstances where the academic's role is still to assist, but while being more passive.

The move towards mass higher education has disrupted this form of learning in many institutions. The definition of 'small' in itself has changed. Many universities now consider any groups with fewer than 25 students to be small and this often correlates with the booking and use of a room (about the size of a school classroom) of which there are more available in the university and on the timetable than large lecture theatres. In part, then, the definition of group size is to do with the way the physical structures of universities were built. The coming of mass higher education and the rapid growth of student numbers means that there is no problem with recruiting student numbers, the challenge is to find suitable rooms to put them in.

You cannot really have a long and profitable discussion with a group of this size. 'Group within group' work takes over. Seminars subdivide into sets of about five students per set and these work on an exercise and/or discussion before feeding back to a plenary.

What makes for a good seminar? Student preparation is often the key to a successful seminar where learning is maximized. Academic staff have to encourage reading and make sure students are fully informed of what reading is necessary before a seminar meets. Some students might be nominated to take the lead in their subsets and are strongly encouraged to do the required preparation.

A virtual learning environment can be used to post links to online reading and to remind students what is happening from week to week. Regular emails and text messages could be used to keep reinforcing these learning disciplines. There is some evidence this makes for better face-to-face learning as a result.

In order to encourage the discipline of preparation, many universities and departments have increased the use of the assessment of seminars. In this situation students are expected to present to all or part of the group, more formally, at least once during the semester course or module. Their presentation is marked against agreed criteria, and these are applied to the presentation by academic staff, listening student peers, or both.

The assessment of such presentations also has the advantage of increasing important transferable skills for students, given that many will have to undertake presentations in the workplace on leaving university.

Online seminars rather than face-to-face groups?

There are two types of online seminar now widely discussed in the literature. These are asynchronous and synchronous. Online seminars frequently are referred to as 'online discussion forums' and the traditional academic word 'seminar' is not always used in this modern context. In our view, there is no particular reason why 'online seminars' or 'online discussion' cannot be used interchangeably to describe identical learning activities.

Within the literature and contemporary historical analysis of online seminars it would appear that more attention has been given to the asynchronous variety. This is online discussion that does not all happen at the same point in time, but where people visit the text-based discussion at different times within a defined period. This is because the asynchronous form of seminar is analogous with the very invention of online learning. These text discussions were the earliest and most common form of online, web-based teaching. Many readers will be familiar with the typical structure and presentation of an asynchronous seminar discussion online, but the basics are covered next.

An asynchronous seminar needs an online resource. This should be easy to use with the absolute minimum of technical complications, otherwise some students will be disadvantaged by the limitations of their private computer equipment and therefore unable to take part (most universities offer students entry to some open-access communal computer pools that would presumably guarantee access when personally owned technology fails). Typically, the online discussion structure and program will be written entirely in xml code so that it can work through any modern web browser, such as Microsoft Explorer or Netscape Navigator. Thus students can navigate and take part by clicking on the web site and using basic web surfing skills and no additional programs and technology or extra skills are needed. Normally it would not be necessary to use email to take part in such a discussion because discussion windows and postings are embedded in the host web site.

Table 5.1 argues that online asynchronous seminars actually have some advantages over face-to-face meetings. They allow a flexible time of entry and departure and usually give students more time to prepare and to plan their own intervention. It is less likely that a student can hide in the discussion and rely on student peers to solve problems and answer questions. In many aspects, asynchronous discussion promotes independent learning.

Salmon (2002; 2004) has documented the need to build an online discussion community before students have the confidence to take part in deep learning. Therefore, some initial socialization and introductions must take place. She suggests a number of key stages in the productive process of an online seminar series. The sensitive moderation of asynchronous seminars becomes critical to their success. The role of the teacher becomes important to encourage and clarify the online discussion (Nunes and McPherson 2003).

Synchronous online seminars

Online seminars where everyone meets at the same prearranged time are not as common in higher education as the asynchronous form, but examples of these forms of communication are growing outside higher education. Younger students are certainly familiar with the technology because these are in effect 'chat rooms' that resemble the well-known, Microsoft

Table 5.1 Strengths and weaknesses of traditional seminars versus asynchronous online seminars

| Traditional face-to-face | | Asynchronous online | |
Strength	Weakness	Strength	Weakness
Resources			
Provides real human contact with possible strong social context	Needs suitable room timetabled.	Flexible entry.	Requires all students to have access to a suitable computer.
Added value			
Students have opportunity to improve social skills	Introverted students disadvantaged.	Students have opportunity to improve IT skills.	Students without IT skills or easy computer access are disadvantaged.
Non-response			
	Students fail to turn up or 'hide' (turn up and do not contribute).		Students fail to contribute.
Preparation			
Preparation instructions given out at beginning of course	Has to be done by a fixed time and explained at previous event or in previous document.	Preparation instructions available asynchronously.	Can be done at student convenience with online (easy access) resources.
Activity			
Gives one or more students leadership and vocal presentational experience	Likely to be dominated by a few students' reflections.	Leadership less important, given an adequate structure and focus in the activity.	All students have equal time and space to contribute, regardless of their leadership or social skills.
Group dynamics			
Allows students to develop face-to-face group skills of leadership and presentation	Possible to make very minimal contribution without consequences.	Students learn to encourage and support each other in a text-based medium.	Possible to make minimal contribution, but it is more obvious that the person has opted out.
Reflection			
Human contact can reinforce reflection	Limited time for personal reflection.	More flexible time for personal reflection.	Reflection has to be text-based.

MSN Messenger experience and in the academic environment are based on similar technologies built into VLEs, such as Blackboard and WebCT.

Currently, there are more likely to be technological problems and barriers with synchronous seminars than asynchronous examples (Kirkpatrick 2005). The main reasons for this are slowness on a large and busy network, and the fact that some small piece of software usually has to be downloaded onto the host computer before it can take part (for example, teenagers wishing to chat with peers normally have to install MSN Messenger on the family computer, otherwise they cannot join in). Part-time and postgraduate/professional courses can become particularly unstuck with this issue of installing software as many big employers such as the UK NHS will not allow staff to install programs for security reasons. Despite these technological barriers in education, which have prevented the format becoming very popular, the technology is advancing fast elsewhere. More mobile technology such as phones and personal digital assistants (PDAs), using G3 mobile wireless, are beginning to carry similar programs, making such streaming of text communication much more likely among the young. Computer-based versions on laptops and desktops are increasingly being linked to video and audio, so that chat rooms are no longer text based, but based on real-time pictures and conversation. Broadband has made this a real and inexpensive possibility. Many are put off by the personal security risks, although vendors such Microsoft have tried to take this seriously when adding video and audio to their Messenger product.

It is common to hear a critical response from academics when the idea of synchronous online seminars are suggested. There is an assumption that all the social and added-value benefits of face-to-face seminars will be automatically lost with synchronous online communication. There is a related assumption that synchronous online communication is of poor educational quality and does not promote any social skills. But some wider reflection is needed before ruling out the use of synchronous online technology as one part of an education and learning environment. One should remember that traditional seminars cannot be assumed to be positive learning experiences if a group of students turn up without preparation and no discussion follows. There are some students who are silent in the traditional classroom experience who produce surprising input when given a keyboard and access to a chat room experience.

Synchronous learning offers its own peculiar benefits that are not replicated in the face-to-face classroom environment. There is an 'alternative' element for some younger students, given the link in youth culture with ideas like Internet chat rooms and mobile phone 'texting'. This does cut both ways in that such students might also use the technology for low-level social peer-to-peer interaction rather than academic learning and reflection.

Synchronous communication develops its own curious and quite different type of narrative when compared with face-to-face discussion, and there is often a text-based 'stream of consciousness'. All ideas are summarized and quickly listed in a rather disorderly stream, often with abbreviations, notations and so on used for speed and practicality. The final output should not necessary be assumed to contain low-quality reflection. Within it can be some very interesting reflections and opinions, these captured precisely because the medium is instant and spontaneous. Similarly, there is a lack of the courtesy of interpersonal reflection (the process of listening to others one at a time in face-to-face seminars) with a strange and disorderly mix of reading others' materials and then typing in new ideas that is not linear and organized in the face-to-face group sense, but emerges as rather cyclic and non-linear. This does mean everyone tends to make some level of creative contribution over time and the outcome can often be surprising in terms of the level of coverage and depth that is reflected in the final captured text file.

There are a number of limitations that might prevent realization of the full learning possibilities. The group cannot be too big if all are to be encouraged to take part. Some level of intimacy is needed. The ratio of group size to intimacy impact looks larger and more tolerant when compared with face-to-face groups, precisely because all the complications of eye contact, seating position and so on are not evident in a chat room so people's barriers potentially come down more quickly.

Dissertations and projects

Many higher education courses finish with an assessment that includes a long period of autonomous self-directed study. Typically this might be a dissertation or a project of between 10,000 and 20,000 words. Such assessments provide real transferable skills for employers in terms of a student demonstrating confidence in working largely alone on a big project, but knowing how to make good use of what supervision and support is available. Skills of acquiring and sorting and ranking relevant information and then summarizing it and synthesizing it are also gained. Finally, the ability to present material, using skills of structuring and writing clearly, are also learnt and evidenced. Most modern professional and technical employment opportunities demand such skills.

What additional benefits can online technology provide to this kind of learning and assessment? Dissertation and project work depends on good initial guidance about what is required and how these skills can be developed by the learner. Online resources can support this by making material permanently available for easy access when the independent learner needs it. Direct links can be made to the growing range of information search engines and information repositories that are used in such learning.

Ongoing tutorial support that is based on short regular contact, where focused questions are asked and draft material is commented on, may be better provided by email and online contact rather than always by face-to-face interviews. The online dissertation tutorial model allows for plenty of time for reflection and thinking before communication is sent and promotes better planning of the use of supervision in independent autonomous learning. The online environment encourages the submission of text-based ideas and drafts to the online tutor.

Tutorial support

Individual tutorial support is another tradition of higher education. Individual and small-group tutorials are not traditionally attributed to child learning at school, where much emphasis is placed on highly structured and directed group work within the classroom. Students often arrive at university bemused when told they will have 'tutorials' and wondering what this means.

Tutorials involve regular meetings between an individual academic and a student (or very small group of students) to consider the student's learning needs and to closely monitor his or her progress in knowledge and skills attained. It is highly individualized and contextual to where the individual is at in any one time or space. Often these activities are fairly self-directed in terms of the teacher asking the student for an account of his or her current learning and how he or she is synthesizing learning into his or her overall knowledge and personal and professional development.

As higher education has moved towards higher student to staff ratios that resemble children's schools rather than universities, higher education has had to radically rethink its policy on tutorial support. Universities in the UK have been reluctant to relinquish the tutor role, seeing it as important, where one individual academic has an overview of each student's progress or lack of it. Indeed, this means the potential of the tutorial is more important than ever before in an age of mass higher education and the growth in numbers of students. But universities are left with formidable challenges about how to provide tutorials in a diminishing resource base.

Online technology can be used to supplement or replace face-to-face tutorials and to help ensure that some form of personal communication at this individual level does take place. Information technology can help institutionalize this one-to-one communication, enabling tutors to keep an up-to-date direct link to their tutor group, by regular emailing and text messaging. This is more time-efficient than writing letters. Links can be made to assessment databases, where the tutor can easily see the tutees profile of marks, rather than having to dig out a file from a dusty filing cabinet. Information technology efficiencies can, we argue, enhance the tutor role and help preserve its great traditions. Students can be encouraged to complete email and online questionnaires to review their learning and personal development, and then submit these to their personal tutor.

The turn to constructivist learning

The criticisms of traditional lectures and seminars promoted by writers such as Laurillard and Bligh have encouraged a growing interest in more active and interactive teaching methods in higher education in recent decades. These new forms post-date seminars and lectures as educational ideas and emphasize adult learning as a creative and experiential process, rather than higher education being based on the teaching of passive students by more knowledgeable academics. In these new processes the emphasis is on students being helped to construct knowledge in their own unique way, given the help of other students and teachers. The teacher becomes a facilitator of learning rather than an autocratic leader. While these relatively newer forms predate online learning, they can, as ideas, be integrated with technology to increase the learning benefits. Examples of such forms discussed below are action learning, problem-based learning and work-based learning. Henry (1994) says clear examples of the experiential approach are personal development, prior learning, placement and project work. In such experiential approaches, skills and knowledge are developed together wherever possible. Constructivism puts slightly less emphasis on real-world experience, but challenges students to make their own uses of information and data placed before them.

Action learning

Action learning can be defined simply as: 'a process in which a group of people come together more or less regularly to help each other to learn from their experience' (Dick 1997) A more detailed working example is available in the form of a case study from the UK NHS National Primary and Care Trust Development Team (at www.natpact.nhs.uk/). In this example the process was specified as below:

Action learning brings together small groups of participants with the following intentions:

- To work on and through organisational/individual issues. This is most effective when the commitment is voluntary.
- To work on real problems. Situations in which 'I am part of the problem and the problem is part of me.'
- To work together to check individual perceptions, clarify (and render more manageable) the issue and explore alternatives for action.
- To take action in the light of new insight. Begin to change the situation.
- Bring an account of the consequences back to the group for further shared reflection.
- To focus on learning, not only about the issue being tackled but also

on what is being learned about oneself. This is essential to turn developing understanding into learning that can be transferred to other situations.

- To be aware of group processes and develop effective ways of working together.
- To provide the balance of support and challenge that enables each person to manage themselves and others more effectively.

In these learning situations an 'action group', or action learning set, is usually led by a facilitator who works with the members to identify what skills they have and what further skills need to be developed. This informs the shared quest for knowledge. But the facilitator is a fairly passive leader who seeks to get the group to lead themselves and to take responsibility for the direction taken.

The nature of action learning, when compared to the traditional academic seminar, is that it moves small-group learning into a more active and dynamic mode. It is also inherently pragmatic in that it starts with identifying problems and challenges, usually within a professional or organizational context. There are difficulties with applying action-based learning to online learning. A key part of the attraction of action learning for professional and experienced workers is that is gives them social contact with like-minded people outside their normal working routine, but contact that is still productive and purposeful. Carrying out the same staged but dynamic process online might not be nearly as attractive to many such people as face-to-face meetings. Online action learning might be used where members of an action group are too geographically dispersed to meet physically. Online action learning is possible through small-group discussion boards and chat rooms, both synchronous and asynchronous forms. In the synchronous form the dynamics can be enhanced if media technologies such as voice and video Internet protocol are used. The difficulties here are that all members of the group need the same high standard of technology. This might be possible if one large geographically dispersed company or organization is organizing and supporting the online activity and it offers a common technological platform and software to all participants.

Problem-based learning

Action-based learning can be difficult to construct for full-time, younger students working in more theoretical areas, when, for example, undergraduates' learning is discipline led rather than problem based. Problem-based learning differs from action-based learning in that the students are present with a predefined problem to explore, rather than exploring what problems exist from their situations and experiences. In this sense problem-based learning has a wider remit in higher education than action-based learning. Teacher's aim to organize the curriculum so that it reflects problem-based scenarios and is not driven by subject and discipline-based knowledge categories (Savin-Baden 2000).

Online learning has much to offer the problem-based approach (Paz Dennen 2000). It can provide structured links to an information repository where a range of information and links are available to the student group to enable it to start exploring the 'problem'. This reduces preparation time and expense, in terms of collecting and copying large amounts of information. Problem learning would seem particularly well suited to a blended approach where groups meet initially in a face-to-face setting, to establish social rapport and then move more to online contact, such as ongoing asynchronous discussion where they explore the problem and share developing insights and the finding of new, related information.

Work-based learning

Work-based learning seeks to encourage the construction of knowledge and creative thinking in the workplace, rather than following the traditional convention of removing a person from the workplace in order to allow them to be reflective and creative.

> Work Based Learning is a modern way of creating university-level learning in the workplace. Its special work-linked features enable learning to take place at, through – and be centred on – the working environment. By using an actual work role and an organisations' objectives as the focus for academic enquiry Work Based Learning is uniquely structured to benefit both the individual employee and the employing organisations.
> (Middlesex University National Centre for Workbased Learning Partnerships, at www.mdx.ac.uk/www/ncwblp/)

This quote, from one of the national centres of excellence for work-based learning, describes clearly what the method is about. But students may struggle with switching into a critical reflective and learning role in the workplace. This might be somewhere they have become accustomed to behaving in a functional managerial or professional manner and much behaviour is subconscious and repetitive. Personal reflection and academic reflection can be much more difficult than first expected.

Glass et al. (2002) found that a key issue for employers in Scotland resulting from the development of work-based learning was the creation of more appropriate support and provision around the actual work-based learning. Although online learning was not explicitly explored by Glass et al., it should be noted that online technology provides a resource which can link knowledge-based content and related learning reflection. Similarly technologies such as online discussion boards, and their application to managed online seminars, allow easier dialogue and personal interaction with learners in the workplace and are key tools to encourage their use of reflection and the exploration of new knowledge and ideas.

We have shown that online learning can play a key part in assisting the turn to constructivist and experiential learning, but the road forward is complex. Bostock (1998), in a review of the use of the World Wide Web, email and video to promote constructivist approaches in a mass higher education course, found that personal interaction was assisted but that it was difficult to promote true collaboration between students. Bostock found that one of the most important strategies to aid success was to design a form of assessment which promoted the learning philosophy of the course.

Assessment methods

In recent years the modernization of higher education in the UK has brought with it a more holistic approach to assessment in terms of its relationship with the curriculum. Attempts have been made to integrate assessment into every aspect of coursework, so that it is not seen as an isolated end point which is dislocated from teaching activity (Boud 1995). This is a key method for encouraging positive experiences of learning (Gibbs 1999).

Many universities now encourage and practise Scriven's (1967) two types of assessment – formative and summative. Formative assessment is in fact an integrated learning activity where students practice what they have learnt independently from the teacher but the feedback obtained does not usually count towards a final grade. Students engaged in activity to inform, practise and improve their skills. In contrast, summative assessment is the more traditional regulated method, where a grade is allocated and formally recorded. Students have to decide about the application and usefulness of new material, they make some individual judgements and reach a conclusion about the value of the knowledge they have gained. Summative assessment can take many forms, including those that encourage strong longitudinal links with ongoing learning and teaching activities, such as portfolios and projects.

The Quality Assessment Agency for Higher Education in England and Wales has encouraged this assessment-modernization approach by requiring that learning outcomes are clearly specified for all courses and their learning and modules. Related to this is the practice that assessment criteria should be given to students in advance for all summative assessment, and that these should be linked by the teacher to relevant learning outcomes. It can be argued that the resulting framework should ensure that all learning outcomes are covered by some type of summative assessment and specific assessment criteria. This systematic approach is argued to be too bureaucratic by some. Critics such as Furedi (2005) argue that higher educational attainment has subtle and critically reflective outcomes that are not easily detectable in a linear and well-organized checklist of skills. Such critics of the new higher education agenda are concerned that much abstract and deep learning cannot be scrutinized in the 'modern' way and learning is in danger of being lost if the new bureaucracy and systematic organization is taken too far.

Online learning adds new dimensions to this modern evolution of assessment. It allows relatively easier access to formative assessment methods when managing large groups, which can help minimize teacher management time. For example, an online multiple choice question (MCQ) test can provide instant and readily analysed feedback for both the student and teacher. Online learning also provides new opportunities for summative assessment by controlled and distant submission, but these methods are not without their own regulatory challenges. It has already been argued in Chapter 3 that much of the current moral panic in mass higher education about regulatory standards and the detection and punishment of dishonesty in assessment is as relevant to conventional face-to-face and paper-based assessments as it is to online methods. No medium it seems is completely secure and fraud proof.

If the modernization of mass higher education is accepted as inevitable to some extent, online learning can become a tool for helping to better integrate assessment into the learning and teaching process. As Garrison and Anderson (2003: 93) conclude: 'the challenge can be mitigated through the effective use of the interactive and collaborative characteristics of e learning'.

The historical method by which the majority of students were assessed in higher education was through unseen examinations. Students would be asked to attend at a specific time and place. They would be carefully segregated and access to books and equipment would usually be restricted. Students would be required to handwrite their answers to a number of questions that were intended to test their knowledge and critical skills across a broader range of the curriculum as possible.

Examinations

In the past ten years much has been said about the disadvantages of unseen examinations. They do not promote group and shared working. Some people cannot cope with the sudden stress and pressure they advance. Almost all academics who have any empathy for other human beings and who have worked in the sector for a few years or more will tell you at least one story of a brilliant and conscientious student they came across who just could not do themselves justice in unseen examinations. The mass expansion of higher education has seen increased access to the sector for those with special needs such as dyslexia and mental health problems – both are conditions that seem in part to be aggravated by stressful educational circumstances like unseen examinations. There is a suspicion that unseen examinations often become a form of memory test and that they do not test students' creative and critical skills particularly well (because students are under an intensive time pressure they do not deliver to the best of their ability on these demanding aspects). Many academics complain that the overall quality of students' work in these circumstances is not good; even basics like handwriting and spelling can suffer. Students find it close to impossible to satisfactorily reference and source influential material. All this might lead us to conclude that the skills gained in unseen exams are not directly related to real-world skills and situations.

On the other side of the argument we might want to concede there are a few advantages. Examinations promote an ability to cope with pressure. There is a clear sense of uniformity and equity about the process; it is difficult to cheat, though not impossible. Certainly there is a high risk of being caught. Teachers can set specimen questions and students can practise these (the examples can be placed online quite effectively), so students can be taught and learn to become better at passing examination questions, and these examples can in some way be linked to knowledge that is useful for the real-world and skills context.

It is hard to imagine online technology having much impact on unseen examinations. As mentioned already, they can be a place for adding the use of past papers and revision methods, like taking specimen papers and seeing specimen answers. It is not impossible that an unseen examination could be taken online. It is hard to imagine how it might replace the predictable standardization and equity of all students being in one room together at the same time.

Seen papers

One assessment method that tries to deal with the weaknesses of unseen papers and has been used by academics in recent decades is the setting of 'seen' papers. In this situation the paper is made public to students a period of time before they enter the controlled environment of the examination hall.

This may reduce stress and anxiety. The student has a period of time, usually a matter of days, to prepare. There may be immediate consequences on learning resources and complaints that all students are chasing a limited book stock. Online resources offer some alternatives and equity to this problem. Revision and preparation is no longer dependent on the conventional library book stock.

An associated issue is whether such an assessment strategy should allow students to bring notes and or other material to the examination. The general lesson seems to be that the more material the assessors allow students to bring to the final examination the greater the problems for them in terms of policing equity and fairness. Even when this is restricted to an aide-memoire, for example one piece of A4 paper, there is the equity issue of students having different size writing and they waste time trying to perfect their ability to write small.

Takeaway examination papers

These are in effect essays, or similar, that have to be completed in a very short space of time (for example, a few days later) and returned. There is some concern that the pressures of takeaway papers results in students being more likely to plagiarize material, in particular from web sites. The advantages are that students do have time to work on a piece while still experiencing the stress created by the time pressure, and this should provide important learning about coping with stress and pressure for future employment.

Clearly takeaway papers can be posted via an online resource, and even submitted to an online resource, and this can minimize expensive and time-consuming university administration. These papers can easily be collected via an online facility, providing there is equity of timing and access. Papers can be submitted online via technologies such as the 'digital drop box' provided by the virtual learning environment, Blackboard.

Although online collection of assessment in this way might have administrative advantages on the day of submission, a more negative trade-off may result if academic staff have to print all the papers before marking, or if they are expected to mark 'on screen' (there are health and safety issues related to long and intense periods reading at the screen).

Essays and short pieces of written work

Essays and similar written pieces such as fieldwork and projects have grown in popularity in recent years. A clear advantage is that they give a student a long and considered period of time to plan carefully, to research and to draft and refine a focused piece of work. Writing and referencing skills can be perfected, as can the ability to be concise and to summarize material. It is argued that the skills used in essay writing are coterminous with the analytical report-writing skills needed in professional and technical employment.

The disadvantage of the growth of this kind of assessment is that it can lead to a student over-specializing on certain aspects of the curriculum. A worst case scenario is that a student chooses essay topics in his or her course that include some overlapping content and knowledge, and the student manages to avoid being assessed on certain aspects of the curriculum. The introduction of learning and assignment criteria closely linked to learning outcomes has sought to curtail this kind of student activity. If followed rigorously and based on an assessment structure that ensures coverage of criteria and outcomes, this will ensure that a student is assessed on all major aspects of the curriculum. Essays and similar written assessment then becomes more generic and less specialized.

There is a separate concern that it is relatively easy to cheat in an essay or piece of writing assessment by getting someone else to do the work for you, or by plagiarizing material from a web site or similar. In such situations there is a relatively low risk of getting caught, although this does seem to be increasing as universities increase their activity of plagiarism detection systems (see Chapter 3).

Multiple choice questions

Multiple choice questions (MCQs) were one of the first forms of assessment to be subjected to new technology. In the 1980s, technology emerged that allowed answer sheets to be submitted into a computer so that results could be automatically obtained without any work from an academic or similar. All the teacher had to do was write unambiguous and appropriate questions, a task that is itself not always easy and less time-consuming! Multiple choice questions are now a key feature of online learning environments such as Blackboard and WebCT. These allow a rich use of formative testing during a period of teaching and learning. If used for summative assessment, there could be concerns that students have obtained assistance in supplying the answers and the results are not necessarily their own scores. The real strength of MCQs in online learning seems to be their formative application. Academics can design and save a bank of questions. Questions can be of many different types. Answers and cohort statistics can be easily viewed and analysed, and students get regular feedback on their performance, as do teachers.

Portfolios

Portfolios encourage students to collect evidence throughout their teaching course that they have achieved certain skills and can demonstrate they have acquired the knowledge required. Portfolio assessment normally works best in applied environments, such as technical and professional degrees and certificates. If academic and other teaching staff (perhaps professional tutors at a placement) are involved in signing off skills chronologically, it will be possible to significantly reduce the risk of fraud or the student obtaining too much help from others. It can almost be guaranteed in such circumstances that most of the work is the original work of the student submitting the portfolio.

The main criticism of portfolios is that they are too skill focused and can be rather fragmented in terms of their ability to test creative and critical abilities to combine elements of knowledge and practice in a flexible and adaptive manner. Aspects of portfolio work can be set to mitigate for these factors, for example, writing a synthesis or overview of all or part of the portfolio and what has been learnt in the process.

Online resources can be used to good effect to assist students in organizing their portfolios, providing templates and creative resources that will assist them (see Woodward and Nanlohy 2004; Currant et al. 2006). Blogs and wikis can be used to contribute to this kind of online process (see Chapter 2).

The patchwork text

This is one of the new and modern forms of assessment that seeks to build on the lessons learnt over recent decades. It looks well suited to blend the human, online and distance learning environments, and seeks to maximize the integration of teaching, learning and assessment. In short, assessment takes place regularly, often as part of the learning and teaching activity. It involves a range of short pieces of writing, and it is argued that it can be more conducive to widening participation and encouraging maximum involvement in ongoing learning and teaching. While it has the potential to increase the organization and marking time for the academic involved, an online learning system can assist with this by collecting student information and possibly even assisting with the marking of some elements. Students might do some of the assessment together in groups, an activity that, again, can be well structured and supported online. Some elements might be peer assessed rather than teacher assessed. Similarly an online system can help organize and collate any peer-assessed element. At the end of the course, unit or module, a student usually completes an integrative piece of writing that finally stitches the patch together and enables the student to see the breadth of his or her learning (Winter 2003: Young 2004).

Goodfellow and Lea (2005) have emphasized the importance of integrating ongoing online discussion that is text based with any final writing assessments submitted by the same students. The students' development of writing needs to be encouraged through the online experience and with a view to the requirements of their final assessment. Examples might be selecting a quotation from a piece of reading and providing an analysis, choosing between different arguments and making a summary case for one perspective, writing a short definitions of key concept, or writing a short book or chapter review. In all these examples of possible online discussions the emphasis needs to be on peer-to-peer or teacher-to-student feedback and dialogue in the online environment that gives feedback to assist in developing an appropriate academic writing style.

There is concern that assessments such as patchwork texts maximize the workload of academic staff because they have to ensure that students are constantly organized and producing quality work, but this can and should be built into regular teaching sessions that enable students to take responsibility for the management of their own work and goals. Again, technology can be used to send out automatic reminders, to clearly link online content material, such as a text or web site, to a very specific writing task.

This ends the section where we have reviewed the constructivist turn in higher education and how it has worked its way into assessment strategies. Specific learning and teaching methods have sprung up to encourage the integration of assessment and teaching, and to encourage and facilitate more student-directed learning. Online resources can play a key part in continuing this change and making it a richer learning environment for all students.

Conclusions

In this chapter we have reviewed the traditional teaching and assessment methods in higher education and the ways in which the academic environment has become more critical of the centuries-old menu of lecture, seminar, tutorial followed by an unseen examination. In recent decades there has been an explosion of creative thinking and fundamentalist criticism of this old diet. Much of great importance has been said and written in this purge, and yet in many ways it is surprising that so much traditionalism has remained.

Certainly the traditions have been challenged and have had to evolve. Many of the reasons for their evolution are pragmatic, also moderately influenced by a fundamental critique of learning and teaching. The change in learning and teaching has been primarily driven by the managerialist modernization of higher education with the imperative from politicians and business that it must find a way of managing and structuring the growth of higher education into a mass active for the majority, rather than it remaining the traditional preserve of an elite minority. Alongside this transformation in size and politico-economic mission, technology has played a key influence. Technology has helped some of the fundamentalist critics to offer radical alternatives that were unthinkable a few decades ago, for example the new idea of asynchronous and adaptive online media presentations that replace the monologue in the lecture hall.

In conclusion, higher education learning and teaching is a boat at sea tossing and turning in an ocean of competing logics and influences. The value base of these logics and influences at times brings creative convergence, but it is also prone to irrationality and this can cause conflict and fragmentation of ideas and practice.

For this reason the continuing rapid pace of change and evolution is unlikely to lead to a singular and idealistic outcome where technology somehow inspires a very large transformation of the quality of learning that empowers students and makes them more mature and self-directed in their use of knowledge. Certainly this is a visionary ideal, but the outcome is less likely to be so tidy. In our view technology will continue to offer some real opportunities to increase the quality of learning and teaching, and to help old methods evolve to the formidable political and economic context challenges that they face. Online learning can successfully be used to promote the constructivist and experiential turn, but it is not unreasonable to note that many academics will respond with a large degree of pragmatism, taking what works in a difficult institutional environment rather than being driven by a fundamental and self-critical idealism. Many of the new entrants to higher education are likely to be lacking in self-confidence when it comes to the demands of the ideals of constructivism and will need a lot of support and encouragement to benefit from these kinds of activities. Induction and preparation for learning are as important as they have ever been. There is likely to be a lot of diversity in what happens and, in the medium term, technology looks set to feed this diversity rather than to deliver a new and higher order of quality, equity and standardization.

6

Applying Online Learning to Teaching Practice in Higher Education

Introduction

In this chapter we give further consideration to the complexities of designing a learning process within an online environment. A case study of a module development team's project, from one of the authors' current work experiences, is used to give a more detailed analysis and synthesis of how learning methods can be applied to online learning. These are illustrated in this chapter as 'learning in action' by the academics involved in the case study project. Different learning methods and philosophies are delved into and evaluated in a two-dimensional manner. On one dimension is the axis of how academics learnt to use ICT, and on the other are the methods and methodologies that can be utilized to optimize learning in an online learning environment. The chapter also provides an example of collaborative, curriculum design using the new technologies and offers guidance on how academics can work through their concerns utilizing theoretical models of practice development.

We explore in this chapter, through the case study, how a team of academics renewed their philosophy of learning through consolidating some of the historical aspects of seminal learning theory and making it explicit within ICT. The experience has prompted a belief that learning theories from a different period of educational development are now coming into their own in their application to online learning. The chapter does not consider in depth the technological aspects of constructing an online learning environment, as this is covered elsewhere in the text (Chapters 2 and 4). Instead, the chapter concentrates on describing how a small group of academics formed a module development team and brought together aspects of online learning in a development that was originally prompted by the trend to consider the global implications of health-care practice. It was deemed by the team that this topic could appeal to students both within and without the university 'walls' and, in conjunction with an increase in international students, the team believed the concept of an online learning mode of delivery had potential. This is turn prompted a voyage of discovery into online learning. Many of the team had little or no knowledge of online learning methods and a sensitive approach to acknowledging each others lack of knowledge was needed and is reflected upon in this chapter in the section on learning for lecturers and collaborating on the curriculum.

The team were working as part of a large, multidisciplinary Faculty of Health graduate programme, which meant that there was also a desire to draw from different disciplinary perspectives on such a module. There were implications for the team that they would need to find a way to work effectively together, while respecting each other's disciplines as well as acknowledging their different levels of competence and understanding of ICT. There was no formal intention to follow a prescribed model of curriculum development, as none could be found that suited the multidisciplinary purpose. However, a framework for collaboration and values clarification was sought to provide a schema in which different disciplines could comfortably articulate their differences, priorities and concerns. It is described in the chapter as the process of creating a community of practice.

This chapter then gives examples of different frameworks for online learning and describes how the team came to choose the relevant frameworks for their module. The team designed different learning activities and these are outlined in this chapter. The difficulties experienced by the team in grappling with the challenges of enabling students to demonstrate a conceptual understanding of the cultural and theoretical perspectives expected at master's level, within an online learning environment, are also included.

Teaching and learning philosophies and methods were examined by the team, their appropriateness for transfiguration to the online learning environment evaluated and new methods considered, which then became part of the 'learning in action' of the project team. The final element was to propose an evaluation strategy for online learning and teaching as a flexible method of learning.

The main focus in this chapter is therefore on the process of learning which is generally understood to involve gaining new knowledge and skills. A characteristic change in the approach towards learning in higher education was significantly indicated in the Dearing report (1997) where the terms 'teaching and learning' were transformed to 'learning and teaching' – shifting the emphasis from teaching onto learning. Academics are now seen as facilitators of learning rather than directors, and these teaching roles have generated a move towards the use of learning outcomes as opposed to teaching objectives (as discussed in Chapter 4 when we were considering the philosophy of design). In Chapter 1 we spoke about the drivers that are influencing changes in higher education, such as globalization and economic, political and social changes. For academics there is an additional ethical driver, and that is the development of educational theory, which is explored in the final sections of the chapter. These developments are responding to a growing and pronounced interest in education

Table 6.1   Case study stages

Stage	
1	Reviewing groups abilities, enthusiasm and motivation to adopt new technologies in teaching and learning.
2	Creating a community of practice.
3	Use of the online learning environment.
4	Evaluation on different dimensions.

processes as well as the content of courses linked to the development of the new learning technologies. Changes in the nature of educational theory will be considered in this chapter through analysis of the case study, which takes the form of four stages (see Table 6.1) alongside practical methods to achieve optimum conditions for learning.

Learning for lecturers

One of the first discussions by the team was their anxieties about the use of ICT and their variable experiences in using these learning methods. While most had mastered ICT to produce learning materials and to communicate, they were not familiar with the variety of approaches that could be used in online learning. Some were also hesitant in adopting an entirely unfamiliar mode of teaching yet had begun to show interest and enthusiasm, and were therefore on the brink of using the new technologies and thus motivated to discover more. They were on the cusp of a pedagogical change first identified by Mason (1998) as the urge to digitize, virtualize and globalize the campus (see also Chapter 2). It is agreed that the importance of interactivity in the learning, the changing role of the teacher, the need for knowledge management skills, team-working abilities and the move towards resource-based learning are all elements that are focal to developing online learning methods (Mason 1998; Hurst and Quinsee 2004). However, the challenge is to assist academics accustomed to traditional teaching and learning modes to think differently about how they teach their subjects in the online learning mode, rather than be reluctantly drawn into facing a wired world that feels alien, distant and beyond their control.

We hear much about the move to online learning that is threatening the traditional mode of classroom education and evolving its own pedagogy (Bourne et al. 1997). Wild (1996) discovered that many novice and experienced teachers did not always fully understand why ICT was being promoted and used. In our experience of introducing ICT to PGCE students this remains the case for many novice teaching students; however, there are an increasing number who are beginning to see the utility of ICT. Moreover, knowledge of the implications of this emerging form of teaching and learning, such as the paradigm shift from teacher-centred to learner-centred approaches or the impact of independent learning and widening

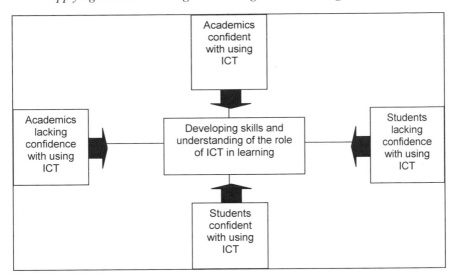

Figure 6.1   Factors levelling the ground between academics and students

participation requires consideration equally with the development of technical skills (Harasim 1990). The duality that this implies, where academics have to embrace the technological skills to use ICT effectively and the opportunities that this form of learning can offer, has been aptly described by Pritchard (2004) in discussing a model for introducing new students to ICT. This implies new learning for both academics and their students (Figure 6.1). This project wanted to stress the wider learning benefits of ICT rather than the future functionality, skills-based approach. This sentiment is very similar to our own views and underpins much of our rationale for writing this book.

There is no denying that understanding and utilizing learning technologies requires specific skills training to use the technology, design materials and computer-based interactions. Haynes et al. (2004) found, in a survey based on an assessment of competency of specific IT skills, that while 86 per cent of staff had access to a computer, 55 per cent of staff were below the benchmark standards. Within these figures, there was a large variation of ICT skills among academic staff, which was comparable to other institutions. Thus, a strategy to build upon enhancing existing skills in the production of learning materials and to build confidence in using ICT was considered more beneficial than strategically introducing industry ICT competencies and compellingly changing embedded academic practices.

We have moved into a new world where wires, screens, gigabytes and megabytes are becoming commonplace. For the technically phobic it remains a frightening time, whereas for the electronically adventurous it is an overdue opportunity. For the team, who were occupying the middle ground, that is, wanting to embrace the new but uncertain of which switch to click, it was a time of searching for the right place to get into the circuit.

For them it was finding out how best to assess what online learning meant and how to go about using what is available to achieve the best outcomes.

The work of Geoffrey Moore on the 'technology adoption life cycle' is interesting here, in terms of the different perspectives of innovators, early adopters, early and late majorities, and the different methods needed to appeal to them and enable them to integrate a new technology into their work and lifestyle. Moore (1999) argues that there is a real chasm to cross between early adopters and the 'early majority' of users (see Figure 2.1 in Chapter 2), and this is relevant in higher education, where innovation in e-learning has been taking place among technology enthusiasts for some years now, and is beginning to spread into the majority of educators (see also Jobbins 2005).

Collaborating on the curriculum

The team were ready to become involved in on online learning and engage in a collaborative, curriculum project. Rekkedal's (1994) model for mapping the emergence of distance and online learning can be used as a guide to establish at what common stage academics are in the process of collaborating:

1   Pre-subject area – no evidence of interest in the area or perceived need or interest.
2   Beginnings – individuals begin to enquire or research or ask questions or issues arise which are triggered by some event or catalyst.
3   Emergence – more interested parties beginning to work in the area and a community begins to develop.
4   Diversification – the area starts to mature, different schools of thought emerge and the area begins to align or take place alongside more established areas.
5   Establishment – the area becomes recognized in its own right, with a defined community, experts, associated journals and conferences, perceived of as 'respected' research with associated professional status, course and career routes.

Stage 1 establishes a level of interest and motivation in the subject. In this case study the experience of collaborating was to gather academics together to work in partnership on a postgraduate module on International Health Dimensions that drew from an eclectic range of epistemologies, political and scientific domains. The unifying factor for the academics was an interest in applying their subjects to the topic of the globalization of health. They had not worked together before and were from different departments. Yet, there was no question that one topic would be more fundamental than another which engendered horizontal collegiality. Colleagues were, however, nervous about using ICT and were self-declared novices in online learning approaches to teaching and learning. Consequently, the catalyst for stage 2 was to identify their own learning needs. They were going to be moving from expert to novice, which was a complete antithesis to their personal career trajectories and current levels of expertise as all were experts in their subject domains. By stage 3, interested parties had begun to explore how their subjects could be represented in ICT, whereas some had fallen into the quagmire of other priorities and needed support and encouragement. It was here that Rekkedal's (1994) model captured both the dynamism of working in an emerging field and helped to normalize the process as one of moving towards new ways of working. However, in order to sustain the team through the development process we had to acknowledge that we were lecturers who were learners.

Creating a community of practice

This means achieving a critical balance between being an expert in a topic at one moment and a novice in another, at a different moment. Wenger's (1998) work on communities of practice (CoP) is relevant here. It forms part of the broader school of socializing theories, which are defined by a number of shared characteristics. In essence, there are four main components of Wenger's model:

- Meaning – in terms of sharing experience;
- Identity – in terms of becoming a person and recognizing individuality;
- Practice – in terms of doing;
- Community – in terms of belonging to a group of like-minded people.

The focus is on the acquisition of membership, defined around CoP with the facility to share understanding and values. To those readers familiar with group process and team-building these will be recognizable features of successful group dynamics. However, few curriculum teams consider how they will work together, or recognize areas where confidence is lacking or explicitly delve into their comprehension of a common purpose that will contribute to successful task completion. A central tenet of CoP is the concept of learning as a social process, through inclusion and participation. The premises which underpin this tenet are that we are social beings and that this is an important aspect of learning. Developing our ability to experience the world and our engagement with it is believed to be the ultimate aim of learning. The novelty for the curriculum team engaged in this process was that they were joining a community that would move towards adopting a shared understanding on a new topic. They possessed a shared commitment to this aspect of the project but the concepts of distance learning using online learning were new and distinctive.

Deciding a framework for the teaching and learning experience

Framework for teaching – the online learning facilitator

The team felt that crucial to students during their online experience is the online presence of an e-moderator. This is a teaching role adapted for online learning and it unites all the skills of teaching and implicates the teacher in a new role that matches the paradigm shifts we have been discussing hitherto. Laurillard (2002) has suggested a conversational framework can be used to engage students online, based on Vygotsky's ideas of the zone of proximal development. This theory maintains that children learn most effectively when they are guided rather than directed. It is a form of facilitated learning adapted to the adult learning domain where talking, in this case through online discussions, and questions from the student to the academic and vice versa promote new ideas to be built or constructed from existing knowledge. It is the basis for current constructivist theories of adult learning as discussed in Chapter 2. Laurillard's model attempts to simulate face-to-face interactions by suggesting the following activities:

- 'Narrative – teacher's conceptions are made accessible to students and vice versa;
- Interactive – the teacher provides feedback to students based upon the outcomes of tasks students undertake;
- Adaptive – the teacher uses this information to revise what learning has taken place and if necessary change the focus of the dialogue;
- Communicative – the teacher supports processes where students discuss and reflect upon their learning;
- Productive – the student and teacher agree learning goals and task goals which can be achieved using media forms suitable for the online learning environment such as PowerPoint presentations.

(Laurillard 2002: 90)

Less time is spent on the transmission of information in online learning and more time is spent on supporting students to achieve the transferable skills discussed earlier, maintain engagement with the module/course, provide feedback on activities, prompt the submission of formative work and respond to queries. Students need to know that someone is there in the same way that they are reassured if they know academics are available at certain times on campus for tutorials. It is easy to think that, because the teaching is taking place online, different conditions exist, but they do not and have to be accentuated so that students do not feel isolated or abandoned. It is as important to communicate to the students with lively banter and chat – such as about upcoming breaks or long weekends – so that students know when to expect either communication from academics or silence with a reason. This also helps students to structure their own time management. Posting messages that are welcoming and informative, and that help to maintain interest and motivation, are a key role for the online teacher. Encouraging students to post similar messages also creates the social dimension of learning necessary to exchange meaningful ideas in discussions. These lines of social communication do need to be separated from the more serious intellectual discussions that are topic centred, but they create a positive self-esteem among group members and promote higher learning activities.

Some of the tasks of the role will be to:

- Continue to find current resources through portals, gateways and search engines;
- Use the VLE or MLE to gain most advantage for the students' online experiences;
- Devise, implement and manage online learning tasks by setting up timed releases of information or activities;
- Manage asynchronous or synchronous discussions;
- Manage assessment tasks, formative and summative;
- Respond to technical questions and forward questions to technical advisers;
- Moderate online discussions according to the agreed protocol – in some instances academics are expected to contribute in order to shape discussions, whereas in others situations students interact and critique each others' contributions; a third approach is to blend the previous two models;
- Monitor students engagement to identify those students who are reluctant, shy, lacking confidence or too overpowering – in the same way that group dynamics are facilitated in a classroom discussion. Individual contact with students who are struggling online or being overbearing may be necessary, either by email or in person depending on the proximity of the students and the nature of situation;
- Maintain the quality and availability of online resources.

All these activities are discussed and described in detail by Salmon (2002; 2004) in her texts on e-moderating and e-tivities. Salmon also provides examples of coping strategies for academics to reduce time spent on e-moderating, such as standard feedback replies to frequently asked questions. Once the approach and role of the e-moderator have been established among those participating in the online module development, then the framework or structure of the learning can be decided.

Framework for delivering online learning

While there was a collective interest in designing the content of the module, in the case study, the module team requested input on the relative merits of online learning modes. There are many specific techniques and research is beginning to emerge on the most effective methods (see, for example, McDonald 2002). Mason (1998), however, provides a useful framework for three different online models which were reviewed by the team for their relative merits.

Content + support model

This is where course content is delivered in print format or as an online package and is combined with tutorial support delivered by email or online conferencing. Course or module content materials are utilized that can be tutored by other academics, including the content authors. Materials can include items such as seminar notes, handouts, directed reading and PowerPoint presentations. This is a model for managing teaching to different groups by educators who have not been directly involved in designing the course content. It can involve elementary collaborative activity between students, perhaps in the form of basic asynchronous conferencing. This creates opportunities for peer comment. In this model, these online elements are added to the course and students might complain of fragmentation because of the range of learning methods and activities on offer. Mason suggests that no more than about 20 per cent of the students' study time should be spent online in this model. This model could be suitable for delivering course materials on different sites in complex course provisions, using intranets and/ or pre-designed packages or learning environments.

Wrap-around model

This is where tailor-made materials (such as study guides, activities and discussions) are 'wrapped around existing materials' (textbooks, pre-designed resources, for example quizzes, CD-ROM resources or tutorials). It is suggested that the aim with this model should be to provide 50 per cent of delivery in each mode, half in the classroom and with face-to-face tutors, and the other half through online materials and interaction. This model can encourage students to explore learning resources more on their own, but with the support of their peers and with less rigid direction from their teacher. This model is suitable for changing fields of practice and can incorporate practice and theory learning. It can also be used for problem-based learning through the use of case studies, simulations and audio or video recordings.

Integrated model

This model promotes online learning more explicitly than do the first two models. Modules or courses consist of students undertaking collaborative learning activities drawing upon different learning resources. The majority of the learning takes place online through asynchronous discussion, evaluating information and learning materials, and doing virtual learning activities. The students have quite a high degree of control over what happens and can determine the path that learning takes. This model integrates content and support, and promotes the creation of a virtual learning community. This model is suitable for autonomous learning that is founded on the theoretical principles of adult learning and andragogy (Hurst and Quinsee 2004).

Deciding which model

The wrap-around model was initially favoured in the case study because the benefits of student interaction were considered valuable for sharing different viewpoints and cross-cultural perspectives. There are some existing resources, such as that offered by the UK Office of Health Economics (www.oheschools.org/), which is a study program with five units and self-tests. However, there are few such programs and even fewer of the required standard. Because the core group would be inviting specialists to donate materials, the content + support model was considered. The advantage would be to gain a wide selection of materials. The disadvantage would be the necessity to ensure the materials were meaningful to the students' own priorities and purposes. The integrated model appealed the most, as students would be adult learners and motivated by their own goals for learning. Tasks would be included in the module, such as analysing texts and responding to questions through online discussion. Students would be given core topic areas such as:

- Articles on the Philosophy of Culture in the Paideia Archive www.bu.edu/wcp/MainCult.htm; or
- Reith Lecturers (1999) by Anthony Giddens on A Runaway World www.lse.ac.uk/Giddens/reith_99/

and then encouraged to utilize the Internet or their own resources to research a topic area related to their own spheres of professional interest. The activity that would be lacking is collaborative learning, as this might not be feasible given the potential distance of students. The team decided this could be reviewed if the numbers of students following the module could ensure learning partnerships to be established. However, students will follow a model, successfully adopted in an existing module, for action learning. The team concluded that the integrated model would require continuous activity, and the module was planned to be available over a 13-week semester but with time for students to consolidate learning between reading and discussion periods. The chosen model was therefore a blend of content support and integrated model.

Technical resources

Critical to the success of any course or modules are the availability of resources to both students and academics. Previous experience had indicated that students had access to computers at work or at home, or from university library facilities, however no exact data was available to support this assumption. However, our previous experience had indicated that 75 per cent of students who enquired about online learning modules were computer and IT literate, based upon their own self-assessment. It was also made explicit in module information that a good level of these skills was required before commencing on the module.

The exact technological requirements for the module were also indicated in the advance module information to indicate that students would have to have equipment that would be able to download documents, develop PowerPoint presentations, view video and audio clips, send and receive emails and have access to the Internet on a line that they could afford. Many have telephone lines to support their Internet browsers, whereas we encourage students to use broadband, but this not always financially feasible and for those students in third world countries is not an option at all. International students would be encouraged to make contact with the British Council to seek out places where they could access computers or local libraries and educational funding bodies. Students in the UK are encouraged to use their own university facilities where possible. Students were given instructions and advice on how to use their time online effectively, that is: to choose the cheapest time tariff to schedule their work online, how to work off-line, to save documents onto the desktop where possible and to download onto floppy disks so that they could take their work with them to alternative computing resources where possible.

In the case study we also considered potential hardware and software compatibility and availability for academics. Not all academics had machines with the same processing power and memory capacity to handle course development. There was also a variation in levels of ICT skills and confidence among the group. In-house training was available for all academic staff and uptake of this was encouraged. Some staff preferred to take online instruction in their own time and at their own pace. Technical advice was available from our central university technological support administrators, however, as we had decided not to design materials using HTML and to keep the level of technological sophistication to a minimum, this did not emerge as a significant issue.

Transforming teaching materials

One area of support that was needed more than others was to assist colleagues in transforming their existing teaching materials into easily accessible and viewable chunks of information. The first step was to change word documents so that the fonts were easy on the eye by changing the font from Times Roman to Verdana. Then changing the font colour to Teal which is softer to read and, finally, to change the background colour of all text documents from white to cream, which is less bright and glaring.

The next step was to advise colleagues on how materials could be displayed and structured and the functionality of the web-based platform explored to provide maximum support for learning. The majority of colleagues were taking previously delivered lecture notes and transposing these into the online environment. This cannot be straightforward transference as while the aim is to re-create a learning environment that captures the communication and interaction of a classroom-based activity but without the conventional 'walls', this cannot be completely reproduced and other, creative methods have to be used. Ragan and White (2001) discuss the difficulties of re-creating communication that happens during a teaching session, such as when teachers are tacit and say things like, 'take a look at this diagram again' or 'try to remember this part as it will have implications for later'. They believe the essential feature of communicating learning in the online environment is to emphasize the desirability of reflective, perceptive and clear communication for the written word. To achieve this they introduce the concept of the golden triangle, which addresses three primary design components (Figure 6.2).

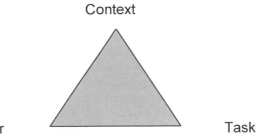

Source: adapted from Ragan and White 2001

Figure 6.2 The golden triangle of online communication

The three corners of the triangle are reminders to academics to situate the learning within the context, consider the needs of the learner and design related tasks. In this case study, the context is the rationale and purpose of the module as well as the design of the learning spaces created in the Blackboard platform. The capabilities and constraints of the context, such as the confines of Blackboard and its structure, have to be borne in mind. Learner characteristics also need consideration, for example the potential drawback that students in financially disadvantaged circumstances may not have to access the Internet for prolonged periods of time. Suitable tasks and activities for structuring ideas are the final component of the triangle and could be online tutorials, exercises, quizzes and guides to further study. Experiential exercises could be studying case-based, problem-based or evidenced-based materials, simulated role plays, fieldwork exercises or following practical demonstrations (Maier and Warren 2000: 76). Ragan and White (2001) suggest the next step is to interrogate the apices of the triangle with questions from the student's perspective such as:

- What is this module all about?
- Why should I care?
- What am I supposed to do?

We have already discussed the implications for online learning and the theoretical propositions that require an acknowledgement of factors such as the opportunity for students' to explore values and beliefs, personal abilities and orientation towards learning, students' levels of dependence relative to independence, readiness to embrace the online learning environment and motivation as an adult learner. A preliminary assessment of readiness to learn (a) the topic and (b) as an online learner has to be undertaken prior to commencing the module, and information about the expectations for student engagement with the learning materials fully explained in materials sent out in advance. In this module it was not necessary to send out packages of learning materials as all the supplementary materials are available online, however, with some courses this may be necessary if students do not have access to libraries, and materials are only available in paper format.

However, the literature suggests (and it is also the authors' experience) that students benefit from at least one face-to-face encounter to orientate to this mode of learning and to meet other students, which is thought to enhance learner engagement and satisfaction. There are difficulties with this in that students who have to travel distances incur extra expenses. Lieblein (2000) designed a comprehensive web-based orientation and eliminated all mandatory trips to the campus for orientation, only to find that student and academic bonding suffered as did identification with the campus and university which engenders a sense of belonging to a wider community. The solution was to create a CD-ROM to cover all orientation topics, sets of literature, on-campus orientation, and so on. The campus-based orientation has become optional and, with the resulting choice of orientation options, the drop-out rate has decreased. Therefore, the compromise of optional attendance and comprehensive web-based orientation was adopted for this module. In the case study, because face-to-face encounters might not be possible with students who accessed the module from a distance, students were expected to participate in an introductory discussion board, post a photograph of themselves and, with the guidance of pre-posted prompts from the moderator, describe themselves and their intentions to study.

Having decided the orientation programme, our approach to deciding learning activities was for each contributor to the module to brainstorm different activities that would enable the students to engage actively with their learning materials. Each academic then buddied up with a colleague, swapped ideas and suggestions, and supported the potential designs for the topics. Core ideas for presentation and structure of each topic were presented by the group facilitator. The academics then worked on their designs for each of their own topics to present in a manner that would lead the student into the topics and with appropriate visual and auditory support.

The first consideration was how the learning outcomes could be met with the learning materials and what activities could be generated from these. The second was to identify at least two tasks for each topic for students to undertake either prior to or after accessing the topic. It was also important to consider additional resources that students could access online that relate to the topic, and for them to give critical feedback on these. The case study team were thinking about whether there should be opportunities for students to combine feedback from studying the topics through online discussions or other ways of sharing information.

Colleagues were asked to consider the order and structuring of chunks of their topics and to present them in at least two different formats, for example word documents and PowerPoint or word documents and related web sites. Academics were asked to provide case examples where possible, or give indications where theory could be applied, and then ask students to provide their own examples of theory application and integration. These discussions led to a map of activities that provided ideas for general learning activities that encompassed and drew together the whole learning experience as well as specific activities for certain topics. The next step was to sew the topics together into a canvas of learning that would bring the whole module into a unified perspective and consider how students would be encouraged to sail through the module during the scheduled 13-week semester.

Designing learning activities

After spending time deliberating about the relative merits of different structures, design methods and teaching materials, the module team decided on specific learning activities to unify the learning and map it against the learning outcomes. These were divided into participatory and individual learning activities.

Participatory and individual learning activities

The module was designed to give students an increased understanding of global influences on health and of organizations such as the World Health Organization, Unesco and international professional bodies. The module learning outcomes were to enable students to:

- Demonstrate scholarly insights into the producers and sources of global health initiatives and an understanding of international trends in health care;
- Demonstrate an understanding of different models of analysis relevant to

the globalization of health and synthesis of the implications for global patterns of health;
- Demonstrate a conceptual understanding of the dominant cultural and theoretical perspectives;
- Critically evaluate the relevant research and available information online.

To achieve these outcomes different learning activities were devised. In order to accomplish the required intellectual standards for study at master's level, the team felt there needed to be a balance of individual and participatory learning. The available media needed consideration before its learning effects could be estimated. Therefore, Laurillard's (2002: 90) taxonomy (Table 6.2) was utilized to assess the worth and learning potential of different forms of media.

Table 6.2   Laurillard's taxonomy of educational media

Learning experience	Methods/technologies	Media forms
Attending, apprehending	Print, TV, video, DVD	Narrative
Investigating, exploring	Library, CD, DVD, web resources	Interactive
Discussing, debating	Seminar, online conference	Communicative
Experimenting, practising	Laboratory, field trip, simulation	Adaptive
Articulating, expressing	Essay, product, animation, model	Productive

Source: Laurillard, D. 2002 *Rethinking University Teaching; a Conversational Framework for the Effective Use of Learning Technologies,* 2nd edn. London: Routledge, p.90, table II.I. Reproduced with the permission of Thomson Publishing Services

All learning experiences in the taxonomy are represented in the module case study except the simulation exercise.

Individual learning activities
- *Personal learning plans* (PLPs). To collate and gain a record of learning activities each student devises a personal learning plan. An online facilitator, a member of the module team, guides the student in constructing the learning plan. The plan identifies the student's personal learning aims and the activities they will be undertaking to achieve these aims.

Participatory learning activities
- *Online action learning sets.* Students collaborate in five, online, action learning sets (ALS) (see Chapter 5 for more detail on action learning). The ALS discussions are asynchronous and open for two weeks. Each student is expected to describe what he or she has achieved towards his or her PLP and submit his or her objective(s) for the following set.

- *Presentations.* Students are expected to provide a presentation on their chosen topics to be available to all students at the culmination of the module. The presentation uses PowerPoint and is accompanied by notes summarizing the points being made in the presentation. These notes are supported by referenced literature. The final ALS is a presentation of the students' topics, assessed by peers and tutors, using the criteria outlined in Table 6.3. The marks from the presentation contribute to 20 per cent of the final mark for the module. A written assignment, on the topic of their choice, is submitted for the remaining marks.
- *Topic summaries.* The module is structured around specific topic areas, for example: Internationalization and Globalization, Theory (sub-topics – Systems theory, Critical theory, Postmodernism and Gaia theory), Philosophy of Culture, Policy and Politics, Social and Health Inequalities (Democracy, Gender Issues), Health Economics, Epidemiology, Health Promotion, Infection Control and Management and Ethics. These topics are presented in a variety of formats following Laurillard's (2002) guidelines (see Table 6.2). The students can work through each topic at their own pace and in any order they choose. However, the introductory topic on Globalization must be completed first. As each topic is completed the student sends to the module coordinator their summary of the topic. This may be in the form of responses to guided questions about each topic. The topic summaries are posted onto the student notice board.
- *Searching and critiquing.* Other activities are to take a virtual tour of web sites of major international organizations and to find and critique information relevant to their individual topics of interest. These critiques are then posted onto the student notice board.

Conceptual levels of learning

We have established universal criteria for marking written studies in our university, however, these are to measure the outcome of learning. The module team felt that the process of learning was just as important and therefore adopted a guiding framework for facilitating students to gain positively from the learning experience (de la Harpe and Radloff 2001). The framework has six stages, each building upon the previous stage to consolidate and integrate learning:

- Adding knowledge to existing understanding.
- Memorizing and storing information.
- Acquisition of knowledge for later application.
- Abstraction of meaning and relevance for application to professional or personal context.
- Interpretative processes which challenge and/or change understanding of subjectivity.
- Personal development.

Table 6.3 Online presentation assessment criteria used in the case study

Criterion	Mark	Guidance notes
1 Accuracy and style of presentation		Spelling, punctuation, typographical errors Use of illustration, sub-headings, bulleted lists
2 Clarity of rationale for presentation		Introduction to topic, relevance and purpose. Indication of who is being persuaded and what is their position?
3 Relevance of presentation to chosen topic		Rationale for presentation, main assertion or thesis. Is it the only reasonable proposition?
4 Coherence of structure		Middle – logical outline of substantive area and its importance, arrangement of evidence Conclusion – explicit articulation of the focus of presentation
5 Rigour of approach to critique		Detail of critical appraisal, use of critical or analytical framework. Opposing views presented fairly. Potential validity of opposing arguments. Soundness of evidence
6 Integration of literature		Relevance and suitability to support points or arguments
7 Analysis of points raised		Specific arguments, alternative views, summary, identification of salient points. Convincing, authoritative, believable and sufficient or emotional, opinionated and rhetorical
8 Quality and currency of references		Breadth, variety and reliability of sources
9 Creativity of ideas		Innovative approach, both to design of presentation and conceptual challenges/insights to topic
10 Either professional relevance or ethical issues		Evidence of personal or professional attitude of presenter, tone of language. Degrees of fairness and open-mindedness, personal bias, breadth of perspective

Notes: Each criterion will be marked out of four. 1 = unsatisfactory, 2 = adequate, 3 = good and 4 = excellent totalling a maximum of 40 marks. This mark will be divided to give a total available mark out of 20 per cent, which will contribute to the final assessment.

The assumption is that while the students do not have prior knowledge of globalization, they have knowledge of their own fields of expertise. Students studying in the university are often qualified professionals undertaking master's level studies to further their career prospects and enhance professional knowledge. Therefore application of knowledge is a priority. The final three stages are where the module team feels the students demonstrate mastery in their chosen topic and this is evidenced in the written study of their topic, which would attract half of the marks. These stages are shared with the students and guide the completion of their PLPs. The final challenge was to agree an evaluation tool.

Evaluation methods for online learning

The final stage in designing the module was to consider evaluation methods. There are many methods for evaluation, however, these were not felt sufficient to capture the process of the module development or its multiple aims. There are four potential areas for the evaluation of web-based e-learning programs suggested by Hoernes and Wallen (2003) that were felt to reflect the development and final outcome of the module delivery:

- Formative;
- Process;
- Outcome;
- Impact.

Formative is where concepts and messages are piloted, and the effects are tested with audiences and then merged with evaluation activities. This development has utilized formative evaluation with some of the module materials, those that have formed part of previous learning experiences, and the methods of learning such as online action learning sets. *Process* is where progress in achieving the project or learning is recorded, successes are reported and any lessons learned are analysed. This is recorded in notes of meetings and the final culmination of materials and learning activities on Blackboard. *Outcome* evaluation is where the lessons learned are summarized, the immediate effects of the program are demonstrated in terms of the conceptual learning framework used and the findings are disseminated. *Impact* is where the module, or project team, look beyond the immediate results at the long-term effects to the program and ask if there are any unintended effects of the program. The final area was felt to be innovative, futuristic and dynamic.

Changes in the nature of educational theory

A feature of working with the new technologies is the attitudes of educationalists towards creativity and their willingness to shift towards using different teaching and learning methodologies. In this case study example, academics were prompted to reflect on learning theory and re-evaluate their theoretical positions. In the authors' experiences we have seen students also prompted to re-evaluate their attitudes towards learning to embrace the process as well as the outcome. Changes in educational theory are indicating an increasing interest in the process of learning as well as the content, as originally espoused by Mezirow (1978). He was a pioneer in transformative learning which embraced a philosophy of learning that included independent learning, experiential learning, collaborative and cooperative learning, examples of which we have seen illustrated in the preceding account of the curriculum design. The following is a discussion of these theories illustrated with examples from students who have taken online learning modules.

Transformative learning

This theory is underpinned by the notion that in order for adults to learn they need to construe meaning from a combination of what they have experienced with what they will learn. It draws upon two domains of learning based upon the epistemology of Habermas's communicative theory. One domain is that of instrumental learning where learning is achieved through tasks such as problem-solving, determining the cause and effects of relationships between phenomena and a process of analytic discovery. The second domain is centred on communication, where understanding the meaning of what others communicate about their values, ideals, feelings, moral decisions (and concepts such as freedom, justice, love, autonomy, commitment and democracy) are fundamental (Mezirow 1991: 8).

The theory of transformative learning explains how our early experiences are located within a cultural context and have thus formed our assumptions about what we know. The aim of transformative learning is to transform perspectives that are embedded in learning structures constructed from meaning schemes and meaning perspectives. *Meaning schemes* are composed of specific elements of beliefs, value judgements and feelings, whereas *meaning perspectives* are general frames of reference, world views or personal paradigms involving a collection of meaning schemes. It is easy to see how in traditional learning methodologies, that utilize small-group seminars to discuss ideas, and express value systems and attitudes towards the nature and construction of knowledge, such transformation can be facilitated in the higher education context. The challenge is to be able to reproduce this discursive and Socratic approach in the online environment.

An essential feature of this theory of learning is its student centredness and if this feature can remain a prevailing philosophy of learning methodologies in online learning then the aims of transformative learning will be realized. For example, offering opportunities and providing exercises for students to follow for collaborative learning through online exercises, which can take place either synchronously or asynchronously, is one method. Another method is to promote independent learning which can be achieved through exercises that expect students to find information and make critical comments upon their findings. Problem-solving and critical reflection are also fundamental features of transformative learning and are methods that, when introduced into the learning environment, enable meaningful as well as deep learning, as opposed to surface learning. An example of this is a student who took an online module, previously designed by one of the authors and not part of this case study, but described here to illustrate the idea. The module was in clinical studies and aimed to develop knowledge and understanding of a problem-solving methodology in health-care practice. This student was provided with theoretical input on decision-making theory (see Figure 6.3 for an example of how this was first introduced). The student was then asked to undertake specific analytical tasks (see Figure 6.4).

This exercise was linked to an asynchronous discussion to be shared with other students on the module illustrated in Figure 6.5. Students are given prior notice of the discussion topic, and the date when the topic is to

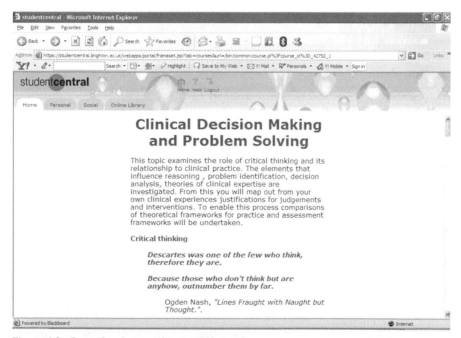

Figure 6.3   Introduction to the module topic

Figure 6.4　Examples of analytical analysis

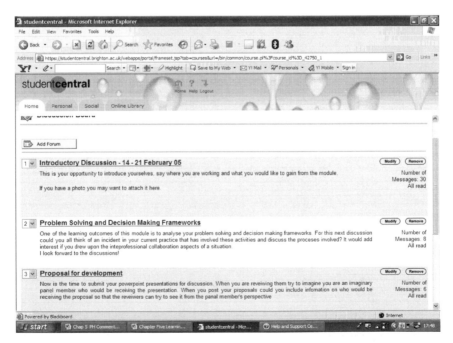

Figure 6.5　Introduction to online asynchronous discussion

be held, in pre-module information and the dates are scheduled in the online calendar. The discussion is opened for one week and students are expected to participate at least twice. The module coordinator acts an e-moderator, ready to interject with clarification and prompts, if necessary, to sustain the critical nature of the discussion and guide thinking to areas that are not being explored. This example is related to forum topic 2 in Figure 6.5.

Box 6.1 illustrates the student's response copied here from the discussion board. In Box 6.1 the student has followed the theory on offer and has searched for her own model of decision-making that she believes has more meaning for her particular field of practice. She has attempted to follow the model and has built in her own critique. Her answer alludes to the cultural expectations of the role of nurses in a particular type of health-care environment. The student then considers the model for other situations and has therefore transformed this learning to other potentially complex circumstances.

Pritchard (2004) provides another example of this activity in his project report on tasks that students on a Postgraduate Certificate in Education were given to familiarize themselves with the online learning environment. The tasks were devised around 'treasure hunt' exercises, in which students were given three sets of clues over a three-week period for three separate hunts. They were encouraged to work in pairs to encourage collaborative learning. To encourage discussion students were advised to ask another member of their group first before contacting a tutor. Experimentation was also encouraged as each task was not of the type that would damage the IT system or software. Feedback from the students indicated that the activities were generally well received and had a positive effect in terms of increased confidence and decreased anxiety. However, it was apparent from the feedback that some students preferred instructional approaches and others an explanatory approach.

Methods to enable transformative learning are only effective if preceded by clear instructions, which if taken out of context may seem over-deliberate, yet in the online environment need to be didactic and specific to overcome any ambiguity or misunderstanding. Added to this is the need to explain the expected outcomes, with examples, that students are to produce when undertaking the activities. Again, this deliberateness overcomes misunderstandings about what is to be the desired outcomes of the activities.

It is also relevant to state clearly what will be shared with other students and what will be personal study, so that students are prepared for the amount of exposure their ideas will be getting. Salmon (2004) suggests that education and training are undertaken for a purpose that is different from casual game-playing for pleasure or leisure. Online learning uses a medium that is similar to that used for game-playing; therefore, the purpose has to be made more explicit in order to differentiate the two. By giving students instructions associated with goals that are provided by the e-moderator, and

Box 6.1 Student's response

I've used the Toulmin Model to analyze a recent clinical experience when I was faced with the decision of what to do about a hypotensive patient. Attached is a copy of how I worked through the model to logically justify my decision that the patient was hypovolemic and required a blood transfusion.

In the book Core Concepts in Advanced Practice Nursing there are two models that can be applied to decision making:

- Focus – find, organize, clarify, understand, and select;
- PDSA – plan, do, study, act.

Similarly, a framework is described in Creative and Critical Thinking:
PHASES IN DECISION MAKING

1   Recognizing and defining a problem.
2   Gathering relevant information.
3   Generating possible conclusions.
4   Testing possible conclusions.
5   Evaluating conclusions.
6   Reaching Decisions.
7   Recognizing and defining a problem.
8   Gathering relevant information.
9   Generating possible conclusions.
10 Testing possible conclusions.
11 Evaluating conclusions.
12 Reaching Decisions.

I think all of these frameworks and models are similar in their concepts in that you begin by identifying a problem and then move on to gathering and assessing all of the necessary information about the problem that will allow for a plan of action to be made. After trying out the plan, an evaluation is needed to see if the plan worked and if further clinical decisions are necessary to stop, continue, or change the plan. These frameworks are essentially the same as the nursing process (assessment, planning, implementation, and evaluation).

For my example of identifying the problem of hypotension, I then followed these steps to reach a conclusion of what I should do about the problem. My nursing assessment included collecting the data of low CVP, low urine output, cool shutdown peripheries, tachycardia, bleeding to dressing/drain, and a low Hb. I also communicated and collaborated with other health care professionals by reading the anaesthetic report about how much blood was lost in surgery, speaking to the surgeons when they came up to review about their opinion of the surgical wound and bleeding, and informing the ITU SHO and nurse shift leader about the cardiovascular status of the patient.

Because ITU nurses have quite a bit of autonomy with a clinical decision such as how to treat hypotension, I was able to independently go ahead and give two units of PRBC that were previously prescribed as a PRN order from the SHO when I informed her earlier in the shift that blood products might be necessary for this patient. I felt that my nursing diagnosis of hypotension due to hypovolemia was correct because the blood pressure responded to the blood transfusion and improved afterwards as did the urine output/CVP. As seen in the Toulmin Model, I did consider other causes for hypotension with appropriate treatment (e.g. septic or cardiogenic shock that may have required inotropes) but these things did not appear valid. If I had evaluated at the end of the process that my clinical decision was not correct or a different solution was needed, I would have again colla-borated with the SHO and shift leader to brainstorm ideas about what the next plan of action should be.

In ICU, I often follow a structured clinical decision making frame-work as seen by the previous example but I think I also use a certain amount of intuition. I remember admitting this particular hypotensive patient after he arrived back from theatres for an emergency AAA repair, and intuitively I knew that I would be giving him a great deal of IV fluids that I had already stocked my bedside drawer full of. As an ITU nurse, my gut feeling without even conducting a physical assess-ment would be that a patient in his condition would need IV fluids and likely even blood products. This type of intuitive process is part of Benner's theory of novice to expert.

As well, my clinical decisions are often guided by local guidelines and clinical protocols that have flow charts to follow. For example, we have specific protocols for ventilation weaning, heparin infusions, enteral feeding, and insulin sliding scale. When I first started thinking about this, I thought perhaps critical analysis is taken away from the decision making process because you are simply following a flow chart without it being 'your' decision of how much insulin or heparin will be administered. But, the evaluation part is just as important and necessary to see if the protocol is working for this particular patient. Following a pre-determined pathway or care bundle may not be appropriate or effective for the clinical problem and part of the decision making process is to decide if a change is needed.

Sources: P. E Benner, (1996). *Expertise in Nursing Practice: Caring, Clinical Judgment, and Ethics.* New York: Springer; P. M. Gray, M. M. Anderson and D. Robinson (2001). Quality management: Implications for nursing. In D. Robinson and C. P. Kish. *Core Concepts in Advanced Practice Nursing*, (eds) St. Louis: Mosby; W. E. Moore, H. McCann and J. McCann (1985). *Creative and Critical Thinking* 2nd edn. Boston: Houghton Mifflin.

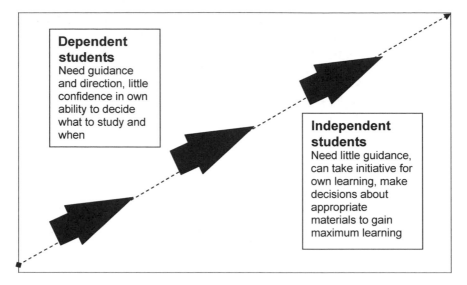

Figure 6.6   Trajectory of learning dependency

structured into the design of online learning activities, the creative potential of the medium can be utilized to its fullest.

Independent learning in the online learning environment

The student example in the case study illustrates the trajectory upon which
students will travel when taking their first steps towards independent
learning in the online learning environment. This takes them on path that
moves them from dependence to independence (Figure 6.6). Each student
will be at a different stage, depending on their personal levels of confidence
with (a) the subject, (b) technology and (c) their usual student classroom
behaviour, for example either extrovert or introvert, a passive or an active
member of a group.

Any creator of the structural designs of online learning environments has
to consider the implications of this trajectory without always taking into
account any detailed previous learning experiences by the student. It is
impossible to expect that academics will have at their disposal detailed
information on each of their students' previous life or educational
experiences. If they do, then it is highly commendable, however, in the
main large cohorts of several hundred students are the norm in most universities. In UK higher education courses today, the students are likely to be
drawn from a wide range of educational backgrounds and do not fit a
stereotypical characteristic of being aged 18 years and immediately post-A-

level. Strategies to widen the participation in higher education from all groups in society and of all ages are outlined in UK government policy drivers (HEFCE 2001) and have been followed. This is not only confined to the UK. Yvonne Taynton, in a paper presented at the ASCILITE conference in Australia gave a valuable student perspective. She claimed that:

> the background of students in higher education is changing from the traditional middle class school-leaver to a complex mix of age, race, gender, ethnicity, socio-economics, and experience. This complexity of student needs, abilities, experience and expectations provides challenges for academic and administration staff as well as for students.
>
> (Taynton 2000: 1)

Moreover, Taynton maintains that:

> Negotiating the steep learning curve for those unfamiliar with computer technology can involve real feelings of anxiety and stress. Coping with unfamiliar study and assessment schedules and the development of the research and writing skills necessary to successful scholarship often means juggling work and family commitments and dealing with accompanying feelings of guilt and frustration ... Under such pressures it is not surprising that students may find themselves struggling to cope with feelings of inadequacy and isolation ... Online learning can mitigate some of the undesirable consequences of university life in the 21st century such as equity of access for distant or working students, it may also exacerbate other issues.
>
> (2000: 1)

Becoming an independent learner is a premise of the current overarching reforms of higher education in the UK. The Dearing report (1997) recommended that preparation for lifelong learning be implemented in HE curriculum and underpinning this concept is the ability to be an independent learner. The intention is not to give students the freedom and opportunity to completely self-educate but is intended to encompass some of the theories discussed above and provide conditions for learning that give students space, support and encouragement to become reflective and confident adult learners.

Adult learning theory

The notion of learning through life is hardly new and is mentioned in ancient Greek history in Plato's *Republic*. The view that education should be lifelong is synonymous with the development of 'adult education'. Interest in how adults learn was stimulated in the 1980s with the introduction of the concept of andragogy. There was limited use of the concept in the 1800s, but Malcolm Knowles (1984) popularized it in the adult education community in the late twentieth century. It was originally used to describe elements of Plato's education theory where andragogy (*andr-* meaning 'man') could be contrasted with pedagogy (paid- meaning 'child' and *agogos* meaning 'leading'). Knowles, argued that andragogy was based on an understanding of four characteristics of adult learners. These, he asserted, were different to the characteristics of child learners as outlined in pedagogy. His precepts were:

1   Self-concept: As a person matures his or her self concept moves from one of being a dependent personality toward one of being a self-directed human being.

2   Experience: As a person matures he or she accumulates a growing reservoir of experience that becomes an increasing resource for learning.

3   Readiness to learn: As a person matures his or her readiness to learn becomes oriented increasingly to the developmental tasks of his or her social roles.

4   Orientation to learning: As a person matures his or her time perspective changes from one of postponed application of knowledge to immediacy of application, and accordingly his or her orientation toward learning shifts from one of subject-centeredness to one of problem centredness.

Knowles later added a fifth characteristic:

5   Motivation to learn: As a person matures the motivation to learn is internal.
            (Knowles 1984: 12; see also www.infed.org/lifelonglearning/
            b-andra.htm and www.infed.org/thinkers/et-knowl.htm)

His work was drawing heavily on an educational philosophy based on humanism similar to those theories of Mezirow and Rogers, but indicates more of the framework for 'how' learning can be achieved with adult learners as well as the 'what', derived from his consideration of the characteristics of adults. This depends upon the maturity of the individual which, if assumed, may or may not be accurate and cannot always be directly or specifically assessed when students begin to learn. Enabling students to carry out in-depth self-analysis prior to undertaking studies is, in our view, something that should be part of an individualized learning programme embarked on with personal tutors and taking place before study begins. That said, the principles identified by Knowles need addressing in the online environment in a manner that also takes account of the situatedness of learning and the changes in consciousness proposed by Mezirow.

Collaborative exercises, providing examples of the application of principles and subject knowledge and the use of experiential learning can enhance learning and contribute to students' generalized motivation to learn. An academic's responsibility is to incorporate these forms of learning in a manner that harnesses the principles of Knowles's theory to give students the ability to learn the transferable skills that will prepare them for future lifelong learning. Fortunately, for online learning this also enables active learning, as opposed to passive learning, which is deemed to enhance overall learning. Active learning has been found to improve learning because (a) students prefer this form of learning, (b) it is equal to lectures in promoting mastery of content and (c) it is superior to lectures in promoting higher-order thinking, analysing and evaluation cognitive abilities (Bonwell and Eison 1991). For academics working in the online environment, this means being creative with ideas, questions, prompts, tasks for analysis and evaluation when providing materials that are to be read, and thus encouraging these active thinking processes rather than passive reading of documents.

Given the changing nature of the student characteristics epitomized by Trayntor above, the work of Knowles could not be less pertinent. However, the Knowles approach demands individualized assessment of each student's previous learning experiences. As we have recognized above, it is problematic to adopt these principles in the current climate where high student numbers are the norm and mitigate against individualized and personalized learning assessments despite an acknowledgement that this is the preferred approach. One solution is to adopt the principle that Knowles embodies, that is, to accept that adult learners have individualized learning needs, which are framed by previous life experiences. Thus, for online learning to be a successful, 'its design, implementation and evaluation must involve taking into consideration those social and equity issues that affect the performance of a changing user base' (Taynton 2000: 1).

To do this completely, the social and cultural context of learning experiences have to be considered as well as the likely influence of individual approaches to learning. These could be considered as barriers to learning online. MacBrayne (1993, cited in Rezabek 2000: 10) found 12 potential barriers that were significant. They are listed here in rank order:

1 Lack of money.
2 Poor academic preparation.
3 Too far to travel.
4 Family responsibilities.
5 Lack of information.
6 Forgot how to study.
7 Low self-esteem.
8 Too old to learn.
9 Lack of interest.
10 Lack of support.
11 No transportation.
12 Lack of childcare.

These research findings from MacBrayne were taken from students who were already enrolled and had overcome many difficulties to get to that point, thus the findings are described as 'potential' barriers. Rezabek notes that research into subjects who had not been able to enrol because of these kinds of barriers would likely be quite different in rank ordering.

MacBrayne and Rezabek discuss how the concepts being dependent or not on the time learning is potentially available, and being dependent or not on the place where learning is carried out (for example, at home or in a library), are key determinants in choice. These factors influence whether or not someone enrols for a classroom, traditional distance or online distance learning type of module or course. Their research also indicates that self-discipline in a more isolated environment is crucial if the student is going to be successful. The finding indicates that the more independent the learning environment the greater the importance of self-discipline to persist with study and learning. These findings suggest that motivational assessments and self-reflective activities can be a very important precursor to online learning, as is any activity to assist induction and self-confidence in the early stages.

If students are assessed, or self-assess, to identify their preferred learning style this will help them to make appropriate decisions about what kind of learning environment is best for them. This will inform them as to the type of learning activities they will appreciate and benefit from the most. It is likely that learners will need to be encouraged to work on aspects of their learning style which they are less favourably disposed to, but if they are aware of their own strengths and weaknesses this can be done self-critically and with support, without necessarily fundamentally undermining their self-confidence.

Both MacBayne and Rezabek discuss the fact that a disproportionate number of women enrol for online learning in the USA compared with the general population. This is seen to be attractive to women who have to take on substantial caring roles more often than men. In this situation, online learning and teaching gives new opportunities for progressing learning when the quality of support is good.

Access to good technology and assistance with training in the basic skills to use such technology are important prerequisites that can undermine self-confidence and possible success if they are not provided.

Rezebek (2000: 11–12) notes the following in his data:

It would seem important to explore accessibility of various technologies, comfort level with those technologies and comfort with the different pedagogies each entails ... Adults may be much more uncertain and fearful initially to use these technologies. During the initial era of audio conferencing it was fear of using the microphone. With interactive television it was fear of the microphone and being 'on-camera'. We need to help create a 'comfort zone' with these new technologies to overcome the negative influences. With the advances in technology and its increasing use in the daily lives of many, the almost mystic aura of technology may eventually disappear. At greatest risk, in the mean time, may be the many adults from ages 30–60 who were past their formative years when the technological revolution began ... school students of today may be of less concern to educators as they are being exposed to computers and other technologies in their schools and homes at an early age.

In designing the module evaluated in this chapter the team did consider our students' access to technical resources and this was discussed above in the section on technical resources.

One means of creating a more familiar environment is to consider the role of the teacher. A major difference for online learning may be that students will be learning without the familiar comfort of a face-to-face encounter with a lecturer. The relationship that is established at this time is crucial and yet has to be difference. The work of Gilly Salmon (2002; 2004) is helpful to consider here as she has evolved a role for educators that is more facilitator than educator. There is a commonly shared myth among some students and lecturers that online learning is a passive experience where materials are posted onto the Internet and students are then left to download and read what has been written. This shows how important it is to create a learning environment where active learning takes place, and this involves the lecturer as much as the student. The role is as an online learning facilitator. Here is yet another challenge for lecturers as they will be expected to adapt to this form of teaching style, which is equally as important as students adapting their learning styles.

Conclusions

We began by talking about learning and the constant need, given the pressures of mass higher education, to remind ourselves about how people learn. The quotation below captures the creativity and excitement of learning, as we aspire to promote it:

> I want to talk about learning. But not the lifeless, sterile, futile, quickly forgotten stuff that is crammed in to the mind of the poor helpless individual tied into his seat by ironclad bonds of conformity! I am talking about LEARNING – the insatiable curiosity that drives the adolescent boy to absorb everything he can see or hear or read about gasoline engines in order to improve the efficiency and speed of his 'cruiser'. I am talking about the student who says, 'I am discovering, drawing in from the outside, and making that which is drawn in a real part of me.' I am talking about any learning in which the experience of the learner progresses along this line: 'No, no, that's not what I want'; 'Wait! This is closer to what I am interested in, what I need'; 'Ah, here it is! Now I'm grasping and comprehending what I need and what I want to know!'
>
> (Rogers 1983: 18–19, cited at www.infed.org/biblio/b-learn.htm)

As every experienced academic knows, a crucial aspect of being a successful teacher is to create conditions that optimize the acquisition of learning. In 1985 Gagné, reported on a study (first published in 1965), that considered the sets of circumstances that are required for learning to occur, that is: 'when certain observable changes in human behaviour take place that justify the inference of learning' (p. 5). From this study he identified eight forms of learning: signal, stimulus response; chaining: motor and verbal; concept learning; problem-solving; learning structures; the motivation and control of learning; learning decisions – that constituted a system he believed was essential to create conditions for learning. This approach may be considered overly mechanistic as we read this in the early part of the second millennium, but it is worth revisiting, if only to remind ourselves that we cannot forget even the simplest of circumstances if we are to create satisfactory conditions for our students to learn inside or outside an online learning environment.

Using Gagné's and Rogers' work from the 1960s nearly 50 years later may seem absurd – more so when we are discussing learning methodologies that were not invented at the time the theories emerged. Yet from this pioneering work, other theorists have derived frameworks to draw together the threads that constitute learning processes and how teachers can best simulate these conditions. Even more so, these theories can help us get to grips with liberating learning in the 2000s. Carl Rogers (1983) originally introduced his pivotal ideas on the student-centred approach in his groundbreaking work *Freedom to Learn* in 1969. Moving away from the behaviourally driven theories of previous years, he stimulated controversy and interest by proposing a humanistic theory of education based upon the notion that individuals should be free to learn in a manner that they devise for themselves. This controversial approach drew attention to the needs of individuals to achieve learning and considered learning to be part of the product of education or as an outcome. More recent thinking in educational theory considers the process of learning to be as equally important as the product.

The teaching methods we use to achieve learning processes are often varied, can depend upon the nature of the students we are teaching or relate to the subjects we teach, and are often supported by a philosophical (implicit or explicit) intent that influences the whole curriculum. The means through which we have acquired our knowledge of teaching methods are equally varied, such as:

- Our personal, professional education in teaching and learning by gaining teaching certificates, and so on;
- Experimentation;
- Responding to evaluations with a critical and creative flair;
- Observing peers;
- Our own personal experiences of what we felt were effective and suitable methods for our chosen subject areas.

Thus we develop a repertoire of teaching methodologies with which we gain confidence and assurance, and which we cultivate during our years of teaching experience. Novice academics, on the other hand, are at the beginning of their learning curves to become teachers and spend time and effort to find appropriate teaching methodologies. This means they are more likely to be amenable to adopting different teaching strategies. It does not, however, preclude novice academics being suspicious of learning technologies and this will depend upon their own experience of ICT. It is therefore understandable that any academic, when faced with the new online teaching and learning methodologies, which in one blow remove many of the features that are deemed to be central to teaching (such as the spoken word, facial expression, voice tonality and sub-vocal and auditory clues), are reluctant to adopt the new methodologies. That is why in this chapter we consider the teacher as learner as well as exploring the methods of learning that ICT can provide.

The momentum for online learning is gaining speed. However, not everyone is convinced of its efficacy. The costs of developing materials are high, and evidence suggests that online learning and teaching may be no better than traditional face-to-face methods (Russell 1999). The opposing view is that the problem lies not with the medium itself but with the approaches of those who use it inappropriately. To counteract these criticisms, this case study development had a clear purpose, was not converting an existing module, nor was it a paper-posting exercise. Students will be expected to engage in learning that involves reading print to assimilate new concepts and ideas. This might be regarded as poor practice for web-based learning as it is a passive and boring form of activity. However, it is balanced with other learning following Laurillard's (2002) advice such as critiquing web-based materials and ALS. In Chapter 4 we argued for a pragmatic approach to the design of learning that allows online learning to connect easily with text-based environments and to allow students to feel at ease about this.

Furthermore, the module case study was not intended as a distribution channel or a vehicle for information which might be found to detract from the learning experience. Neither was it intended to create a view among lecturers that the use of information technology is an additional burden (Sosabowski et al. 1998). It is designed as an interactive experience for students and a satisfying teaching opportunity for lecturers.

The strategies explored in this chapter are undergoing constant revision and evaluation. Models of delivery may have to be re-engineered if students find the balance of activities do not meet their personal learning plans. The use of the PLPs will be fundamental in the eventual evaluation strategy. The community of practice has succeeded in enabling the commitment of the team to the project and is evidenced by its completion.

There cannot be a discussion of learning without considering the potential barriers to learning in the online environment. We have already explored the individual's self-esteem, the potential of technological fear and misunderstanding of the difference between passive and active learning engagement in online learning. The negative effect of anxiety and low self-esteem, that have always had a negative effect on learning, may manifest themselves in an online situation, and we have to be wary of it being any worse than in the traditional learning context. Those students who find face- to-face learning difficult in seminars for example, may be happier with online learning. But, similarly, ICT is an extra barrier for some mature students. Those that find IT threatening will decline in number in the next decade or so. There are many creative opportunities that online learning gives, argued throughout our book, but at the same we are honest about some of the limitations for some individuals in some circumstances, for example rural or impoverished communities, or those who are anxious about using ICT and are studying alone.

The sharing of values among individuals with lecturing roles who are receptive to the work of Knowles (1980) and Wenger (1998) has provided a common platform. Methods to assess the conceptual levels of learning are an innovation that have yet to be tested in the process and outcome eva-luation areas. The impact area of evaluation may prove to be the most exciting and will requite longitudinal follow-through of students. In the final analysis, care will have to be taken to ensure that all critical elements of the module case study are equally identified and weighted for importance and relevance. The experience of designing online learning and the exci-tement of seeing this mode of learning come to fruition is a stimulating development in our teaching careers. The opportunity that online learning brings is a chance to renew and re-energize teaching methodologies and techniques. It is also especially an opportunity that offers a potential advantage to those who may have been disenfranchised by lack of access to learning.

7

Conclusion

This book has sought to take both a wide-ranging and pragmatic approach to the arrival of online learning in higher education. In historical terms, online learning is still in its infancy. We have seen in this book how its arrival was characterized by predictions that much of global higher education would be rapidly disrupted as a result. But predictions of university closure and a dramatic shift towards distance learning courses have not come to fruition.

The prediction that students would be less willing to be attached to a physical place and instead would demand a self-determined and e-based mode of learning consumption also seem far from realized. What we have, however, argued in this book is that online learning is a significant and important development that slowly but surely is pushing the evolution of higher education towards a different future. An important aspect of this evolution is the mix of factors that are driving change, of which technological change is only one.

It has been argued that technology is interacting with other major social and political transformations; in particular, globalization and the demand for mass higher education. It is the mix of these social forces that determines the future of higher education, not technological change alone. Globalization itself is driven by a number of features, but arguably the strongest feature is the dominance of international markets over political and ideological forces, and the growth in consumerism and market values. These features have had their own strong impact on higher education and its commodification.

It is tempting to try and find one overarching word or concept to describe this synthesis of change. We could talk of the modernization of higher education, and this does capture some of it, but the term 'modernization' is too attached to a particularly Western political project wedded to the 'third way' and ideas of a permanently happy marriage between the political state and the marketplace.

In our view it is better to talk of the 'post-industrial revolution' and higher education. It can be argued that Bell's (1999) thesis on post-industrialization was seminal in being ahead of its time, and indeed now much of his description is coming to pass (Bradley et al. 2000). 'Post-industrial' captures the collision of higher education – a sector that has always been defined by knowledge – with the recent idea of the *knowledge economy* and *knowledge management*. Higher education has been crafting and debating aspects of knowledge and its management for centuries, but in the past 25 years it has increasingly had to come to terms with the fact that an explicit focus on knowledge and its value is driving much of the developed world outside of the university environment. In one sense, this has always been the case. Scientific knowledge led to inventions, these inventions went to market and then business and capital markets took over. This was the industrial revolution, and universities played some part in it, creating the beginnings of a knowledge revolution. But in the post-industrial revolution it was no longer just physical resources and physical inventions arising from these resources that form people's economic lives, but the culture of consumption and technology that began to take over. Information technology has enabled information and knowledge to become stronger commodities in their own right. This has driven the growth of the Internet (the so-called information revolution), and the rapid growth of higher education. People are aware of information and its relationship with knowledge; they know how complex and difficult it is to manage these commodities. They see universities as being able to teach them many things that will enable them to take part in this social and market transformation, not least they need to be able to handle and manage information via the new technologies that allow this to be done. Post-industrialism, then, means a greater demand for university education.

Paradoxically among all this very real bonding of information with technology is a continuity. Knowledge and its management are still as much about people as they ever have been. The communication between people, the conflicts and collaborations, the debates and contests about what is useful and applied, is still as important to knowledge management as the actual technological materials that underpin the information revolution. There are human communication aspects here that information processes can never replace. Information technology may improve such processes of communication but will never replace the higher human task of conceptualizing and formulating knowledge, this through creative thought and interaction. Blended learning is therefore likely to be central to future developments.

This is exactly the point with online learning. It does not somehow take over learning and replace it. It is a process of evolution. It is not as if 'old learning' is converted to 'new learning'. It is, rather, an evolution in the process of learning, a new method by which people may choose to learn, and many will find they can learn more efficiently, alongside other methods. Online learning has a central part to play in assisting the development of modern approaches to learning such as constructivism.

Some have tried to suggest that this new learning process is somehow 'better' than the 'old' processes; that schoolchildren will no longer go to schools; that students will no longer go to universities, hence the term 'from bricks to clicks' has entered the contemporary phrasebook. The suggestion was that learning institutions will lose their sense of place and that students will sit at multimedia terminals and construct process and interactions with many different peoples and places. But in so many ways this seems to miss the point. The traditions of learning via human interaction are as old as human civilization itself. Such cultural processes will have to continue to evolve alongside human civilization and its cultures and material progress, but such strong histories cannot and will not be revolutionized overnight. Place will still have a strong presence in learning, and online learning may in some cases strengthen this link as much as it undermines and challenges it. Much online contact is local. Arguably it can add to local communities and their interactions as it strengthens traditional bonds and communication.

We see online learning as an important evolution. We also see it as inevitable. It is possible to debate whether it is a good thing or not, but we see this as rather futile. Like so much technological change in human civilizations it is predetermined, inevitable – the issue that needs debating is how we should manage it and get the best from it. Cultural, economic and commercial pressures outside universities dictate that it will continue to happen, so how is the higher education community going to manage it?

Online learning does bring gains and losses; it does have strengths and weaknesses. Let us consider some of the weaknesses first. It seems that online learning is associated with a reduction in face-to-face contact between students and academics. Many have reservations about this. Certainly we should be cautious and will continue to want to place a high value on good quality human interaction in the educational environment. But this is where it gets more complex. We cannot assume that all face-to-face learning is of higher quality, just because people are in the same room. Failures can occur because of a lack of confidence within the learner, from too much power and control being given to the teacher. Furthermore, the biggest driver in the reduction of face-to-face contact in universities is not online learning facilities, but the move towards higher student numbers, the demand for mass higher education. This reduces the number of hours of face-to-face contact. It increases the group size of face-to-face contact that is offered. We think that online learning is often a response to a drop in face-to-face contact, rather than a primary cause of it. It can help to rebuild more personal contact, through virtual contact that is in small groups or encourages one-to-one communication.

A similar weakness is that online learning might be seen as an easy teaching method, a cheap way of coping with large student groups. This is indeed a risk. Online learning will fail if it is not managed correctly: if there is no induction to online learning and resources, no provision of the proper equipment and computer access, a lack of strategic thinking for the continued investment and renewal that the rapidly developing technologies require, no opportunity to develop first the skills that are necessary, and no support and positive reinforcement when staff and students make their first steps. In these circumstances, a sudden move to online learning will be a low-quality experience for large student groups and their teachers. Modern universities have to defend their implementation of online learning as a method for coping with large-group teaching. They have to show that it is being used as a high-quality learning tool and not as a cheap and ill thought out option merely to display basic knowledge content.

In the UK, one of the faster expanding universities is Kingston University, situated in south London. It has been trying to defend a change in learning strategy recently. The QAA noted that the university had recorded a 20 per cent rise in student numbers in a five-year period. It questioned whether the university could really use a VLE as a quick method for coping with this steep rise in numbers. The university strongly defended its e-learning strategy arguing that its use of the VLE was 'pedagogically sound' (Baty 2005: 6). This kind of debate about the good management and use of online learning is likely to be a growing international feature as universities increase their student numbers and try to implement quality learning strategies under difficult resource constraints.

Universities might see online learning as a strategy for pursuing an economy of inputs, for increasing staff to student ratios, or as a method for accepting deteriorating staff to student ratios. While we have argued in this book that online learning can be a good idea for coping with such a problematic environment it seems doubtful that such a circumstance is ideal. In any event, there should be a timescale for implementing such a fundamental change of approach. There should be time to assess what technology is best to use, and what training and support strategies should be implemented. A rush to use online learning in pursuit of an economy of inputs seems to us to be likely to result in the wrong decisions being taken owing to a pressurized environment. A circle of stress is likely to result where both academic staff and their students grow anxious about the rapid implementation of new technology and new learning methods. Better for such an evolution to take a sustained period of time, to be evaluated regularly, and with time given for suitable but significant changes of direction where necessary. Such an implementation of online learning via a VLE is likely to take about five years if it is to be done alongside a positive evolving of the learning culture of staff and students. A very rapid implementation over one or two years is unlikely to achieve its goals, and is in danger of being based on short-term targets and output goals that ignores longer-term outcomes and value-added dimensions.

In those places where there has been a rush to online learning it can be argued there has been a loss of student and professional confidence in the institution and its methods. Examples are attempts to implement technology without adequate consultation and reflection on what kind of system is needed. We heard of one university where expectations were high and rather hyped by the institution, but the system frequently failed and could not cope with the number of people trying to use it. Intentions that the VLE would quickly become the main source of routine communication with students were not achieved. Students felt cut adrift from content and asynchronous learning, leaving them more anxious and dependent on limited traditional lectures and seminars.

Given the kinds of negatives discussed so far in this chapter, it is perhaps understandable why some people are ideologically opposed to online learning. But there are always some people opposed to such changes. Small numbers of academics were opposed to the introduction of email in their institutions and refused to use it. Similarly, some staff tried to refuse the offer of desktop computers and the requirement to word-process records and teaching materials. Many have a sense of respect and sympathy for such individuals; after all the majority know only too well the stress that comes with such changes in working practice and the real danger that there is more workload rather than less as result, certainly in the short term, while people adapt.

But in time many begin to notice the benefits. Despite all its frustrations, email does allow quick and direct communication with most other staff and students. Word-processing gives staff increased efficiency in creating both teaching resources and publishable articles. The majority would not want to give up those benefits. There comes a point when you can no longer swim against the strong tide of such changes – when you have to have a computer, or access to one, when you have to have an email address – otherwise you undermine your own ability to take part in the academic community. Compared with private companies, universities are timid about forcing academics to swiftly adapt to such technological change, but it is interesting that most do accept the change and evolve with it. The same will surely be true of online learning.

Another criticism of online learning is that it allows more managerial control. In this book, the managerial changes in higher education associated with the New Public Management ideology were explored and noted to be a significant driver for change in many countries. These forces have driven higher education towards a more short-term business-orientated model where long-term benefits and wider public value is sometimes ignored. Online learning can easily be manipulated for crude business management – to count the number of students, to perform simplistic evaluations and argue that large quantities of content have been dispensed to students. These tools can be appealing to business managers who must argue using basic statistics that their universities are making money and performing well. These activities should always be viewed with some cynicism. While in the modern university they have their place, such reductionist-based performance management can easily be taken too far. There are ethical dilemmas here for those academics who are fundamentally concerned with the long-term qualitative integration of online learning into the culture and customs of higher education.

Another concern is that the online agenda has brought with it a loss of control over one's educational materials and a danger that both other academic staff and students can more easily plagiarize another person's materials without giving that person proper citation. In Chapter 3 these concerns were discussed in some detail. There does appear to be a real concern that such dishonesty is easier in the online environment. Good institutional policies and procedures including protecting a university network system so that a large majority of detailed material is more self-contained and secure can go a long way to overcoming these problems. Certainly careful institutional risk analysis and management is needed.

Finally, there is a concern that the increasing move towards online learning will reproduce a digital divide, a separation of the technological rich from the technological poor. Will technology become a further barrier to the most disadvantaged groups in society and reinforce traditional barriers to higher education? But it does not necessarily have to be the case that a technological divide automatically reinforces a learning divide. Governments and educationalists need active polices to use technology to promote learning and access to higher education via technology. There is no deterministic reason why technology should become an additional barrier to entry. There are opportunities for it to become a gateway to entry, given the falling of technology prices and the increased number accessing online and similar communications. A good example of this is how the mobile phone leapfrogged other communication technologies in poorer countries and began to create new communication networks for poor and disadvantaged peoples. Technology should be used actively and creatively to overcome socio-economic barriers of entry to higher education. Wireless and mobile technologies are rapidly increasing the possibilities for the delivery of online learning.

We now progress to summarize the main gains and advantages of online learning.

Online technology offers a new creative medium and a different mode of learning. This medium has different time and space characteristics. It introduces the notion of asynchronous learning and communication, and can assist learning in a diverse and fragmented higher education world where students struggle with busy lives and increasingly face the pressure to work in paid employment while studying. In addition, the asynchronous learning method can promote greater reflection and higher levels of involvement from students who find that face-to-face seminar group contact is difficult and impersonal, especially in larger groups. Internet communication does not easily replace face-to-face contact, although this is possible in distance learning courses, but the great advantage of asynchronous learning is that it can offer a new level and approach to higher education teaching and learning that widens the scope and appeal of learning and increases the breadth of the learning experience for the majority of students.

As new technology becomes increasingly available, online learning looks like assisting in widening access to different social groups, because it aids considerably both the distance and part-time forms of learning. It can reduce travel and time costs while maintaining the quality of content and learning for these types of students. There are increased opportunities to contribute for some students who do not normally find traditional face-to-face environments conducive to participation.

Similarly, it enhances student autonomy via its preference for self-directed and experiential learning, where the learner has more direct control over the pace and use of self in learning activities. Students are taught to be less dependent on the teacher and to make their judgements about the source of materials and how these can be put to use. The academic has less direct control of students and their experience of educational provision. Online learning can assist the constructivist turn in higher education.

There is the added value of the gain in technological and online skills developed while taking part in online learning. Online learning promotes an extraordinary gateway to information sources that continues to grow rapidly. The learner has ease of access and the ability to make autonomous judgements about what information to use and develop. There is an added value here of the development of information and knowledge management skills that are highly transferable in the knowledge economy.

Online learning methods also encourage a new type of creativity in terms of the design of materials and application of related software. These skills, when required of students in the online environment are also highly transferable in the new media and ICT age.

There are many positive aspects with regard to the quality of learning processes and interfaces when online learning is used. Materials are usually much more transparent and shared than in the traditional lecture hall mode. Online learning through the use of ICT does much to promote a higher quality of learning materials and learning exercises. Online learning offers a wide range of creative medium and opportunities. Materials can easily be seen by colleagues and this can also promote shared learning and shared use of materials. It can encourage a more collectivist approach to teaching and a stronger local academic community.

A number of advantages can be identified with online learning when it comes to assessment strategies. Online learning provides excellent formative assessment tools whereby academics can easily be up to date and appraised of the realities of learning and the pace of development experienced by their current students. It can also be useful with integrated summative assessment methods, where students need a clear structure and purpose for project work and similar portfolio approaches.

Online learning may be more a phase transition than a revolution, but the rapid growth of electronic information on the Internet is exponential. Changes of such quantity do not necessarily lead easily to qualitative change. The prediction that e-books would replace hard copies now looks unlikely. Indeed, the fall in publishing costs, with small runs of specialized publications, seems to be increasing the number of books published each year, not reducing them. Nevertheless there is a rapidly growing amount of quality electronic material available for academics and students, and signs that the journal industry will increasingly move to electronic dissemination. Newspaper editors are also grappling with reductions in circulation while their web-site hits increase. Good quality news and information web sites are becoming an increasingly popular mode of receiving news.

Even if one decides that the idea that online learning would drive the closure of traditional universities was seriously over-hyped, the information revolution looks real enough. More and more information is in digital form, rather than solely available on paper. The management of all this new electronic information is a formidable challenge to the higher education sector, given that its bread-and-butter existence is the use of information to develop knowledge in its various forms. But the knowledge abstraction activities that follow from the availability of information will not necessarily have to be undertaken online. 'Face to face' will still have its place, but online learning will also become a key medium for managing all this information and helping to create and refine it into knowledge.

> Too much emphasis has been put on the delivery of materials and using that to define e-learning. There should be a much broader approach. Far more important than the on-line delivery of materials is the use of communication systems to underpin learner encourage-ment, care and motivation. We are only at the start of the way in which ICT can enrich the tutor/learner transactions and learner/learner transactions.
>
> (Mauger 2002: 11)

When taking part in online learning, students and academics are at the forefront of a new world of using information to construct knowledge. The use of information has always been central to the higher education mission, but it is now undergoing a sea change, driven in large part by technology. This gives students more direct and immediate access to information but does not guarantee that they will have the ability to formulate it into knowledge. Academics are anxious about students misusing information from the Internet and not learning appropriately from it. Academics will indeed continue to play a very central role in helping to steer students through this new information world to form useful knowledge outcomes. Much of the historical learning process is similar, but the activity has entered a new and exciting phase where the potential for the student to be more proactive is real. Knowledge constructs and their applications may be renewed more rapidly than in the past and academics will be daunted by this large flow of information and their students' use of it.

The online environment is here to stay and with it come some new and exciting challenges for higher education. Academics will play a key role in assisting students in developing the skills to effectively search, critically evaluate and assimilate information and acquire knowledge for a later application. They will help students to use analytical interpretative processes which challenge or change their understanding of subjectivity and objective epistemologies, and abstract the meaning and relevance of this knowledge for application to specific and differentiated contexts. This will further strengthen the higher education community's confident tradition of critical reflection about how knowledge is used to create a better and more productive world.

Glossary

Asynchronous Communication that does not all happen in the same time or place, but over a period of time.

Bandwith The capacity of a network service.

Blended learning This refers to a mixture of traditional face-to-face learning concurrent with the use of online learning (sometimes called augmented learning or hybrid learning).

Broadband The capacity of an Internet network. Broadband represents a significant improvement in bandwidth, so that larger files can be transferred at greater speed because the total network has improved capacity. Connections to broadband are always available and do not have to be dialled.

Browser A piece of software that displays HTML code, so that web pages can be displayed on a hardware device such as a PC, laptop, PDA or mobile phone.

Digital A system that uses binary numbers for the storage of information. Digital information is of higher quality because it is subject to less interference and distortions when compared with other audio and visual information systems.

Hyper Text Mark-up Language (HTML) This is the program language that dictates the Internet and World Wide Web. HTML code specifies how text and images will appear in browser software. Different versions of browsers may interpret and present the code slightly differently.

Hyperlink A link in an HTML document that either leads the reader to somewhere else in the same document (an anchor) or to a different page elsewhere on the computer network.

Internet The global connection of computers via interlinked networks across the World Wide Web.

Managed learning environment (MLE) Like a VLE, this is a single platform and gateway that connects students and academics to a network of ICT that can be used for learning materials and activities. In addition a MLE offers, where appropriate, links to other platforms such as student and university records.

Microprocessor   An tiny eletronic and digitial computer component that includes micro transistors and a semiconductor integrated circuit. It is at the core of comptuer hardware devices and is an invention that promoted much of the information revolution.

Multimedia   A computer file or similar that communicates a variety of types of information and media including text, audio and still and moving images.

Online   When a computer, or similar hardware device, is connected to a network, allowing it to communicate with potentially very large numbers of other computers.

Online learning   The idea that interactive education can take place via a sophisticated network of computers.

Platforms   A hardware framework on which network systems, or similar, are run.

Portable document format (PDF)   This is a common text file format now widely used in the publishing industry and on the Internet.

Search engine   A web-site directory that specializes in directing people to other web sites and allows them to search millions of other web sites for suitable specialist material.

Synchronous   Communication that occurs at the same time.

Uniform Resource Locator (URL)   This is a web address: a text code that when entered into a browser will take the user to a specific web site. An example is http://www.google.com

Virtual   A place that does not physically exist, but that exists on a computer network.

Virtual learning environment (VLE)   A single platform and gateway that connects a student and academic to a network of ICT that can be used for learning materials and activities.

Web cam   A small and inexpensive camera that is portable and easy to use that can be connected to a hardware device such as a PC and laptop. It allows asynchronous network communication on the World Wide Web, to show simple video footage of the person using the computer and sending messages. Web cams can also be used to show running footage of a fixed place, such as tourist location or a place where there are issues of security.

Wireless network   Computer network communication or similar that does not need physical wires, but that can operate via radio transmission.

Bibliography

Adam, S. (2004) Using learning outcomes, *UK Bologna Seminar*, Vol. 2005, Heriott-Watts University, Edinburgh. Available at www.bologna–edinburgh2004.org.uk/library

Alexander, B. (2006) Web 2.0: A new wave of innovation for teaching and learning? *EDUCAUSE Review*, 41(2): 33–44. Available at www.educause.edu/

Allen, I.E. and Seaman, J. (2005) *Growing by Degrees: Online Education in the United States, 2005*, Olin and Babson, Sloan Consortium. Available at www.sloan-c.org/resources/survey.asp

Argetsinger, A. (2001) Technology exposes cheating at U-Va, *Washington Post*- 9 May, p. A01. Available at www.washingtonpost.com

Barker, K. (2002) Canadian recommended e-learning guidelines (CanRegs). Available at www.futured.com/

Baty, P. (2003) Virt-u dies with nothing to show but cheap porn, *Times Higher Education Supplement*. Available at www.tes.co.uk/

Baty, P. (2005) Kingston bursting, says QAA, *Times Higher Education Supplement*, August.

Beaty, L., Hodgson, V., Mann, S. and McConnel, D. (2002) Understanding the implications of networked learning for higher education, *ESRC Seminar Series, Dissemination Event*, University of Sheffield, UK.

Becher, T. and Trowler, P.R. (2001) *Academic Tribes and Territories*. Buckingham: Open University Press.

Bell, D. (1999) *The Coming of the Post-Industrial Society*, special anniversary edn. New York: Basic Books.

Bernard, R.M., de Rubalcava, B.R. and St Pierre, D. (2000) Collaborative online distance learning: issues for future practice and research, *Distance Education*, 21(2): 260–77.

Biggs, J. (1999) *Teaching for Quality Learning at University*. Buckingham: Open University Press.

Blake, N. (2000) Tutors and students without faces or places, in N. Blake and P. Standish (eds) *Enquiries at the Interface: Philosophical Problems of Online Education*. Oxford: Blackwell.

Blake, N. and Standish, P. (eds) (2000) *Enquiries at the Interface: Philosophical Problems of Online Education*. Oxford: Blackwell.

Bligh, D. (2002) *What's the Use of Lectures?* 5th edn. Bristol: Intellect Books.

Bonwell, C.C. and Eison, J.A. (1991) Active learning: creating excitement in the classroom, *ERIC Digest*, ED340272. Available at www.ericdigests.org/1992–4/active.htm

Bostock, S.J. (1998) Constructivism in mass higher education: a case study, *British Journal of Educational Technology*, 29(3): 225–40.

Boud, D. (1995) Assessment and learning: contradictory or complimentary? in P. Knight (ed.) *Assessment for Learning in Higher Education*. London: Kogan Page.

Bourne, J.R., McMaster, E., Rieger, J. and Campbell, J.O. (1997) Paradigms for on-line learning: a case study in the design and implementation of an asynchronous learning networks (ALN) course, *Journal of Asynchronous Learning Networks*, 1(2): 38–56.

Bradley, H., Erickson, M., Stephenson, C. and Williamson, S. (2000) *Myths at Work*. Cambridge: Polity Press.

British Learning Association (2001) 10 steps to getting started in e-learning, Leitchworth: BAOL. Available at www.baol.co.uk

Brown, J.S. (2000) Growing up digital: how the web changes work, education, and the ways people learn, *Change*, March–April, pp.11–20.

Brown, J.S. and Duguid, P. (2000) *The Social Life of Information*. Boston, MA: Harvard Business School Press.

Bruce, B. (1999) Education online: learning anywhere, anytime, *Journal of Adolescent and Adult Literacy*, 42(8): 662–65.

Bruce, B.C. (2000) 'Credibility of the web: why we need dialectical reading', in N. Blake and P. Standish (eds) *Enquiries at the Interface: Philosophical Problems of Online Education*. Qxford: Blackwell.

Buczinski, J.A. (2005) Using information retrieval technology to combat IT mediated plagiarism, *Internet Reference Services Quarterly*, 10(2): 95–9.

Cann, A.J. (1999) Approaches to the evaluation of online learning materials, *Innovation in Education and Teaching International*, 36(1): 44–52.

Castells, M. (1996) *The Rise of the Network Society*, Vol. 1. Cambridge, MA: Blackwell.

Clarke, J. and Newman, J. (1997) *The Managerial State*. London: Sage.

Cole, G. (2005) Pocket power, *Times Educational Supplement Online*, 7 January.

Cowan, J. (1998) *On Becoming an Innovative University Teacher: Reflection in Action*. Buckingham: Open University Press.

Creswell, J.W. (1998) *Interpretive Inquiry and Research Design: Choosing among Five Traditions*. Thousand Oaks, CA: Sage Publications.

Cross, K.P. (1998) Why learning communities? Why now? *About Campus*, 3(3): 4–11.

Csikszentmihlayi, M. and Robinson, R.E. (1990) *The Art of Seeing: An Interpretation of the Aesthetic Encounter*. Los Angeles, CA: J. Paul Getty Museum.

Currant, N., Higgison, C. and Murray, C. (2006) Learners' experiences of using e-Portfolios (eP) in raising aspirations for higher education and supporting their transition into HE. Paper presented to the JISC UK Innovating e-learning conference (online), 27 March.

CVCP and HEFCE (Committee of Vice-Chancellors and Principals and Higher Education Funding Council for England) (2000) *The Business of Borderless Education: UK Perspectives*. Warwick: CVCP.

Daniel, J.S. (1996) *Mega-Universties and Knowledge Media: Technology Strategies for Higher Education*. London: Kogan Page.

De la Harpe, B. and Radloff, A. (2001) The importance of lecturer conceptions of teaching and learning for facilitating student learning online, Improving Student Learning Symposium, Edinburgh, September.

Dearing, R. (1997) *Report of the National Committee of Inquiry into Higher Education.* London: HMSO.

(*DfES*) Department for Education and Skills (2002) Young people and ICT. Available at www.dfes.gov.uk/research/data/uploadfiles/ACF2AB1.pdf

Dick, B. (1997) Action learning and action research. Available at www.scu.edu.au/schools/gcm/ar/arp/actlearn.html

Disability Rights Commission (2004) *The Web: Access and Inclusion for Disabled People.* London: TSO.

Dixon, K., Pelliccione, L. and Dixon, R. (2005) Differing student views of online learning modes across two programs in an Australian university, *Campus-Wide Information Systems*, 22(3): 140–7.

Donabedian, A. (2003) *An Introduction to Quality Assurance in Health Care.* Oxford: Oxford University Press.

Downes, S. (2005) E-learning 2.0, *eLearn Magazine*, 17 October. Available at http://elearnmag.org/

Drennan, J., Kennedy, J. and Pisarski, A. (2005) Factors affecting student attitudes toward flexible online learning in management education, *Journal of Educational Research*, 98(6): 331–8.

Edwards, R., Raggatt, P., Harrison, R., McCollum, A. and Calder, J. (1998) *Recent Thinking in Lifelong Learning – A Review of the Literature.* Sudbury: DfEE.

Eurostat (2002) *The Social Situation in the European Union 2002.* Brussels: European Commission.

Finch, J. (2006) HMV boss is first victim as internet price war batters the high street, *Guardian*, 13 January. Available at www.guardian.co.uk/

Fuchs, T. and Woessmann, L. (2004) Computers and student learning: bivariate and multivariate evidence on the availability and use of computers at home and at school, *Brussels Economic Review*, 47(3–4): 359–85.

Fuchs, T. and Woessmann, L. (2005) Computers and student learning, Royal Economic Society's 2005 Annual Conference, University of Nottingham, UK. Available at www.res.org.uk/econometrics/504.pdf

Furedi, F. (2002) Why I think consistency is not always a virtue, *Times Higher Education Supplement*, 5 July.

Furedi, F. (2005) You'd better make some noise while you can? *Times Higher Education Supplement*, 11 February.

Gagné, R.M. (1985) *The Conditions of Learning and Theory of Instruction*, 4th edn. London and New York: Holt, Rinehart and Winston.

Gagné, R.M., Briggs, L.J. and Wager, W.W. (1992) *Principles of Instructional Design*, 4th edn. Fort Worth, TX: Holt, Rinehart and Winston.

Garrison, D.R. and Anderson, T. (2003) *Online Learning in the 21st Century: A Framework for Research and Practice.* London: Routledge Falmer.

George, P. L. (1999) Assessing student perceptions of Internet-based online learning environments, *International Journal of Instructional Media*, 26(4): 397.

Gibbs, G. (1999) Using assessment strategically to change the way students learn, in S. Brown and A. Glasner (eds) *Assessment Matters in Higher Education: Choosing and Using Diverse Approaches.* Buckingham: Society for Research into Higher Education/Open University Press.

Gibson, O. (2005) Gates unveils his vision of a future made of silicon, *Guardian*, 28 October. Available at www.guardian.co.uk/

Glass, A., Higgins, K. and McGregor, A. (2002) *Delivering Work Based Learning Training and Employment Research Unit.* Glasgow: University of Glasgow Scottish Executive Central Research Unit.

Goodfellow, R. and Lea, M. (2005) Supporting writing for assessment in online learning, *Assessment and Evaluation in Higher Education*, 30(3): 261–71.

Hanson, J. (2002) Staff development for ICT and e-Learning: skills or pedagogy? Available at www.ltsn.ac.uk/genericcentre

Harasim, L. (ed.) (1990) *Online Education. Perspectives on a New Environment.* New York: Praeger.

Harris, M. (1996) *Higher Education Funding Council for England Committee of Vice-Chancellors and Principals Standing Conference of Principals Review of Postgraduate Education (Reference M 14/96).* London: HEFCE.

Haynes, P. (2005) Demystifying knowledge management for the public services, *Public Money and Management*, 25(2): 131–5.

Haynes, P., Ip, K., Saintas, P. et al. (2004) Responding to technological change: IT skills and the academic teaching profession, *Active Learning in Higher Education*, 5(2): 152–65.

Heathcote, E. (2006) Learning design templates – a pedagogical just-in-time support tool. Paper presented to the JISC UK Innovating e-learning conference, 27 March.

HEFCE (Higher Education Funding Council for England) (1999) *Communications and Information Technology Materials for Learning and Teaching in UK Higher and Further Education.* Bristol: HEFCE. Available at www.hefce.ac.uk/pubs/1999/99

HEFCE (Higher Education Funding Council for England) (2001) *Strategies for Widening Participation in Higher Education: A Good Practice guide. 01/36.* Bristol: HEFCE.

Henley Centre (2001) *The Second Internet Age: Online Culture.* London: Consignia.

Henry, J. (1994) Managing experiential learning: the learner's perspective, in N. Graves (ed.) *Learner Managed Learning: Practice, Theory and Policy.* London: Routledge.

HEQC (Higher Education Quality Council) (1997) *Managing Quality Standards in UK Higher Education: Approaches to Self-Evaluation.* London: HEQC.

Hilton, J. (2006) The future for higher education: sunrise or perfect storm? *EDUCAUSE*, 41(2): 59–71.

Hodson, P. and Thomas, H. (2003) Quality assurance in higher education: fit for the new millennium or simply year 2000 compliant? *Higher Education*, 45(3): 375–87.

Hoernes, P. and Wallen, G. (2003) *We can Build It: Developing Responsible Web-based Health Care Education for the Public.* Bethseda: Department of Health and Human Services, National Institutes of Health.

Honey, P. and Mumford, A. (1992) *The Manual of Learning Styles.* Maidenhead: Peter Honey.

Hope, A. (2001) Quality assurance, in G. Farrell (ed.) *The Changing Faces of Virtual Education.* Vancouver: Commonwealth of Learning.

Howarth, N. (2004) Motivating the individual at the core of learning, *Inside Learning Technologies*, December. Available at www.learningtechnologies.co.uk

Hrachovec, H. (2000) Electronic texts are computations are electronic texts, in N. Blake and P. Standish (eds) *Enquiries at the Interface: Philosophical Problems of Online Education.* Oxford: Blackwell.

Hughes, O. (2005) *Public Management and Administration*, 3rd edn. London: Macmillan.

Humphrey, R.M.P. (1997) High debt and poor housing: a taxing life for contemporary students, *Youth and Policy*, 56 (Spring): 55–63.

Hurst, J. and Quinsee, S. (2004) A quality framework for producing clinically competent nurses through distance education, *European Journal of Open, Distance and E-Learning*. Available at www.eurodl.org/materials/contrib/2004/Hurst_Quinsee.htm.

Huxham, M. (2005) Learning in lectures: do interactive windows help? *Active Learning in Higher Education*, 6(1) 17–31.

JISC (Joint Information Systems Committee) (1996) *Five Year Strategy 1996–2001*. Available at www.jisc.ac.uk

JISC (Joint Information Systems Committee) (2002) MLEs and VLEs explained, Briefing Paper No. 1, *JISC MLE Information (Briefing) Pack*. Available at www.jisc.ac.uk/uploaded_documents/bp1.pdf

JISC (Joint Information Systems Committee) (2005a) Vision and infrastructure: changing to a wireless world, *Innovative Practice with e-Learning – Case Studies*. Available at www.jisc.ac.uk/

JISC (Joint Information Systems Committee) (2005b) *Learning and Teaching: Issues Standards*. Available at www.jisc.ac.uk/

JISC (Joint Information Systems Committee) (2006) *Designing Spaces for Effective Learning: A Guide to 21st Century Learning Space Design*. Available at www.jisc.ac.uk/

JISC (Joint Information Systems Committee) e-Learning and Pedagogy Team (2004) *Effective Practice with e-Learning: A Good Practice Guide in Designing for Learning*. Bristol: Higher Education Funding Council for England.

Jobbins, D. (2005) From add-on to necessity, *Times Higher Education Supplement*, ICT in Higher Education(6): 14–15.

Juwah, C.I. (2002) Using information and communication technology to support problem based learning: a commissioned article by the Institute for Learning and Teaching in Higher Education (ILTHE). Available at www.ilt.ac.uk/

Kearsley, G. (2002) Is online learning for everybody? *Educational Technology*, 42(1): 41–4.

Keller, J.M. and Dodge, B. (1982) *The ARCS Model of Motivational Strategies for Course Designers and Developers*. Fort Montrose, VA: Training and Developments Institute.

Khan, B. (2000) A framework for e-learning, *Distance Education Report*, 15 December.

Kirkpatrick, G. (2005) Online chat facilities as pedagogic tools, *Active Learning in Higher Education*, 6(2): 145–59.

Knowles, M. (1980) *The Modern Practice of Adult Education*. Chicago: Association Press.

Knowles, M.S. et al. (1984) *Andragogy in Action: Applying Modern Principles of Adult Education*. San Francisco, CA: Jossey-Bass.

Knowles, M.S., Holton, E.F. and Swanson, R.A. (1998) *The Adult Learner*, 5th edn. Woburn, MA: Butterworth-Heineman.

Kolb, D. (2000) Learning places: building dwelling thinking online, in N. Blake and P. Standish (eds) *Enquiries at the Interface: Philosophical Problems of Online Education*. Oxford: Blackwell.

Kukulska-Hulme, A., Evans, D. and Traxler, J. (2005) *Landscape Study in Wireless and Mobile Learning in the Post-16 Sector – Summary*, May. Available at www.jisc.ac.uk/

Lankshear, C., Peters, M. and Knobel, M. (2000) Information, knowledge and learning: some issues of epistemology and education in a digital age, in N. Blake and P. Standish (eds) *Enquiries at the Interface: Philosophical Problems of Online Education*. Oxford: Blackwell.

Laughton, D. (2003) 'Why was the QAA approach to teaching quality assessment rejected by academics in the UK HE? *Assessment and Evaluation in Higher Education*, 28(3): 309–21.

Laurillard, D. (1987) The different types of learning in psychology and education, in J.T.E. Richardson, M.W. Eysenck and D.W. Piper (eds) *Student Learning: Research in Education and Cognitive Psychology*. Milton Keynes: Open University Press.

Laurillard, D. (2002) *Rethinking University Teaching: A Conversational Framework for the Effective Use of Learning Technologies*, 2nd edn. London: Routledge.

Leon, P. (2004) Wireless warnings, *Times Higher Education Supplement*, 30 April. Available at www.tes.co.uk/

Leopold-Lusmann, B.D. (2000) Virtual learning environments and student learning styles, *International Online Seminar: Teaching and Studying in Virtual Learning Environments*. Available at http://seminar.jura.uni-sb.de/

Lewis, D. and Allan, B. (2005) *Virtual Learning Communities: A Guide for Practitioners*. Maidenhead: Open University Press.

Lieblein, E. (2000) Critical factors for successful delivery of online programs, *Internet and Higher Education*, 3(3): 161–74.

Lipsky, M. (1980) *Street-level Bureaucracy: Dilemmas of the Individual in Public Services*. New York: Russell Sage Foundation.

Lyotard, J.F. (1984) *The Post-Modern Condition: A Report on Knowledge*. Minneapolis, MN: University of Minnesota Press.

Maier, P. and Warren, A. (2000) *Integrating Technology in Learning and Teaching: A practical guide for educators*. London: Kogan Page.

Marton, F. and Saljo, R. (1997) 'Approaches to Learning', in F. Marton, D. Hounsell and N.J. Entwistle (eds) *The Experience of Learning*. Edinburgh: Scottish Academic Press.

Mason, R. (1998) Models of online courses, *Asynchronous Learning Networks*, 2(2). Available at www.aln.org/publications/magazine/v2n2/mason.asp

Mauger, S. (2002) E-learning is about people not technology, *Adults Learning*, 13(7): 9–11.

McCrum, R. (2006) E-read all about it, *Observer*, 15 January.

McDonald, J. (2002) Is 'As good as face to face' as good as it gets? *Journal of Asynchronous Learning – Special Issue on Nursing*, 6(2).

McKie, J. (2000) Conjuring notions of place, in N. Blake and P. Standish (eds) *Enquiries at the Interface: Philosophical Problems of Online Education*. Oxford: Blackwell.

Mezirow, J. (1978) Perspective transformation, *Adult Education*, 28(2): 100–10.

Mezirow, J. (1991) *Transformative Dimensions of Adult Learning*. San Francisco, CA: Jossey-Bass.

Modern Languages Association (1977) *Handbook for Writers of Research Papers, Theses and Dissertation*. New York: Modern Languages Association.

Moon, J. (2004) Linking levels, learning assessment and assessment criteria, *UK Bologna Seminar*, Heriot-Watts University, Edinburgh. Available at www.bologna–edinburgh2004.org.uk/

Moore, G. (1999) *Crossing the Chasm: Marketing and Selling High-Tech Products to Mainstream Customers*, 2nd edn. New York: HarperCollins.

Moos, R.H. (1974) *The Social Scales: An Overview*. Palo Alto, CA: Consulting Psychologist's Press.

Morgan, C. and Murgatroyd, S. (1994) *Total Quality in the Pubic Sector: An International Perspective*. Buckingham: Open University Press.

MORI (Market and Opinion Research Institute) (2002) *Clicking with Confidence?* London: MORI. Available at www.mori.com/

MORI (Market and Opinion Research Institute) (2004) *eMORI Technology Tracker.* Available at www.mori.com/

Morkes, J. and Nielsen, J. (1997) Concise, SCANNABLE, and objective: how to write for the web. Available at www.useit.com/papers/webwriting/writing.html

Muirhead, B. (2004) Research insights into interactivity, *International Journal of Instructional Technology and Distance Learning,* 1(3). Available at www.itdl.org/Journal/Mar_04/article05.htm

Muirhead, B. and Juwah, C. (2004) Interactivity in computer-mediated college and university education: a recent review of the literature, *Educational Technology & Society,* 7(1): 12–20.

Nielsen, J. (1999) *Designing Web Usability: The Practice of Simplicity.* Indianapolis, IN: New Riders Press.

Nielsen, J. (2001) *E Learning Post,* 16 January. Available at www.elearningpost.com/features/archives/001015.asp

Noble, D.F. (1999) Digital diploma mills. Available at www.firstmonday.org/issues/issue3_/noble/index.htm

Nunes, M.B. and McPherson, M. (2003) New tutoring skills for online learning: a constructive view, in V. Uskov (eds) Proceedings of *IASTED Computers and Advanced Technology in Education International Conference.* Greece: Acta Press.

O'Leary, R. (2002) Virtual learning environments. Available at www.ltsn.ac.uk/genericcentre

Oblinger, D.G. and Hawkins, B.L. (2006) The myth about online course development, *EDUCAUSE Review,* January/February, 1. Available at www.educause.edu

Open and Distance Learning Quality Council (2000) Standards for open and distance learning outcomes. Available at www.odlqc.org.uk/index.htm

OECD (Organisation for Economic Co-operation and Development) (2001) *The Hidden Threat to E-government: Avoiding Large Government IT Failures. PUMA Policy Brief No 8.* Paris: OECD.

Osborne, D. and Gaebler, T. (1992) *Reinventing Government: How the Entrepreneurial Spirit is Transforming the Public Sector.* New York: Penguin.

Palloff, R.M. and Pratt, K. (1999) *Building Learning Communities in Cyberspace: Effective Strategies for the Online Classroom.* San Francisco: Jossey-Bass.

Palloff, R.M. and Pratt, K. (2001) *Lesson from Cyberspace Classroom: The Realities of Online Teaching.* San Francisco: Jossey-Bass.

Panitz, T. and Panitz, P. (1998) Encouraging the use of collaborative education in higher education university teaching: international perspectives, in J.F. Forest (ed.) *University Teaching: International Perspectives.* New York: Garland.

Parlett, M. and Dearden, G. (eds) (1977) *Introduction to Illuminative Education: Studies in Higher Education.* Cardiff-by-the-Sea, CA: Pacific Soundings Press.

Parlett, M. and Hamilton, D. (1972) Evaluation as illumination: a new approach to the study of innovatory programmes, *Centre for Research in the Educational Sciences.* Edinburgh: University of Edinburgh.

Pawson, R. and Tilley, N. (1997) *Realistic Evaluation.* London: Sage.

Paz Dennen, V. (2000) Task structuring for on-line problem based learning: a case study *Educational Technology and Society,* 3(3): 329–35.

Pearson, I. and Winter, C. (1999) *Where's IT Going?* New York: Thames and Hudson.

Pena-Shaff, J., Altman, W. and Stephenson, H. (2005) Asynchronous online discussions as a tool for learning: students' attitudes, expectations, and perceptions, *Journal of Interactive Learning Research,* 16(4): 409–30.

Pettigrew, M. and Elliott, D. (1999) *Student IT skills.* Aldershot: Gower.

Pritchard, A. (2004) Introducing new students to ICT: giving a purpose to it all, *Active Learning in Higher Education*, 5(3): 248–62.

Quality Assurance Agency for Higher Education (QAA) (1999) Guidelines on the quality assurance of distance learning. Available at www.qaa.ac.uk/public/dlg/contents.htm

Race, P. (1999) *2000 Tips for Lecturers*. London: Kogan Page.

Ragan, T.L. and White, P.R. (2001) What we have is a failure to communicate: the criticality of writing online instruction, *Computers and Composition*, 18(4): 399–409.

Randall, J. (2001) Defining standards: developing a global currency for higher education qualifications. Paper presented at 6th biennial conference of the International Network for Quality Assurance Agencies in Higher Education, 21 March, Bangalore, India.

Rekkedal, T. (1994) *Research in Distance Learning Education – Past, Present and Future*. Norway: NKI Distance Education. Available at www.nettskolen.com/pub/

Rezabek, R. (2000) Online focus groups: electronic discussions for research, *Qualitative Social Research*, 1(1). Available at www.qualitative-research.net/fqs-texte/1-00/1-00rezabek-e.htm

Rhodes, F. (2001) *The Creation of the Future: The Role of the American University*. Ithaca, NY: Cornell University Press.

Roffe, I. (2002) E-learning: engagement, enhancement and execution, *Quality Assurance in Education*, 10(1): 40–50.

Rogers, C.R. (1983) *Freedom to Learn for the 1980s*. New York: Merrill.

Rosie, A. (2000) Online pedagogies and the promotion of 'deep learning', *Information Services and Use*, 20(2–3): 109–16.

Russell, T. (1999) *The No Significant Difference Phenomenon*. Montgomery, AL: International Distance Education Certification Center.

Ryan, S., Scott, B., Freeman, H. and Patel, H. (2000) *The Virtual University: The Internet and Resource Based Learning*. London: Kogan Page.

Salmon, G. (2002) *e-Tivities – The Key to Active Online Learning*. London: Taylor and Francis, Routledge.

Salmon, G. (2004) *e-Moderating – The Key to Teaching and Learning Online*, 2nd edn. London: Taylor and Francis, Routledge.

Savin-Baden, M. (2000) *Problem-based Learning in Higher Education: Untold Stories*. Buckingham: SRHE/Open University Press.

Scott, P. (1995) *The Meanings of Mass Higher Education*. Buckingham: Open University Press.

Scriven, M. (1967) The methodology of evaluation, in R.W. Tyler (ed.) *Perspectives of Curriculum Evaluation*. Chicago, IL: Rand McNally.

Segal, B. (1995) A short history of Internet protocols at CERN. Available at http://.ben.home.cern.ch/

Shepherd, J. (2006) 1 in 6 admits cheating, *Times Higher Education Supplement*, 5 May. Available at www.thes.co.uk/

Sims, R., Dobbs, G. and Hand, T. (2002) Enhancing quality in online learning: scaffolding planning and design through proactive evaluation, *Distance Education*, 23(2): 135–48.

Smith, D. (2006) E Ink, *Observer*, 15 January.

Sosabowski, M.H., Herson, K. and Lloyd, A.W. (1998) Identifying and overcoming staff resistance to computer based learning and teaching methods: shedding millstones to achieve milestones, *Active Learning*, 9: 26–30.

Standish, P. (2000) Fetish for effect, in N. Blake and P. Standish (eds) *Enquiries at the Interface: Philosophical Problems of Online Education.* Oxford: Blackwell.

Stiglitz, J. (2002) *Globalization and its Discontents.* London: Penguin.

Sutherland, J. (2005) Ivory towers will fall to digital land grab, *Guardian,* 4 November.

Szabo, A. and Underwood, J. (2004) Cybercheats: is information and communication technology fuelling academic dishonesty? *Active Learning in Higher Education,* 5(2): 180–99.

Tait, A. (1998) Guidance and counselling in the Open University, in M. Crawford, R. Edwards and L. Kydd (eds) *Taking Issue: Debates in Guidance and Counselling in Learning.* London: Routledge.

Tam, M. (2000) Constructivism, instructional design and technology: Implications for transforming distance learning, *Educational Technology and Society,* 3(2): 50–60.

Tarafdar, M. and Zhang, J. (2005) Analyzing the influence of web site design parameters on web site usability, *Information Resources Management Journal,* 18(4): 62–80.

Taylor, D. (2005) Governing through evidence: participation and power in policy evaluation, *Journal of Social Policy,* 34(4): 601–18.

Taynton, Y. (2000) Online learning: a student perspective, ASCILITE 2000 Conference. Southern Cross University, 10–12 December. Available at http://ascilite.org.au/conferences/coffs00/

Terrell, S.R. (2005) A longitudinal investigation of the effect of information perception and focus on attrition in online learning environments, *Internet and Higher Education,* 8(3): 213–19.

Testone, S. (1999) On-line courses: a comparison of two vastly different experiences, *Research and Teaching in Developmental Education,* 16(1): 93–7.

Tett, L., Crowther, J. and O'Hara, P. (1998) Collaborative partnerships in community education, *Journal of Education Policy,* 18(1): 37–51.

Thiele, J.E. (2003) Learning patterns of online students, *Journal of Nursing Education,* 42(8): 364–6.

Thorpe, M. (2000) Online learning – not just an e-university idea, *Adults Learning,* April, pp.11–12.

Tomes, N. and Higgison, C. (1998) *Exploring the Network for Teaching and Learning in Scottish Higher Education. TALiSMAN Training Needs Analysis: A Report to the Scottish Higher Education Funding Council.* Edinburgh: Scottish Higher Education Funding Council.

Ulmer, G.L. (1985) The object of post-criticism, in H. Foster (ed) *Post-Modern Culture.* London: Pluto Press.

Urry, J. (2003) *Global Complexity.* Cambridge: Polity Press.

Watson, D. (2000) *Managing Strategy.* Buckingham: Open University Press.

Web-Based Education Commission (2000) *The Power of the Internet for Learning: Moving from Promise to Practice. Report of the Web-Based Education Commission to the President and the Congress of the United States.* Washington, DC: Web-Based Education Commission.

Wenger, E. (1998) *Communities of Practice: Learning, Meaning and Identity.* Cambridge: Cambridge University Press.

White, K.W. and Weight, B.H. (2000) *The Online Teaching Guide: A Handbook of Attitudes, Strategies and Techniques for the Virtual Classroom.* Needham Heights, MA: Allyn and Bacon.

Wild, M. (1996) Technology refusal: rationalising the fear of student and beginning teachers to use technology, *British Journal of Educational Technology*, 27: 134–43.

Williams, M. (2001) E-commerce inquiry to business 2000, *Economic Trends*, July, 572: 29–36.

Winn, S. and Stevenson, R. (1997) Student loans: are the policy objectives being achieved? *Higher Education Quarterly*, 51(2): 144–63.

Winter, R. (2003) Alternative to the essay, *Guardian*, 10 June.

Woodward, H. and Nanlohy, P. (2004) Digital portfolios: fact or fashion? *Assessment & Evaluation in Higher Education*, 29(2): 227–38.

Wray, R. (2005) Wellcome boost for open access, *Guardian*, 15 December.

Young, P. (2004) The patchwork – an alternative form of assessment for social policy, *SWAPltsn news*, Spring, 6.

Zywno, M.S. and Stewart, M.F. (2005) Learning styles of engineering students, online learning objects and achievement, *ASEE Annual Conference and Exposition, Conference Proceedings*, Portland, Oregon, 12–15 June.

Index

academics
  attitude towards ICT, 54–6, *56*
  ICT proficiency, 150–52, *151*
  role in online learning, 63–4, 78, 152–3
  see also tutors
action learning
  value to online learning, 137–8
activities, learning
  design of, 119–20, *120*, 161–5, *162*,
    164
Adam, S., 79
adult learning
  characteristics and theories, 49–50,
    173–7
Allan, B., 99
Allen, I., 27
America On Line, 11
Analysis
  analytical, 167, *168*
  asynchronous, *170*
Anderson, T., 78, 141
andragogy
  characteristics, 49–50, 173–7
ARCS model of learning motivation, 94
assessment, online learning
  creation of virtual materials, 39
  criteria for, *164*
  impact of new technology, 140–46
assurance, quality
  definition and characteristics, 65–6
  guidelines for online learning, 82–3,
    82, *84–6*
  methods of, 66–7
  pre-requisites for online learning,
    67–8

teaching and learning evaluation,
  59–61
see also indicators, performance;
  outputs and outcomes; standards,
  academic
asynchronous online seminars', 132, *133*
attendance' (virtual learning
  environment)
  role in online learning, 79

Barker, K., *82*
Beaty, L., 50
Bell, D., 182
Berlin Communiqué (2003) (on online
  learning quality assurance), 68
Bernard, R., 33
blended learning', 102, 105, *106–8*
Bligh, D., 124, 137
blogs (internet), 39–40
boards, online
  group discussion, 38–9
  message, 36
British Learning Association, 70–71, *72–5*
Brown, J., 16
Bruce, B., 57
Business of Borderless Education (2000), 23
businesses
  impact of internet, 7

Cann, A., 59–60
capital, social
  impact of internet usage, 8
case studies
  module development team, 150–77,
    151, *159*, *162*, *164*, *167–8*, *170–72*

change, technological
  as driver for online learning, 8–9
  impact on academic roles/attitudes,
    54–6, *56*
charters, student, 76
collaboration
  as means of technology maximisation,
    28–30
Committee of Vice-Chancellors and
  Principals, 23
communication, virtual group *see* blogs;
  boards, online; emails; wikis
communication theory (Haberma), 166
communities, virtual learning
  characteristics, 98–9
communities of practice' (COP)
  (Wenger), 153
computers
  usage impact of new technologies, 8–9
  see also internet; online learning;
    online learning environments
content and support' model of teaching,
  156
co-operation
  as means of technology maximisation,
    28–30
courses, online
  role and development, 22–6
  stages of preparation, *101*
critiquing and searching'
  as learning activity, 163
Cross, K., 98–9
Crossing the Chasm (Moore), 56
Csikszentmihalyi, M., 58
cultures, technological
  challenge within higher education,
    17–19
curriculums
  need for technology resources, 157–8
  role of academics in developing,
    152–3

Daniel, J., 12
Davis, J., 115
Dearing, R., 26–7
deep and surface level' learning, 52
de la Harpe, B., 163
dependency, learning
  trajectory of, *172*
de-professionalization

impact within academe, 54
Disability Discrimination Act (1995), 121
Disability Rights Commission, (DRC),
  121–2
discussion, asynchronous
  case study, 167–9, *168*
discussion boards, group, 38–9
dissertations
  role of online learning, 135–6
distance learning
  role and development, 22–6
documents, storage
  virtual methods, 37–8
Donabedian, A., 65
Dot Life (BBC programme), 115
Disability Rights Commission, (DRC),
  121–2
Dodge, B., 94–6
Drennan, J., 47–8
Duguid, P., 16

E-Learning *see* online learning
e-moderation/moderators
  characteristics and role, 78, 154–5
E-universities
  historical fortunes, 25–6
  quality assurance methods, 66–7
  see also name eg Phoenix
E-University, the (UK), 25
Ealing Further Education College, 18
education *see* learning; teaching
education, higher
  challenge of ICT provision, 14–19
  history (1990s), 9–10, *10*, 12–14
  impact of new technologies, 32–3
  international competition within,
    22–6
  quality assurance within, 66–7
Electronic Learning *see* online learning
Electronic universities
  historical fortunes, 25–6
  quality assurance methods, 66–7
  see also name eg Phoenix
Elliott, D., 19
emails, 40
environments, virtual learning *see* online
  learning environments
European Bologna Process (online
  learning quality assurance), 68
evaluation, online learning

characteristics and criteria, 59–60, *164*
methods, 165
examinations
receptivity to online methods, 141–3

face-to-face' learning
online learning support, 105, *109–11*
facilitation, online learning
tutor roles, 154–5
filing cabinets', online, 37
forums, online discussion, 38–9, 131–5, *133*
frameworks and models
asynchronous analysis, *170*
motivation, 94
quality assurance, 82–3, *82, 84–6*
teaching and learning, 94–6, *95,* 154–61
see also name eg communities of practice'
Freedom to Learn (Rogers), 178
Furedi, F., 140

Gagné, R., 177–8
Garrison, D., 78, 141
Gates, W. (Bill)., 15
Glass, A., 139
globalization
socio-economic influences, 10–11
Goodfellow, R., 145
government and politics
impact of internet, 7–8
groups, discussion
online group discussion boards, 38–9
see also seminars, online
guidelines
online learning quality assurance, 82–3, *82, 84–6*

Haberma J., 166
Hamilton, D., 59
Hanson, J., 55–6
Harris, M., 27
Haynes, P., 150
Heidegger, M., 97–8
Henry, J., 137
higher education *see* education, higher
Higher Education Funding Council of England, 23, 65
Hoernes, P., 165

home pages, 36
Honey, P., 49
Hope, A., 82–3, *82*
Howells, K., 25
Hrachovec, H., 46
Hughes, O., 13

ICT (information and communications technology)
challenges within higher education, 14–19
provision and use, 14–19, 28–40
skill enhancement, 20–22, 150–52, *151*
independent learning
role in online environment, 172–3
indicators, performance, 81
Indira Gandhi National Open University, 67
information, online
quality of, 57
information and communications technology (ICT)
challenges within higher education, 14–19
provision and use, 14–19, 28–40
skill enhancement, 20–22, 150–52, *151*
instruction and instructors
development of techniques, *95,* 154–61, *159,* 163, 165
evaluation of quality, 59–60
impact of new technologies, 127–30
qualities required, 44, 49–50
role in learning experience, 58, 112–13
theories of, 166–77, *167–8, 170–72*
see also andragogy
integrated' model of teaching, 156–7
interactivity (concept)
requirement with online learning, 112–13
International Union of Crystallography, 15
internet
developmental history, 5–8
educational opportunities provided by, 32–3
usage, *6*
see also blogs; home pages; links;

navigation, internet; web pages;
    wikis
Internet 2, 28

Joint Academic Network (JANET), 28
Joint Information System Committee
    (JISC), 15, 28, 68–9, 88
Juwah, C., 94, 112–13

Keller, J., 94–6
Kingston University, 184
knowledge
    impact of ICT on philosophies of,
        50–51
    need for technical knowledge, 157–8
knowledge management
    challenge within higher education,
        16–17
Knowles, M., 49, 173–5, 180
Kolb, D., 47, 97–8

LAMs (learning activity management
    systems), 36
Lankshear, C., 51
Laurillard, D., 47, 124–5, 127, 130, 137,
    154, 162
Lea, M., 145
learning
    development of techniques, 154–61,
        159, 163, 165
    evaluation of quality, 59–60
    impact of ICT on philosophies of,
        50–51
    outputs and outcomes, 79–83, *82*
    planning and process of, 47–9, *50, 93,*
        94–7, *95*
    theories, 166–77, *167–8, 170–72*
    see also curriculums; tutors
    see also methods and levels eg deep and
    surface level'; distance learning; face-
    to-face' learning; independent
    learning
    see also type eg action learning; lifelong
        learning; online learning; total
        learning'
learning, adult
    characteristics and theories, 49–50,
        173–7
learning activity management systems
    (LAMs), 36

learning management systems (LMSs),
    36
lectures
    challenge of online learning, 124–30
Leopold-Lusmann, B., 49
Lewis, D., 99
libraries, online
    need for, 68
Lieblein, E., 160
lifelong learning
    importance of ICT, 52–4
lifestyles, student
    changing nature, 21–2
links (internet), 39
LMSs (learning management systems),
    36
Lyotard, J., 50, 51

MacBrayne, P., 175–6
McCrum, R., 16
McKie, J., 58, 97, 118
management, knowledge
    challenge within higher education,
        16–17
management, time
    importance in online learning design,
        96–7
managerialism, new public
    impact on higher education, 13–14
markets, global
    socio-economic influences, 10–11
markets, higher education
    international competition within,
        22–6
Marton, F., 52
Mason, R., 150, 156
materials, learning
    creation of, 158–61, *159*
Mauger, S., 188
media, educational, *162*
message boards, 36
Metcalfe's Law, 57
Mezirow, J., 174
minimum standards'
    as quality assurance measure, 66
Miniwatts Marketing Group, 5, 11
models and frameworks
    asynchronous analysis, *170*
    motivation, 94
    quality assurance, 82–3, *82, 84–6*

teaching and learning, 94–6, *95*,
  154–61
see also name eg communities of
  practice'
modules, curriculum
  case study of development, 150–77,
    151, 159, 162, 164, 167–8, 170–72
monitoring
  learning quality, 59–60
Moore, G., 56, 57, 152
Moore's Law, 57
Moos, R., 93–4
motivation, learning
  models of, 94
Muirhead, B., 112
multiple choice questions
  receptivity to online methods, 144
Mumford, A., 49

National Committee of Inquiry into
  Higher Education, 26–7
navigation, internet
  design requirements, 118–19
Nielson, J., 114–15, 122
new public managerialism (NPM)
  impact on higher education, 13–14
new technologies *see* technologies, new
Next Generation Internet (NGI), 28
NHS University, 25
Noble, D., 64, 70
NPM (new public managerialism)
  impact on higher education, 13–14

online action learning sets', 162
online learning
  application in adult education
    environment, 174–7
  case study of module development,
    150–77, *151, 159, 162, 164, 167–8,*
    170–72
  challenges of delivery, 40–44, *42,*
    63–4, 99–108, *100, 101, 103–5,*
    106–8
  design and methods of delivery, 77–9,
    108, 111–13, 119–20, *120,* 155–7
  establishment of methods, 70–71,
    72–5
  governmental reviews, 26–8
  history and role, 22–6, 40–41, *41*
  modes and levels of, 33–4, *34*

outputs and outcomes, *82*
  purpose and drivers, 8–9, 70–71
  strengths and weaknesses, 44–7, 183–7
  see also assessment, online learning;
    attendance'; standards, academic
online learning environments
  characteristics and management of,
    71, 75–7, *77*
  content, 116, *117*
  design of, 97–9
  historical development, 35–41, *34, 41*
Open Learning Australia, 26
Open University (UK), 24
Open University of Australia, 26
Open University of Hong Kong, 67
outputs and outcomes, learning
  characteristics, 79–83, *82*
  see also plagiarism; standards,
    academic

Palloff, R., 22, 60
Parlett, M., 59
patchwork [assessment] test', 145–6
peer review, 62–3
personal learning plans' (PLPs), 162
Pettigrew, M., 19
Phoenix University (E-university), 26
plagiarism, 87–90
PLPs (personal learning plans'), 162
politics and government
  impact of internet, 7–8
portfolios, student
  receptivity to online learning, 144–5
post-industrialism
  impact on higher education, 182–3
Pratt, K., 22, 60
presentations, student, 163
Pritchard, A., 169
problem-based learning
  value to online learning, 138–9
projects
  receptivity to online learning, 135–6,
    143–4
public satisfaction'
  as quality assurance measure, 66

quality assurance *see* assurance, quality
Quality Assurance Agency (QAA) for
  Higher Education, 62–3, 65, 140, 184
questions, multiple choice

receptivity to online learning, 144

Radloff, A., 163
Ragan, T., 159
Randall, J., 67–8, 81
Rekkedal, T., 152
resources, learning
   creation of, 158–61, *159*
resources, technical
   curriculum design need, 157–8
review, peer, 62–3
Rezabek, R., 175–7
risk
   role in ICT maximisation, 28–30
Robinson, R., 58
Roffe, I., 64, 68, *69*
Rogers, C., 174, 177–8

Saljo, R., 52
Salmon, G., 78, 111–12, 132, 155, 169
satisfaction', public/user
   quality assurance measure, 66
Scriven, M., 140
Seaman, J., 27
searching and critiquing'
   as learning activity, 163
Segal, B., 8
seminars, online
   challenge and role, 130–35, *133*
skills, information technology
   need for, 17–19
   teaching of, 19–21
social capital
   impact of internet usage, 8
Special Educational Needs and Disability Act
   (2001), 121
staff, higher education
   IT skill enhancement opportunities,
   21
   see also academics; tutors
standards, academic
   challenge of online learning, 68–9,
   82–7, *82, 84–6*
standards, minimum
   as quality assurance measure, 66
Standish, P., 98
Stiglitz, J., 11
storage, document
   virtual methods, 37–8
students

expectation of VLEs, 76
ICT skill enhancement opportunities,
   20–22
impact of online learning methods
   on, 64
university expectations of, 46–7
students, special needs
online learning requirements,
   120–22, *121*
summaries, topic
   as learning activity medium, 163
synchronous online seminars', 132,
   134–5
systems, information
   challenges within higher education,
   14–19
   provision and use, 14–19, 28–40
   skill enhancement, 20–22, 150–52,
   151

Tam, M., 80
Taynton, Y., 173, 175
teaching and teachers
   development of techniques, *95,*
   154–61, 163, 165, *159*
   evaluation of quality, 59–60
   impact of new technologies, 127–30
   qualities required, 44, 49–50
   role in learning experience, 58,
   112–13
   theories of, 166–77, *167–8, 170–72*
   see also andragogy
teams, module development
   case study, 150–77, *151, 159, 162, 164,*
   167–8, 170–72
technologies, information *see*
   information and communication
   technology
technologies, new
   developmental history, 5–8
   impact on teaching, 127–30
   role and challenges, 14–19, 63–4
Testone, S., 58, 60, 112
Tett, L., 53
text, online, 115–16
Thorpe, M., 108, 111
time, management of
   importance in online learning design,
   96–7
Time Warner, 11

total learning'
  challenges of delivery, 100–102, *101,*
    103–5
total quality management, 65–6
Toulmin, S., *170*
transformative learning
  case study, 167–72, *167–8, 170–72*
  characteristics, 166–7
tutorials
  role of online learning, 136
tutors
  qualities required for online teaching,
    44, 49–50
  role in learning experience, 58,
    112–13

universities, electronic
  characteristics of quality assurance,
    66–7
  historical fortunes, 25–6
  student capability expectations,
    46–7
University for Industry, 25
user satisfaction'
  quality assurance measure, 66

virtual learning *see* online learning
virtual learning environments (VLEs) *see*
  online learning environments
Vygotsky, L., 154

Wagner, J., 11
Wallen, G., 165
Ward, M., 114
Web Accessibility Initiative (WAI)
  (Worldwide Web Consortium), 121
Web-Based Education Commission
  (USA), 18, 20, 26
web pages
  design requirements, 113–19, *117*
Weight, B., 60
Wenger, E., 153, 180
White, K., 60
White, P., 159
wikis, 39–40
Wild, M., 150
Williams, M., 7
work-based learning
  value to online learning, 139–40
worldwide web
  developmental history, 5–8
  educational opportunities provided
    by, 32–3
  usage, *6*
  see also blogs; home pages; links;
    navigation, internet; web pages;
    wikis
wrap around' model of teaching, 156

zone of proximal development'
  (Vygotsky), 154